THE INTERNET COMPANION

A Beginner's Guide to Global Networking

Second Edition

TRACY LAQUEY

Foreword by Vice President Al Gore

AN EDITORIAL INC. BOOK

Addison-Wesley Publishing Company
Reading, Massachusetts • Menlo Park, California • New York
Don Mills, Ontario • Wokingham, England • Amsterdam
Bonn • Sydney • Singapore • Tokyo • Madrid • San Juan
Paris • Seoul • Milan • Mexico City • Taipei

Many of the designations used by manufacturers and sellers to distinguish their products are claimed as trademarks. Where those designations appear in this book, and Addison-Wesley was aware of a trademark claim, the designations have been printed in initial capital letters or all capital letters.

The authors and publishers have taken care in preparation of this book, but make no expressed or implied warranty of any kind and assume no responsibility for errors or omissions. No liability is assumed for incidental or consequential damages in connection with or arising out of the use of the information or programs contained herein.

Library of Congress Cataloging-in-Publication Data
LaQuey, Tracy L., 1963–
    The Internet companion : a beginner's guide to global networking /
Tracy LaQuey. — 2nd ed.
        p.   cm.
    Includes index.
    ISBN 0-201-40766-3
    1. Internet (Computer network)   I. Title.
TK5105.875.I57L37   1994
384.3'3—dc20   94-12954
                                                      CIP

Sponsoring Editor: Keith Wollman
Project Editor: Eleanor McCarthy
Production Coordinator: Lora L. Ryan
Cover Design: Virginia Evans and Rob Day
Text design: Arisman Design
Illustrations: Steven Ackerman
Set in Meridien and Futura type by Cathleen Collins

1 2 3 4 5 6 7 8 9-DOH-9897969594
First printing, July 1994

Addison-Wesley books are available for bulk purchases by corporations, institutions, and other organizations. For more information please contact the Corporate, Government and Special Sales Department at (800) 238-9682.

Contents

Foreword

Computer networks have been around for over twenty-five years, and in that time they have gone from being a laboratory curiosity to a tool used by millions of people every day. The first network, ARPANET, was used primarily by a few thousand computer scientists to access computers, share computer files, and send electronic mail. Today, scientists, engineers, teachers, students, librarians, doctors, businesspeople, and even a few members of Congress rely on the Internet and other networks to communicate with their colleagues, receive electronic journals, access bulletin boards, log onto databases, and use remote computers and other equipment.

In the last few years, we have witnessed the democratization and commercialization of the Internet. Today, the network connects not only the top research laboratories and universities but also small colleges, businesses, libraries, and schools throughout the world. The growth of commercial networks has enabled much broader access to the government-subsidized portions of the Internet. And that growth is accelerating because the telecommunications and computer industries have recognized the commercial potential of high-speed, interactive networking and have invested hundreds of millions of dollars in developing new switching technology and new applications for networks.

Since I first became interested in high-speed networking almost seventeen years ago, there have been many major advances both in the technology and in public awareness. Articles on high-speed networks are commonplace in major newspapers and in news magazines. In contrast, when as a House member in the

early 1980s I called for creation of a national network of "information superhighways," the only people interested were the manufacturers of optical fiber. Back then, of course, high-speed meant
56,000 bits per second. Today we are building a national information infrastructure that will carry billions of bits of data per second,
serve thousands of users simultaneously, and transmit not only
electronic mail and data files but voice and video as well.

Unfortunately, it is not easy to keep track of all the new developments in networking. According to some recent estimates,
the amount of traffic on the Internet has been increasing 10 percent per month, and the number of new applications and services has been growing almost as quickly. You can now access
thousands of different databases and bulletin boards on everything from medieval French literature to global warming. Since
the Internet is a network of networks, there is no one place to go
for information on what's available and how to access it. Most
users have to rely on friends and colleagues for information on
the Internet.

That is why I welcome the revised edition of *The Internet Companion*. It provides a valuable primer on the Internet, explains the
"rules of the road," and provides step-by-step instructions on accessing many of the information resources available through the
Internet. It should help both new and experienced Internet users
learn how to make the best use of the network.

For too many people the Internet has been uncharted territory, and as a result they have hesitated to explore the vast potential of networking. I trust this book will change that.

July 1994   *Vice President Al Gore*

Preface

The Internet Companion was the first computer trade book to introduce the world to the wonders of the Internet. When it made its
debut in 1992, it immediately became a best-seller. Even though
today there are other sources of information about the Internet,
including training classes and videotapes, new users still look to
the *Companion* for guidance and help in getting to know and use
this "network of networks."

How times have changed! Back in 1992, few predicted the great
Internet wave, which ever since has been building momentum,
gathering speed. Not long ago, you could recite the "anonymous
FTP" sites from memory, whereas today, there are hundreds of
thousands of places to download files, retrieve software, and access
online books and services. Only five years ago, people cited IP addresses instead of host names, and there were no graphical user interfaces presenting the Internet as "the Emerald City." Now, in
many cases, you don't even need to know computer names, let
alone addresses; you just point and click on colorful icons. Although
previously you could only complain about the government in online political forums, now you can send email to the president and
vice president in Washington, as well as retrieve the latest White
House press releases and initiatives. It used to be that you could
only talk about movies in online forums; today the Internet transmits live video broadcasts and radio shows, as well as movies.

In short, the Internet is continuously changing, growing, and
improving, and it is having a tremendous impact on our lives. It's
not just a physical computer network anymore, but a publishing
medium, a communication channel, and a library. Yet it's both
advanced and primitive. As Bruce Sterling, a science fiction

writer and Internet philosopher once said, "Everyone has a different Internet." What it is to you depends on your expectations, the networking resources available to you, and your motivation to use it. Whatever your fancy, this book will get you started. It introduces you to Internet concepts, applications, and idiosyncrasies and offers you glimpses of how people are using it for the mundane and the marvelous.

This book contains numerous examples and sample commands to try. In general, computer names and email addresses by themselves appear in italic, while new terms are introduced in boldface. Some of the commands are a mixture of bold and italic; in those cases, you should type anything in bold or italic exactly as it appears. The italic represents variable input that only you can supply, such as your email address or your login name.

Keep in mind that although many instructions and examples are given in these pages, this book does not offer step-by-step directions for every case. Remember also that new services are being made available daily, and that even though the resource information was up-to-date when the book went to press, it is very likely that some of it will have changed by the time you read it. Always read any instructions that are given when connecting to an online database, and if you have problems, consult your Internet provider's helpdesk or consulting services.

You may feel as though you're about to be thrown into the ocean with your shoes tied together. But come on in—the water's fine! Millions of people are surfing on the Internet, and you can too. And while you're hanging ten, don't forget to drop me a line: *Tracy@editorial.com*. Numerous Internauts have written to tell me how *The Internet Companion* helped them and how they use it, and I look forward to hearing about your Internet adventures.

Many people helped make this book a reality. In particular, I wish to thank Patrick D. Parker, Laura Fillmore, Tim Evans, Eugene Bailey, Mic Kaczmarczik, Guy Steele, Ed Kozel, Virginia Bechtold, David O'Leary, Susan Estrada, Susan and Peter Rauch, Al and Sheri LaQuey, Gerald and Valerie Parker, and all the people who sent me stories about how they use the Internet.

July 1994   *Tracy LaQuey*

Chapter 1

WHAT IS THE INTERNET AND WHY SHOULD YOU KNOW ABOUT IT?

*T*he Internet is a loose amalgam of thousands of computer networks reaching millions of people all over the world. Although its original purpose was to provide researchers with access to expensive hardware resources, the Internet has demonstrated such speed and effectiveness as a communications medium that it has transcended the original mission. It has, in recent years, grown so large and powerful that it is now an information and communication tool you cannot afford to ignore.

Today the Internet is being used by all sorts of people and organizations—newspapers, publishers, TV stations, celebrities, teachers, librarians, hobbyists, and business people—for a variety of purposes, from communicating with one another to accessing valuable services and resources. You can hardly pick up a newspaper or magazine without reading about how the Internet is playing a part in someone's life or project or discovery.

To appreciate what the Internet has to offer you, imagine discovering a whole system of highways and high-speed connectors that cut hours off your commuting time. Or a library you can use any time of the night or day, with acres of books and resources, and unlimited browsing. Or an all-night, nonstop block party with a corner table of kindred souls who welcome your presence at any time. That's the Internet, and this chapter will tell you why you should know about it.

1

WHENCE IT CAME

The Internet universe was created by an unassuming bang in 1969 with the birth of ARPANET, an experimental project of the U.S. Department of Defense Advanced Research Projects Agency (DARPA). It had a humble mission, to explore experimental networking technologies that would link researchers with remote resources such as large computer systems and databases. The success of ARPANET helped cultivate numerous other networking initiatives, which grew up intertwined; 25 years later, these have evolved into an ever expanding, complex organism comprising tens of millions of people and tens of thousands of networks.

Most users describe the Internet (or the "Net") as a "network of networks"; it appears to stretch forever. It doesn't just connect you and another computer; it connects you and all other Internet-connected computers. Don't think of the Internet as just a bunch of computers, though. It is a perpetually expanding universe with its own geography, "weather," and dynamic cultures. In this cyber-sphere, people in geographically distant lands communicate across time zones without ever seeing each other, and information is available 24 hours a day from thousands of places.

The Internet is inhabited by millions of regular folks, "non-techies" who use it daily to communicate and search for information. When this book was first written in the spring of 1992, the Internet population was mostly researchers and academics, and there weren't many applications and interest groups of relevance to the general public. Two years later, mainstream services dominate use of the Internet. As a result, the Internet is overflowing with useful resources—and with people climbing aboard.

IT KEEPS GOING AND GOING . . .

It's important to understand the significance of the Internet's growth and popularity. In one sense it could be compared to the proliferation of fax machines in the late 1980s. Our worldwide "fax system" wasn't built overnight; it started with a trickle of a few fax machines here and there. As businesses realized their usefulness and power, fax machines became more commonplace.

The value of each fax machine increased as more and more became available.

Similarly, stand-alone computers are useful, but their potential is limited by isolated applications—word processors and spreadsheets, for example—and the amount of money you have to spend on disk drives and CD-ROMs. A mere direct (full-time) or dial-up connection to the worldwide Internet gives you access to more info-goods, services, and people than you'll ever find on your own isolated computer or local-area network. The Internet is already the largest computer network in the world and, in terms of connected networks, people, and resources, it's getting larger, and therefore more "valuable," literally by the minute.

How large is the Internet? According to the Internet Society (ISOC), a professional organization of Internet developers, influencers, and users, as of spring 1994 the Internet reached 75 countries directly and 146 countries indirectly, and consisted of 35,000 networks and 3 million computers. (An email gateway is a special connection that allows only electronic mail to transfer between two or more networks.)

The bulk of Internet computers and networks still belongs to the research and education communities. This is not surprising, given that the Internet arose from the primordial research ooze. However, many universities are teaming up with businesses to develop online catalogs and archives. And, according to the ISOC journal, 31 percent of the networks belong to businesses. Of the number of registered—but not necessarily connected—networks, 51 percent were commercial. There's definitely a rising trend in commercial activity and connectivity; many businesses have realized that they can link their enterprise networks to the Internet and gain instant access to their customers. Some market research indicates that online services—in general—make up almost a billion-dollar industry, with an estimated 25 percent per year growth, so it stands to reason that providers of these services are migrating to the Internet, where the action is.

The types of resources accessible via the Internet are growing at an astounding rate. The term *resource* describes anything you can access on the Internet, no matter where it's physically located. Examples of some Internet resources are a database of regularly updated weather information in Michigan, an online magazine, a cartoon, and an archive of daily newspaper articles. A resource can also be a mailing list or a newsgroup that brings together people from all over the world to discuss shared interests such as soccer, cooking, and poetry. Suffice it to say that there are literally tens of thousands of servers, archive sites, mailing lists, newsgroups, and databases available on the Internet.

The Success of the Internet

It's hard to imagine how the Internet has grown so fast and been so successful without some ambitious organization or individual managing the project. Yet no one has a monopoly on access to or use of the Internet; there's no monolithic empire called Internet, Inc., controlling accounts and application development or roping off the backstage parts of cyberspace. One of the reasons the Internet is so successful is the commitment of its developers to producing "open" standards. The specifications or rules that computers need to communicate are publicly and freely available— published so that everyone can obtain them. The standards that the Internet uses are known as the TCP/IP protocol suite.

Although you may not think about it often, standards play a big part in your everyday life. Camera film always fits in your camera, and loose-leaf paper bought at the drugstore fits in your binder. Libraries catalog books according to a standard system, so that once you learn it, you can walk into any library and find the books you need. On the contrary, things that don't conform to standards can make your life miserable. Standards are just as important in the computer and networking world. Without open standards, only computers from the same vendor could talk to one another, creating an electronic Tower of Babel. Computers and networks that conform to the same communications standards are able to "interoperate," regardless of brand.

Cooperation is a major ingredient of interoperability. The Internet nervous system does not have a central brain, such as a powerful supercomputer that controls its operation by feeding it commands and directing its limbs to perform key functions. Rather, all the networks and computers act as peers in the exchange of information and communication. The technology that makes it happen is known as **internetworking**; it creates a universality among disparate systems, enabling the networks and computers to communicate.

Fundamentally, the Internet revolves around the concept of a **packet**, a basic building block or a digital brick. All information and communication transmitted on the Internet are broken into packets, each of which is considered an independent entity. The packets are then individually routed from network to network until they reach their destination, where they are reassembled and presented to the user or computer process.

This method of networking is very flexible and robust. It allows diverse computers and systems to communicate by means of networking software, not proprietary hardware. If a network goes "down"—meaning it isn't available to transfer information—the packets can be rerouted to other networks in many cases. This dynamic alternate routing of information creates a very persistent means of communication. Indeed, that was the intent of the network engineers developing this technology during the height of the Cold War. They wanted a network that would continue to function even if parts of it were destroyed during an enemy attack.

While most neophytes probably don't care about these standards and technical details, an understanding of the underlying infrastructure will help in learning to use the Internet properly and in taking full advantage of its powerful capabilities. It goes deeper than that though; understanding from the bottom up how separate computers and networks fit together will give you an appreciation for the Net culture—the sharing, cooperative spirit that is inherent in the Internet. Chapter 2 further defines these concepts of interoperability and open standards, as well as explaining how the protocols and networks come together to make the Internet work.

THE EQUALIZER

You can see how open standards enable businesses and individuals to compete on a level playing field in developing networking software and products. But open networking extends beyond the development of networking protocols and products. Once you, an Internet user, are "jacked in," you have access to the same resources as the rest of the millions of Internet users, whether you're located in Sydney or Stockholm.

The phrase "democratization of communication" often comes up in discussions about the Internet, which is, indeed, a truly democratic forum. The network doesn't care if you're president of a Fortune 500 company or a warehouse clerk, a potato farmer or a molecular biologist. Your tidings and opinions are handled the same way, and it's the worth and wit of what you have to say that determines who's willing to listen—not your title.

It's also never been so easy to be both a consumer and a producer of services. If you're ambitious enough and aspire to be an electronic entrepreneur who provides commercial services or Internet access, there's nothing to prevent you—no long lines, no paperwork, and no regulations. (Okay, it's not *that* easy; you do need to read this and a few other books first.) Once your network is *directly* hooked into the Internet, all the computers on that network are accessible from every other Internet-connected computer. (Chapter 7 explains of the different types of Internet connections.)

This environment empowers the individual; it encourages and stimulates participation, imagination, and innovation. There are numerous stories of how just one or two people have leveraged the Net to do great things, whether it's to publish a newsletter, make a name, or develop contacts. If you don't have access to a whiz-bang, high-speed Internet connection or to a large multi-user computer, that's not a problem. Already there are businesses offering rental space on their Internet-connected computers and disks. You can lease "office space" from "office parks" in cyberspace and set up shop. Your virtual storefront may be thousands of miles and two countries away, but it's probably a few seconds hyperdrive from every location. Convenience is a given on the Internet.

Communication

What distinguishes the Internet (and other global networks) from traditional communication technologies is the level of interaction and the speed at which users can broadcast their messages. No other medium gives every participant the capability to communicate instantly with thousands and thousands of people. Consider this: it is possible for you, on your very first Net-surfing expedition, to send a message containing your thoughts to several thousand people. What other communication medium gives you that power? Instantaneously? Without prior editing?

The Internet certainly has people talking; everyone has an opinion, and all opinions seem to end up on the Internet. The Internet functions as an ongoing consumer report, with people continuously offering up views, experiences, recommendations, and warnings. You can use the Internet's communication applications (explained in Chapter 3) to ask for help from thousands of people, broadcast an announcement of an event or a new service, offer your analysis of a situation, or just muse in an interest group. The Internet is a perfect tool for alerting and assembling large numbers of people electronically. Information relating to a certain event can be transmitted immediately, making it a very effective rousing device. Plenty of forums exist for this very purpose—announcing late-breaking bulletins about an event or sparking a debate about the most recent controversies.

Now, this online free-for-all doesn't come without a few "netiquette" rules. As in any social situation, there is an accepted mode of behavior, and you will do well to make note of it before diving in and instantly distinguishing yourself as a barbarian. Chapter 3 contains a must-read guide to some well-known network conduct codes.

SatelLife

Physicians in Africa are practicing medicine and dealing with some of this century's most serious medical challenges in the midst of staggering "information poverty." In the mid-80s, the problem caught the attention of Dr. Bernard Lown, founder of International Physicians for the Prevention of Nuclear War, which won the Nobel Peace Prize in 1985, who felt the high frontier of space should be used for humanitarian rather than military purposes. He started Satel-Life, a non-profit organization committed to promoting health in the developing world by providing improved communication and exchange of information. SatelLife's Health-Net is a computer network linking medical centers in the Southern Hemisphere in much of the developing world with an initial focus on Africa. Using two microsatellites—Health-Sat I & II—simple ground stations, and dial-up in-country networks, HealthNet enables physicians and healthcare workers in rural as well as urban areas to communicate via electronic mail and to reach data bases at research centers in the industrialized world via remote access.

For example, a physician treating a patient with cerebral malaria in Zambia, Africa, where it remains a deadly malady,

(Continued)

Information

President Bill Clinton said in May of 1993: "We are moving very rapidly in all forms of production and services to a knowledge-based economy in which what you earn depends on what you can learn. Not only what you know today, but what you are capable of learning tomorrow." What you can learn depends on the information resources to which you have immediate access. The people who will succeed in today's and tomorrow's world will be those who can effectively use the resources and tools available to them. The Internet is there to help you.

could better treat his patient by communicating with physicians and researchers in other African countries as well as with colleagues in other parts of the world. Through Health-Net News, he can receive abstracts, summaries, and full-text articles selected from a variety of leading medical journals throughout the world or an update from any of the leading malaria research centers in Africa. A leading medical journal may cost more than the annual salary of many physicians, and even communication by fax or telephone is beyond the reach of most health professionals in Africa. Using the HealthNet system, a physician like the one in Zambia can ask colleagues about recent developments in prevention, diagnosis, or treatment. He might use the system to query nearby hospitals about availability of medicine.

Located in Cambridge, Massachusetts, SatelLife has received major corporate support for HealthSat I & II from NEC Corp. in Japan. There are now HealthNets in sixteen countries in Africa and four countries in the Americas, and expansion into Asia will begin by 1994. All HealthNets connect to the Internet through a gateway maintained by the Telemedicine Center at Memorial University in Newfoundland, Canada.

Based on an interview with Charles Clements, M.D., Executive Director of SatelLife.

There is an ever-growing number of valuable information resources being made available via the Internet. These include free and public archives, library catalogs, government services, and commercial databases. The Internet is liquid, changing every second; as news rains down, differing views, reports, and opinions irrigate archives and forums. Powerful search tools, with names like Gopher, WorldWideWeb, and WAIS (all explained in Chapter 4), can help you find and bring home these resources.

These digital devices give you the power to bypass the middleman on your way to the source. It's not good enough anymore to turn on the 24-hour news service on your radio or TV and *wait* for the local weather forecast. On the Internet, you can check the latest weather and order goods and services online when you need them. For example, you can browse online real-estate guides looking for properties thousands of miles away instead of first going to a realtor. You can form your own opinion based on the sources, not the summaries. The Internet can help you make intelligent choices. However, be aware that no network will show you the best path; it's up to you to compile and analyze what's available, and then make the intelligent decision.

Virtual Communities

The Internet excels in bringing people closer together. Since geography is no longer a delimiter, people from different countries and varied backgrounds are able to join together according to common interests and projects. The Internet is responsible for an untold number of associations between people and groups; this kind of interaction on such a wide scale without a computer network is impossible.

The concept of digital colonies and online civilizations is fairly new, yet it is quickly becoming a way of life for many Internet travelers. In this hectic world of two-income households and work-study lifestyles, building communities of interest within a school, neighborhood, or city is difficult. The problems with "reality-space" communities include lack of local involvement, geography, and inflexible schedules. The Internet transcends these barriers. It's a lot easier to join an ongoing discussion with people who share a common interest when *you* are available, no matter *where* you are.

For example, a group of busy, young professionals and students in Seattle, Washington, take advantage of the Internet's flexibility by using an email list to alert everyone to volleyball games, ski trips, and nights out on the town. They also check ski and weather reports on the Internet, and participate in online volleyball and skiing interest groups. Several of them travel, but they keep up with local happenings by accessing the Internet and reading their email on the road. This group could not be as organized without the Internet; at least one dedicated friend would be needed to call everyone and coordinate activities. No one in this group has time to play cruise director. The Internet for them has become a necessary social tool.

Internet "netizens" have circled their computers around virtual campsites, communing and cultivating friendships. Because it's so simple to join or leave a group, your own virtual village may change on a daily or hourly basis. You are a native to your own web, your own cyber-sphere of influence, but it is easy to be a tourist, visiting and interacting in other communities. Beaming yourself around incognito is also possible; you can become a digital cyborg, assuming other personalities. As a well-known cartoon proclaimed in 1993, "On the Internet, no one knows you're a dog."

PEELING BACK THE LAYERS: DIFFERENCES BETWEEN NETWORKS

People have to make many conceptual leaps in order to understand computer networking. Trying to understand the differences between the Internet and other online services and networks is just one of them. It's especially difficult if you've had experience with one but not the others. There are literally thousands of different "networks" that you can access. Some of them have been around for almost twenty years. What makes the Internet different from all the others? Companies like Prodigy and CompuServe are not really networks in the sense that the Internet is; they're commercial providers of information services. To get access, you call up the company, provide your credit card number, and set up an account. You can then use your computer and modem to dial a local or 800 number and get access to the service. The services are documented, support is available, and the pricing structure for usage and access is well defined. Each of these services is owned, controlled, and run by a business.

Not so with the Internet. Remember, it's a network of networks, a transport service, an information highway, *not*, as a

whole, a commercial information service. It's a distributed, an-
archic system, and much larger in terms of people and diversity
of services than all the commercial information systems put together. Support, quality, and pricing for Internet connectivity
and services are not regulated or defined throughout. The on-
ramps are numerous; there are many ways to get access from
local, national, and international Internet transport providers or
from dial-up commercial access systems.

This flexibility has advantages and disadvantages. In most
cases you're not limited to one solution. If you don't like one
Internet provider's service, you can easily get access to the
Internet another way. This can be frustrating, though, because
there are so many choices in providers that sometimes it's difficult to make a decision.

Another difference to keep in mind is the diversity of services
you get on the Internet. For example, to provide an information
service through a commercial information provider, a person or
organization most likely has to get permission and make special
arrangements with the company that owns the service. The
Internet, on the other hand, doesn't have a controlling organization that denies or approves involvement. As a result, individuals
and companies are making new resources available every day. In
fact, many of the commercial databases you might access through
a commercial information service have already made (or are planning to make) direct connections to the Internet. The Internet is
basically providing the highway connections for you to get to
these services. (Be aware, though, that you may still need to set up
an account with each commercial database provider to use them.)

CONVERGENCE: A TRAFFIC CIRCLE ON THE INFORMATION HIGHWAY

The Internet is providing the common ground for information
service providers to do business. It's also blurring the lines between what used to be separate and distinct applications.

On May 23, 1993, a historic moment occurred when a cult movie entitled *Wax: Or the Discovery of Television Among the Bees* was broadcast over the Internet to a small worldwide audience who watched and listened to it live on their computers. The video was fuzzy and in black and white, and the audio sputtered in and out, but this digital moonwalk marked another small, yet significant, step toward the much-heralded convergence of audio, video, and data. The movie was about a beekeeper who ends up being kept by the bees, and perhaps this is poetic justice, as today many Internauts are held captive by the digital bits buzzing through wires and telephone lines.

To understand what this convergence craze is all about, let's back up a bit and consider the different types of communication. Most televisions and telephones transmit information (your voice, the evening news, and so on) using an analog signal; that means the information is represented by a continuous signal of varying strength.

Computers, on the other hand, work with binary digits, or bits. A bit is simply a 1 or a 0. That's it. Computer, or digital, information is simply represented by patterns of these ones and zeros. By digitizing communication—representing everything in ones and zeros—computers can deal with multimedia and data in the same way. Furthermore, if computers are connected to a network, they can enable interactive digital audio and video communication between people. Your computer can become an all-purpose communications appliance that combines the functions of a telephone and TV, and also lets you use applications like a word processor or electronic mail program.

Digitizing multimedia technologies has the communications, broadcasting, and publishing industries all aflutter and ushers in the chaotic days of convergence mania. The traditional roles of the telephone, television network, and cable companies with which we're so familiar are rapidly ceasing to exist, and ultimately, all of these companies will be in the same business, either providing the content—entertainment, *interactive* communication, and information services—or access to these. The broadcast and entertainment industries have only just begun warming up by advertising possible new interactive services, while communication companies consider new alliances and mergers. The publishing industry is also repositioning itself.

And through it all, the Internet has been a testing ground, in a sense amalgamating everything in its path by bringing technologies together and letting them play in a digital sandbox. The Internet may not be providing 500 TV channels, but it is possible today to participate in interactive video and audio conferencing from your computer, and to share the same "whiteboard" for illustrations and notes. You can listen to Internet radio shows while simultaneously downloading software. You can read online articles or books with hyperhooks that "mind-bind" you on-demand to text, video clips, still images, and audio. All of these applications have only recently been made available, but they're rapidly becoming more popular, and are making up a significant percentage of the traffic and use on the Internet. Unfortunately, many of these applications demand powerful workstations and a high-speed connection to the Internet—requirements beyond what most people by themselves can meet. So if you want to see the future, go to a university or a research lab. But it's important to know that these things *are* possible, because it probably won't be long before you can participate.

MRS. SMITH CONNECTS TO WASHINGTON

The merging of communications media, the popularity of the Internet, and the convergence of information technologies have gotten the attention of the U.S. government, and have made everyone take a step back to review regulations. In the United States, regulations apply to each communications industry separately, based on the information or entertainment that is broadcast (TV and cable), or on the type of interactive communication (telephones). However, since digital bits can represent voice, video, and data, redefining policies to standardize or eliminate regulations altogether in order to level the playing field and promote competition is the next step.

The Big Crunch

"I'm reminded of an idea of Stephen Hawking, the British physicist. . . . Hawking has speculated about a distant future when the universe stops expanding and begins to contract. Eventually all matter comes colliding together in a "Big Crunch," which scientists say could then be followed by another "Big Bang"—a universe expanding outward once again.

"Our current information industries—cable, local telephone, long-distance telephone, television, film, computers, and others—seem headed for a Big Crunch/Big Bang of their own. The space between these diverse functions is rapidly shrinking—between computers and television, for example, or interactive communications and video."

From a speech given by Vice President Al Gore on January 11, 1994, at Royce Hall, UCLA, Los Angeles, California.

Noting the convergence trends, the incredible success of the Internet, and the future of interactive multimedia communication, U.S. Vice President Al Gore has called for the formation of the National Information Infrastructure, the NII. The NII will connect more than just computers; it will also link televisions, telephones, and, most likely, "appliances" that combine all three technologies. Many countries' governments are starting to follow the lead of the United States.

Vice President Gore's involvement in the NII is not by chance; he has been an enthusiastic supporter of a national information highway for many years. Most notably, his High Performance Computing and Communications (HPCC) legislation was passed into law in December 1991, while he was a senator representing the state of Tennessee. The HPCC Act defines several components, including providing all researchers with access to powerful supercomputer resources and valuable information

services, and coordinating and combining several federal agencies' individual networking efforts into one high-capacity, high-
speed network known as the National Research and Education
Network (NREN). The NREN exists today as more of a concept or
vision than a physical network; its purpose is to extend the
Internet beyond universities to primary and secondary schools
and to libraries. The NREN vision still exists, but has been
adopted into the goals of the NII. Vice President Gore has chal-
lenged businesses and organizations to connect schools and
libraries in order to provide access to information and interactive
communication facilities by the year 2000.

While the Clinton/Gore administration further defines the
national information highway and the role government should
take, it's using the Internet to disseminate major initiatives and
to receive electronic mail comments. In many countries, governments are the largest producers and users of information, so it
makes sense for them to review the latest information technologies. Many people believe that broad access to government
information is a right—not a privilege—and that tax-supported
projects that produce information should warrant its free electronic availability. In the United States, for example, an increasing number of agencies are beginning to make public archives
accessible over the Internet. Today you can obtain the latest
White House press releases, as well as the text of speeches made
by the president and vice president. The White House has also
made itself more accessible to government watchdogs by estab-
lishing a presidential email box (*president@whitehouse.gov*).

BUSINESS USE

There are myriad reasons why the business community should
be connected to the Internet; indeed, one of the fastest-growing
segments of the Internet today is commercial. The Internet is
providing a wonderful environment in which to do business;
there are many stories of small and big businesses that have
leveraged their relatively small investment in connection costs to

search the Internet for information, keep in contact with customers, or provide online services and operate virtual storefronts. Businesses that claim they listen to their customers' needs can now do so on the Internet. Companies exploring telecommuting options for their employees should definitely evaluate the Internet's capabilities.

Because so many organizations are linked, with more being added every day, connecting to the Internet is a very attractive alternative to building a private network. Many companies justify joining the Internet to be more accessible to customers, and to have the ability to consult with experts around the world. Just providing Internet connectivity services, consulting, and training is a big business. A growing number of Internet providers—large and small—are competing to connect businesses and schools to the Internet.

Just as there is a "Net Code of Conduct," there is also an accepted way of doing business over the Internet. The basic tenet of participation is "you should give as well as receive," but emailing direct-mail advertisements in hopes of receiving more sales is not considered "giving" by members of the Internet community. Businesses that do well provide information in a "passive" manner—that is, by making available an archive of their information and catalogs so people can search when they want to. People definitely don't appreciate being bombarded with glowing descriptions of products, but an outsider giving an objective review or recommendation is considered okay.

Demand for online interactive services is definitely heating up. The types of virtual corporations that are emerging include online bookstores that let you peruse or download online books or order a hardcopy book. There are similar services for record stores and online magazines. An online florist service lets customers first view an arrangement and then click a button to order. Other companies and individuals are selling jewelry, music, software, and support, and providing consulting and training, all online. Not only can you use the Internet to provide a service or distribute a product, but you can also use it to find out the latest business news. Stock reports, the *NASDAQ Financial Executive Journal,* and *Commerce Business Daily* are just some of the useful information resources available—for free—via the Internet.

Businesses should pay attention to the Internet because of the power the consumer now has to shape their products and services. A negative comment is not heard locally anymore—it's blasted around the world, announced on mailing lists, or forwarded via email. Some people are maintaining databases of reviews and complaints about products and services—accessible and searchable by anyone on the Internet. Consider this a true story: A man who was researching a real-estate investment called for comments via an Internet public interest group devoted to concerns and issues in Austin, Texas. Within days, many people had responded with recommendations and complaints about various agencies and real-estate professionals. The man compiled a report based on these comments and circulated it. The whole process took two weeks.

BACKING OUT OF THE DRIVEWAY

The Internet is "The Great Equalizer," but unfortunately, the first hurdle is the highest—that is, actually getting on the level playing field. A transport provider will give you access to the Internet and, as you'll soon learn, there are many ways to get "connected." Whether you have a PC or a supercomputer, a gigabits-per-second speed network or a plain old telephone line, you can get connected to the Internet. Two basic methods of access are available for individuals: through an organization's network, or through a computer, modem, and telephone line. The basic costs are explained below. Chapter 6 discusses some of the available options in more detail, and also tells you the general steps to take if you wish to connect your organization's network.

For many people, the Internet is an all-around good deal. People who have access to it through an organization, such as a university or a large company, don't have to worry about how much they use the Internet. Their communications with people

> "It does not require a crystal ball to predict that business use of the Internet will expand significantly over the next few years. . . . The electronic highway is not merely open for business; it is relocating, restructuring, and literally redefining business in America."
>
> Source: Mary J. Cronin, *Doing Business on the Internet* (New York: Van Nostrand Reinhold, 1994).

from all over the world and accesses to most information resources are not going to show up itemized on a long-distance bill, because the leased lines or network links are already paid for. (This is the way it was in the past, at least. One major Internet provider is starting to investigate "volume charging"— meaning it'll charge each user for the amount of information that's transferred.) For members of networks that don't charge by the packet (a packet is a unit of information), the Internet is like an "all-you-can-eat" buffet.

Even though you may not be charged a long-distance fee to reach a resource, the service on the other end may charge by the minute, by the hour, or by the job. Think of a highway with no tollbooths. You can drive all you want on the highway (the Internet), but you pay for most of the services and goods you stop for along the way. Right now, most of the rest stops on the Internet are free, but more and more "mom-and-pop" diners are springing up.

Individual users who don't have the benefit of organization apron-string links must get their access from commercial Internet providers, public-access Internet sites, or a digital-rich uncle who gives away access through public accounts. Access for those with a computer and a modem is usually through a local telephone call to a modem-pool/terminal server or to another computer. The costs can vary, but many commercial providers charge a flat-rate monthly fee that isn't bad considering the potential gain of instant worldwide communication. Some providers charge as little as $30 U.S. per month for unlimited electronic mail. But, just as the telephone system still doesn't quite reach everyone worldwide, Internet access is not always easily available or reasonable. Many people in remote areas or countries outside the United States must make expensive long-distance calls to send and receive electronic mail or to access resources. Often isolated, and desiring human contact and access to information, they find the extra cost worth it—if they can afford it.

THE FUTURE

The Internet's crystal ball doesn't yield many clues to what will happen in the future. The developers of the early ARPANET envisioned it as a way to bring expensive hardware resources closer to researchers. What they didn't expect was that electronic mail would become so heavily used by researchers at geographically distant sites who want to talk and collaborate with each other. Other high-speed networks that were built to connect supercomputers are now used more for collaboration and access to information.

Today communication and access to information are still the most popular applications, but the Internet is getting a face-lift. We are starting to see more user-friendly interfaces that make this worldwide web "transparent." That is to say, the network and computer are becoming integrated in the home and office, performing important, vital functions without making users aware of the nitty-gritty details.

One such interface is known as Mosaic, and it's been referred to as the new "killer application" of the Internet. Mosaic has worked wonders for the Internet's user-unfriendly reputation, but it is considered a wide load on the infobahn—meaning, it's hogging the road. It requires a lot of transfers of sometimes large amounts of data across the networks, and this can cause congestion, not unlike the traffic jams we experience on today's streets and highways.

"The Internet in particular and the global telecommunications infrastructure in general are expanding at an historically unprecedented rate. Prices are plummeting, bandwidth
is rising, connectivity is spreading, providers are proliferating,
access is becoming more and more available to people with
an increasing diversity of technical capabilities and funding
appetites, and interoperability is being recognized as a crucial
element in nearly every major provider's business strategy.
All of these things are good, and are happening naturally as a
consequence of the natural forces technological evolution
and the marketplace."

Source: Chip Morningstar, Electric Communities, 3339 Kipling, Palo Alto, CA
94306, (415) 856-1130, *chip@netcom.com*.

Our experience with Mosaic is providing us with insight into
the future. Tomorrow's applications will require faster networking technology, and network researchers are working on building higher-speed networks. High speed in the future will be
gigabit-per-second speeds. For example, an entire encyclopedia
could be transferred in a few seconds on a gigabit-per-second
network.

The encyclopedia metric is often used to describe how fast
the network will be, but it's important to realize that although
some advanced applications, such as video conferencing, will require high speeds, this increased capacity will also be used to
handle the growing number of people who will be using the network. You can compare this additional capacity to a ten-lane
highway. The number of lanes does not enable you to drive ten
times faster. It just allows more cars to travel at the same time.

We will need to widen the road, especially if the Internet
continues to grow at its present rate (and it doesn't show any
signs of slowing down). It's estimated that in a few short years,
there will be 100 million people interconnected via the Internet.

The Internet and Business Success

According to Alvin Toffler, the well-known futurist, the economic well-being of the United States depends on the continuing development of the networks. "Because so much of business now depends on getting and sending information, companies around the world have been rushing to link their employees through electronic networks. These networks form the key infrastructure of the 21st century, as critical to business success and national economic development as the railroads were in Morse's era."

Source: Alvin Toffler, *Power Shift* (New York: Bantam Books, 1990), p. 102.

Most likely, they will be communicating with one another by using interactive video and audio applications or email that incorporates multimedia; already there are such applications being used in schools, universities, research labs, and some businesses.

With that, you're probably revving your engines and ready to race toward your computer. However, before you start typing, there's some background material and a few fundamental concepts you have to learn before graduating from Junior Birdsman to Internet Top Gun. So on to Chapter 2, for the "lowdown" of the Internet.

Chapter 2

INTERNET: THE LOWDOWN

Ask an *Internet wizard* what this network is all about, and you'll probably get a long and dusty discourse studded with acronyms and techspeak. It's friendly if you approach it right, but potentially huge and terrifying, especially to people who don't know its special ways. This chapter will explain some of the basic principles that underlie the Internet. Fortunately for you, the most important principle of all is that you don't have to *fully* understand how the Internet works to use it. Plenty of blissfully unaware Internet users are pounding away at keyboards and communicating merrily, with absolutely no knowledge of how the Internet fits together. But, although ignorance may be bliss, the more you know, the more doors are open to you. So here goes.

A NETWORK OF NETWORKS

The Internet is a worldwide web of interconnected university, business, military, and science networks. Why the term *web*? Isn't the Internet just one network? Not at all! It is a *network* of networks. The Internet is made up of little Local Area Networks (LANs), citywide Metropolitan Area Networks (MANs), and huge Wide Area Networks (WANs) that connect computers for organizations all over the world.

These networks are hooked together with everything from regular dial-up phone lines to high-speed dedicated leased lines,

What the Experts Are Saying . . .

"It's a biological phenomenon. The Internet is not a vertebrate. It acts a lot like slime mold, growing in all directions without anyone in charge. Every time I try to describe the Internet to anyone, everyone assumes I'm having a hippie mystic vision!"

—John Perry Barlow, National Net '93

"I'm starting to think of the Internet as a kaleidoscope. It is just so much broken glass and trinkets. Users turn the mirrors and lenses and suddenly, meaning snaps into place for them, where before there was only chaos. My job at NYSER-Net is tuning the mirrors and polishing the lenses."

—Jean Armour Polly, Manager of Network Development and User Training, NYSERNet, Inc.

satellites, microwave links, and fiber optic links. And the fact that they're "on" the Internet means that all these networks are interconnected. This network web extends all over the world, but trying to describe all of it and how it fits together is a bit like trying to count the stars. In fact, so many networks are interconnected within the Internet that it's impossible to show an accurate, up-to-date picture. Some network maps show the Internet as a cloud, because it's just too complex to draw in all of the links. To complicate matters, new computers and links are being added every day. It's estimated a new network is added every 20 minutes.

So think of the Internet as a "cloud of links." The cloud hides all the ugly details—the hardware, the physical links, the acronyms, and the network engineers. Remember that you don't actually need to know all the details to communicate and use resources on the Internet.

Overall, the Internet is the fastest global network around. Speed is often referred to as **throughput**—how fast information can be propelled through the network. The Internet isn't just *one* speed because, as explained above, it can accommodate both slow networks and the latest technology. There are networks on the Internet that are capable of transmitting 45 megabits (about 5,000 typescript pages) per second. The most typical network connection speeds are 56Kbps, which are popular for small organizations, and T1 (or 1.544Mbps) for larger organizations. Gigabit-per-second network speeds currently being tested will allow even more advanced applications and services, such as complex weather prediction models produced by supercomputers and transmitted to weather centers. Or transmitting extremely large (tens or hundreds of megabytes) databases—for example, earthquake data transferred from a collection site to the Institute of Geophysics and Planetary Physics for analysis. Or video conferences including people from all over the world.

IN THE BEGINNING

The Internet was not born full-blown in its present worldwide form of thousands of networks and connections. It had a humble—but exciting—beginning as *one* network called the ARPANET, the "Mother of the Internet." The ARPANET, described in Chapter 1, initially linked researchers with remote computer centers, allowing them to share hardware and software resources, such as computer disk space, databases, and computers. Other experimental networks were connected with the ARPANET by using an internetwork technology sponsored by DARPA. The original ARPANET itself split into two networks in the early 1980s, the ARPANET and Milnet (an unclassified military network), but connections made between the networks allowed communication to continue. At first this interconnection of experimental and production networks was called the DARPA Internet, but later the name was shortened to just "the Internet."

Access to the ARPANET in the early years was limited to the military, defense contractors, and universities doing defense research. Cooperative, decentralized networks such as UUCP, a worldwide Unix communications network, and USENET (User's

Network) came into being in the late 1970s, initially serving the university community and, later, commercial organizations. In the early 1980s, more-coordinated networks, such as the Computer Science Network (CSNET) and BITNET, began providing nationwide networking to the academic and research communities. These networks were not part of the Internet, but later special connections were made to allow the exchange of information between the various communities.

The next big moment in Internet history was the birth in 1986 of the National Science Foundation Network (NSFNET), which linked researchers across the country with five supercomputer centers. Soon expanded to include the mid-level and statewide academic networks that connected universities and research consortiums, the NSFNET began to replace the ARPANET for research networking. The ARPANET was honorably discharged (and dismantled) in March 1990. CSNET soon found that many of its early members (computer science departments) were connected via the NSFNET, so it ceased to exist in 1991.

HOW COMPUTERS TALK

The computers on a network have to be able to talk to one another. To do that they use **protocols**, which are just rules or agreements on how to communicate. Standards were mentioned in Chapter 1 as an important aspect in computer networking. There are lots of protocol standards out there, such as DECnet, SNA, IPX, and Appletalk, but to actually communicate, two computers have to be using the *same* protocol at the *same* time. TCP/IP, which stands for Transmission Control Protocol/Internet Protocol, is the language of the Internet. You may speak Japanese and I may speak English, but if we both speak French, we can communicate. So any computer that wants to communicate on the Internet must "speak" TCP/IP.

Developed by DARPA in the 1970s, TCP/IP was part of an experiment in internetworking—that is, connecting different types of networks and computer systems. First used ubiquitously on the ARPANET in 1983, it was also implemented and made

available at no cost for computers running the Berkeley Software
Distribution (BSD) of the Unix operating system. TCP/IP, developed with public funds, is considered an open, non-proprietary
protocol, and there are now implementations of it for almost every type of computer on the planet. "Non-proprietary" means
that no one company—not IBM, not DEC, not Apple—has ex-
clusive rights to the products needed to connect to the Internet.
Any number of companies, including those just mentioned,
make the hardware and software necessary for the network
connection.

TCP/IP isn't the only protocol suite that is considered "open."
Since the early 1980s, the International Organization for Standardization (ISO) has been developing the Open Systems Interconnection (OSI) protocols. While many of the OSI protocols and
applications are still evolving, a few are actually being used in
some networks on the Internet, and more are planned. So even
though most of the computers speak TCP/IP, the Internet is officially considered a "multi-protocol" network.

The whole idea of protocols and standards can get complicated, but as an Internet neophyte, all you need to be concerned
with are the applications that TCP/IP offers. The difference
between applications and protocols is that you don't actually *see*
the protocols (they're invisible to the end user), but you will access the Internet using the applications that conform to these
standards.

The Internet Toolbox

Three TCP/IP applications—electronic mail, remote login, and
file transfer—are the Internet equivalent of the hammer, screw-
driver, and crescent wrench in your toolbox. There are plenty of
fancier applications using variations on or combinations of these
basic tools, but wherever you roam on the Internet, you should
have the Big Three available to you. The three basic Internet services, as well as the more powerful and colorful applications, are
covered in later chapters, but here's a quick introduction to get
you on your way.

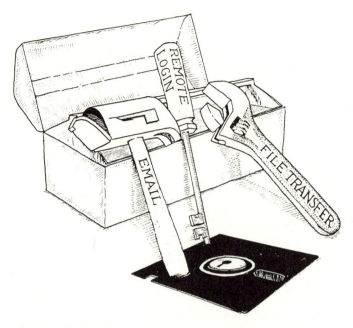

Electronic Mail, File Transfer, and Remote Login are the three basic applications you'll use
on the Internet.

Electronic mail, also known as **email** or **messaging**, is the
most commonly available and most frequently used service on
the Internet. Email lets you send a text message to another person or to a whole group of people. For example, a third-grade
student in Texas can send an email message to a third-grader in
Japan to ask how kids spend their free time there. Or a group of
teachers can have an email conference on using the Internet in
the classroom.

Remote login is an interactive tool that allows you to access
the programs and applications available on another computer.
For example, say Sven, a student at the University of Oslo, is
heading out to a ski vacation in the Rocky Mountains and wants
to check the weather conditions and snowfall there. An Internet
computer at the University of Michigan houses a weather database called the Weather Underground, with temperatures, pre-
cipitation data, and even earthquake alerts for the entire United

States. Sven uses the remote login tool to connect to this computer and interactively query the Weather Underground for the information he needs.

File transfer, the third of the "Big Three" tools, allows files to be transferred from one computer to another. A file can be a document, graphics, software, spreadsheets—even sounds! For example, you may be interested in information on Chernobyl from the Library of Congress's "Glasnost" online exhibit of documents from the former Soviet Union. Using file transfer, you can download those articles from the computer where they're stored onto your own personal computer, where you can read them, print them out, or clip and incorporate parts of them into a paper you're writing.

There are quite a few applications available today that use a combination or variation of these three tools to hide details even further. These operate on a client/server model—that is you use the client on your computer, and it contacts servers for directions and information. Clients and servers don't have to be located in the same geographical area, and in many cases on the Internet, they aren't. This technology is very flexible; during one session, your client may access servers all over the world to help you find information. The client/server concept is explained further in Chapter 4.

As the Internet grows larger, locating the information you need will become difficult unless you're using information discovery and retrieval tools. The major resource-browsing applications, which operate on the client/server concept, include archie, Gopher, WorldWideWeb (WWW), Wide Area Information Servers (WAIS), and Mosaic. Chapter 4 provides explanations for all of these and gets you started in using them.

How Does TCP/IP Work?

When you're actually using the above-mentioned tools, information of various types is being transferred from one computer to another. TCP/IP breaks this information into chunks called **packets**. Each packet contains a piece of the information or document (several hundred characters, or **bytes**), plus some ID tags, such as the addresses of the sending and receiving computers.

Suppose that you wanted to take apart an old covered bridge in New England and move it lock, stock, and barrel to California (people *do* do these things). You would dismantle the sections, label them *very* carefully, and ship them out on three, four, maybe even five different trucks. Some take the northern route and some the southern route, and one has to go through Texas. The trucks get to California at various times, with one arriving a little later than the others, but your careful labels indicate which sections go up first, second, and third.

Each packet, as TCP/IP handles it with its addressing information, can travel just as independently. Because of all the network interconnections, there are often multiple paths to a destination. Just as you might drive a different route to work to save a few minutes here or there, the packets may travel different networks to get to the destination computer. The packets may arrive out of order, but that's okay, because each packet also contains sequence information about where the data it's carrying goes in the document, and the receiving computer can reconstruct the whole enchilada. That's why the Internet is known as a **packet-switched network**. The switches are computers called **routers**, which are programmed to figure out the best packet routes, just as a travel agent might help you find the best flights with the fewest layovers. Routers are the airport hubs of the Internet; they connect the networks and shuttle packets back and forth. The packet is just a chunk of information; it doesn't care (or know) how fast it travels. So it can travel over a "fighter-jet" network—running at Mach-whatever speeds and connecting supercomputers—that interconnects with a "biplane" network operating a lot slower.

The Networks That Make Up the Internet

The Internet network connections don't follow any specific model, but there is a hierarchy of sorts. The high-speed central networks are known as **backbones**. The electronic equivalent of an interstate highway system, they accept traffic from and deliver it to the mid-level networks. An example of such a backbone system is Canada's CA❀net, a nationwide network that connects all its province networks. Australia's Academic and Research Network (AARNet) is a nationwide network connecting its member organizations. Mid-level networks, in turn, take traffic from the backbones and distribute it to member networks, the neighborhood roads of the networking world. For example, the Texas Higher Education Network (THENet) is a mid-level network, connecting over 100 universities and research facilities in Texas. The organizational networks that connect to these nationwide and mid-level backbones may be very big networks themselves. For example, Vienna University in Austria has a large campus network that connects its university departments.

Each of the network links has speed limitations, but speeds are determined by the technology used (not by some "packet policeman"). Wide-area connections are slower than local-area networks. A WAN link is typically 1.544Mbps or 56Kbps. (More and more wide-area networks, however, are starting to operate at 45Mbps.) Local-area networks are much faster. Ethernet, a popular LAN technology, runs at 10Mbps. Compare that with another local-area networking technology, Fiber Distributed Data Interface (FDDI), which runs at 100Mbps. An easy way to understand these speeds is to imagine each of these technologies as a system of water pipes. More water can be pumped through bigger pipes during a given period of time, so they have more bandwidth. Local-area network pipes are usually pretty large, and therefore more water (or data) can be blasted through them than can be pumped (transmitted) during the same amount of time through a wide-area network pipe.

Seamless Worldwide Networking

Once all the pipes—networks—are in place, the Internet, which is actually tens of thousands of networks, looks seamless to the user. By means of internetworking—that is, by connecting networks together to enable communication and information exchange—all the details are hidden from you: the packets, the routers, and all those interconnections. Despite legions of different computers and disparate networks, somehow the whole web works, and any computer directly connected to the Internet can talk to all the other computers on the Internet. So you, working on a computer in your office in Israel or in your spare bedroom in Los Angeles, can communicate with a colleague in South Africa or a friend in Calgary. It's as if you are directly connected by one wire.

WHO RUNS THE INTERNET?

Who controls this web, this cloud, this network of networks? Well, no one, really. The Internet seems to be both institutional and anti-institutional at the same time, massive and intimate, organized and chaotic. In a sense the Internet is an international cooperative endeavor, with its member networks kicking in money, hardware, maintenance, and technical expertise.

The U.S. government has had a big influence on the federally funded parts of the Internet. The National Science Foundation (NSF), as mentioned, initiated the NSFNET in the mid 1980s, a nationwide backbone in the United States that connected many mid-level networks, which in turn connected universities and other organizations. At the time of this writing, the NSFNET production backbone is being phased out and connectivity will be offered by other providers, including commercial networks, in the near future. But you may still hear people refer to the NSF and its influence on the Internet. The NSF funds an experimental high-speed network and will continue to provide funding for a short time to assist universities and schools in getting Internet connections.

The Internet Society

The standards process of the Internet is more centralized, but no less exciting. Development and improvement of TCP/IP protocols is sanctioned by the Internet Society (ISOC), a nonprofit professional organization run by its members (both individuals and

Context Is All

Explaining the magic of networks, Mike Bookey of Digital Network Architects asks you to imagine a car plunked down in the jungle. Checking it out, you might find it a very useful piece of equipment indeed. A multipurpose wonder, it would supply lights, bedding, radio communications, tape player, heat, air conditioning, a shield against arrows and bullets, and a loud horn to frighten away fierce animals. In awe of the features of this machine, you might never realize that the real magic of a car comes in conjunction with asphalt.

For the first 10 years of the personal computer era, according to Bookey, we have used our computers like cars in the jungle. We have plumbed their powers for processing words and numbers. All too often, home computers have ended up in the closet unused. We have often failed to recognize that most of the magic of computing stems from the exponential benefits of interconnection.

Excerpted from "The Issaquah Miracle" by George Gilder (George Gilder's Telecosm), *Forbes ASAP,* June 1993, pp. 114–123.

organizations in various communities, including academic, scientific, and engineering). ISOC is dedicated to encouraging cooperation among computer networks to enable a global research communications infrastructure. The society sponsors several groups that determine the needs of the Internet and propose solutions to meet them. One of these groups is the Internet Architecture Board (IAB), which provides direction to two principal task forces: the Internet Engineering Task Force (IETF), and the Internet Research Task Force (IRTF). The IETF is concerned with operational and technical issues of the Internet, and the IRTF is involved in research and development matters.

Anyone interested in promoting the Internet can become involved in ISOC. Similarly, anyone with great ideas for protocol development and improvement can join the IETF. All you need is desire, the ability to travel to meetings three times a year, and the willingness to volunteer your time in working groups.

The Commercial Internet

Of particular interest to business users are the commercial Internet providers that have sprouted up around the world—in the United States, companies such as UUNET Communications Services, Performance Systems International (PSI), Advanced Network & Services, Inc., Sprintlink, NETCOM On-line Communications Services, and the California Education and Research Federation Network (CERFnet). Many of the commercial networks, such as UUNET, PSI, Sprintlink, and CERFnet, have interconnected their backbone networks to form the Commercial Internet Exchange, or the CIX (pronounced "kicks"). In addition to connecting organizations' networks, all of these commercial providers offer users with modem-equipped PCs and Macs individual access to the Internet. The United States is not the only place where commercial Internet providers have appeared. Quite a few commercial ventures have sprouted up in Australia, Europe, and Japan, for example.

Other projects have the interests of businesses in mind. These include the Enterprise Integration Network (EINet), spearheaded by Microelectronics and Computer Technology Corporation (MCC). EINet offers value-added services, creating an infrastructure purely in support of business and commercial applications. EINet addresses sensitive and complex issues that face organizations who do business online, including security and enhanced electronic mail services.

Another group interested in electronic commerce on the Internet is CommerceNet, a coalition of Silicon Valley (Northern California) organizations. CommerceNet's focus is on commercial use of the Internet, with an emphasis on reliability, security, and ease of use. The coalition hopes to accomplish these goals by developing protocols that address business requirements. Third-party providers can then develop business applications based on these protocols.

(See the Appendix for information about contacting these organizations.)

ACCEPTABLE USE

As you can imagine, with all the people, networks, and government agencies participating in the Internet, there are bound to be rules, restrictions, and policies for parts of it. Probably the best-known document outlining some rules is NSFNET's Acceptable Use Policy (AUP), which basically states that transmission of "commercial" information or traffic (any for-profit activities) is not allowed across the NSFNET backbone, whereas all information in support of academic and research activities is acceptable.

The NSF's AUP is rapidly becoming a non-issue as the networking landscape changes in the United States; the NSFNET production backbone is being phased out, and all the mid-level networks will be obtaining Internet connectivity from other providers. Then it won't matter what type of traffic is sent across it—commercial, research, or academic. But you will probably hear the NSF AUP referenced from time to time, so it's good to know the history behind it.

The situation is changing in places, but the country or network where you get your Internet access may have specific restrictions (such as no commercial use) and acceptable use guidelines (for research and education use only). The Internet as a whole continues to move to support—or at least to allow access to—more and more commercial activity. Users may have to deal with some conflicting policies while that process evolves, but at some point in the near Internet future, free enterprise will likely prevail, and commercial activity will have a defined place, making the whole issue moot. In the meantime, if you're planning to use the Internet for commercial reasons, make sure that the networks you're using support your kind of activity.

Even though the Internet is becoming more commercial, there are still "unwritten" laws that frown upon certain activities, such as direct email advertising. Chapters 3 and 5 discuss some common mistakes to avoid if you're planning on using the Internet for business.

INTERNET CONCEPTS

You'll soon learn how to plunge into the Internet, but before then—as with almost any new adventure in a foreign land— you'll need to acquire a bit of new vocabulary. The basic concepts are simple, and because the network protocols do much of the work, you don't have to become an Internet wizard to travel its highways and byways.

Names and Addresses

If you've ever traveled in a country where you couldn't read the street signs or figure out how they numbered the houses, you'll understand the wisdom of learning the Internet's name and address system. Most computers on the Internet can be identified in two ways. Each computer, or **host**, has a name and a numerical address (both unique), just as most of us can be located by our names or numerically by our phone numbers. It's easier to remember a name than a phone number, and it's the same on the Internet. An Internet computer name is usually several words separated by periods, such as *planet10.yoyodyne.com*. An Internet address—technically an **IP address**—is four numbers also separated by periods, for example, 161.44.128.70.

When you're saying these names and addresses out loud, you should substitute "dot" for "period" to sound as though you belong. This is known as **dotspeak**, and there's a whole lot of it in the Internet. In the examples above, you would say "planet10 dot yoyodyne dot com" and "161 dot 44 dot 128 dot 70."

The idea is for people to use the computers' names when accessing resources, and to let the computers and routers work with the IP addresses. Each Internet-connected organization keeps a database of the names and addresses of all the computers connected to its own networks. Because there are so many computers on the Internet and there is no real central authority, name assignment is best left to the local networks. Imagine if everyone had to get their new phone numbers from Washington, D.C.!

Actually, if you need to register for an IP network number or a domain name (explained below), you'll get close to D.C. The InterNIC Registration Services, run by Network Solutions, Inc., of Herndon, Virginia, provides a central registering authority in the United States for organizations' second-level domain names and network numbers. The InterNIC also registers countries' top-level contact information. Each organization or country then assumes responsibility for assigning names and numbers to its computers.

There are registries for Canada, Europe, Asia-Pacific, and Australia (see the Appendix for contact information). If you're outside the United States, you can contact the U.S. InterNIC, which will forward your request to your country's registration services. You can also query the InterNIC's WHOIS database to find out the contact yourself. Chapter 5 explains how to do this.

If you're an individual user with a PC or Mac and a modem, you probably don't have to worry about registering anything; your Internet provider will take care of that for you. The Inter-NIC does more than register networks and domains, though; Chapter 5 explains about other InterNIC offerings, including user services, resource guides, and training. See the Appendix for InterNIC contact information.

So how does this hostname/IP address stuff work? Suppose you want to learn your way around the subway system of major cities. There's a Subway Navigator on the *metro.jussieu.fr* computer to which you can connect using the remote login tool (you'll learn about Telnet in Chapter 4, but the exact command is **telnet metro.jussieu.fr 10000**). Before you can access this service, a database in France is consulted to find out the IP address of that computer. The address (not the name) is passed on to the routers so that they can make the connection. This is done quickly, automatically, and transparently to you.

Why, then, do you need to know about IP addresses when the system was designed so that you shouldn't ever need to concern yourself with them? The answer, as you may suspect, is that things don't always work perfectly, and there may come a time when you will need to know an IP address to access a resource. For this reason, many resources are often listed with the computer's name and its IP address. The recommended practice is always to use the computer name, since IP numbers—like telephone numbers—can change, while names tend to stay the same.

For those occasions when you need to get a computer's IP address, you might be able to look it up yourself using a "directory assistance" tool like *nslookup* and *dig*. To use either, just invoke them with the name of the computer. For example, **nslookup glas.apc.org** will return the IP address: 193.124.5.33, or the command **dig mtv.com** will return 164.109.15.16 (unless those numbers have changed, which is entirely possible).

Domain Name System. There's actually a method to these names and addresses—a naming system known as the Domain Name System, or DNS. The DNS is also the worldwide system of distributed databases of names and addresses. These databases provide the "translation" from names to numbers and vice versa, a sort of international *Who's Who* of computers. DNS names are constructed in a hierarchical naming fashion, which you can think of as a worldwide organization chart. At the top of this chart are top-level specifications, such as EDU (educational), COM (commercial), GOV (government), MIL (military), ORG (organizations), and NET (networks), and also two-letter country codes, such as US for the United States and CH for Switzerland.

An organization can register for a **domain name**, selecting one of the top-level specifications mentioned above that describes it best, and then preceding it with a recognizable version of its name. For example, the Yoyodyne Software Systems company will have a domain name like *yoyodyne.com*. From there, it can divide itself into subdomains, extending the organization chart to department levels, or it can just give all of its computers names in the *yoyodyne.com* domain.

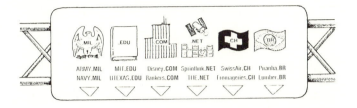

Computer names on the Internet are organized according to the Domain Name System.

Once you understand how this naming system works, you can remember names more easily, and you can also tell things about a computer, such as to what organization it belongs. The names do not, however, always indicate geographical location. For example, *planet10.yoyodyne.com* may be the main computer at the home office in Grovers Mill, New Jersey, *mars.yoyodyne.com* may be at the Hong Kong branch, while *venus.yoyodyne.com* might be located at the Santa Cruz division.

Many U.S. organizations and companies use the three-letter designations mentioned above (for example, EDU, COM, and ORG). However, most countries have stipulated that organizations use their two-letter country codes for top-level domains. For example, an actual computer name, *quake.think.com,* refers to a commercial (COM) enterprise: the computer's name is *quake* and it belongs to Thinking Machines Corporation (*think*), a

"Enough of White Man's ASCII"

Dave Hughes, who is kind of an Internet evangelist, took to the foothills of the Rocky Mountains to work with a group of Native American teenagers at the American Indian Science and Engineering Society's summer school in physics. According to Dave, the kids, who were from the Navajo, Zuni, Crow, Tohono, Sioux, and Picurus Pueblo tribes, "showed polite, quiet interest as I explained the technology and made a local call to the Internet (Colorado Supernet). They laughed a bit, read, and responded to email sent especially to them by Dr. George Johnston, physicist at MIT, whom I asked to directly 'welcome' them to the world of mathematics and physics by telecom.

"Then I said, 'enough of white man's ASCII,' and started calling up the Indian art, the Crow Dance poetry, the new pieces by Lorri Ann Two Bulls, via modem, at 2400 baud. They *really* got excited! Putting questions to me, walking

(Continued)

supercomputer manufacturer in the United States. Another example is *fujitsu.co.jp,* a computer at the Fujitsu Company in Japan (*jp* is the two-letter country code for Japan).

Now you probably have a few questions. After learning about the DNS, every new Internet user first wants to get a list of all the computers on the Internet. After all, you have a telephone directory of all the people in your home area. But there is no exact, up-to-date Internet name and address list available in hard copy or online anywhere.

In the early days of the ARPANET, a list was maintained, but the Internet grew too rapidly to keep up with all the additions and changes. The distributed domain name system has replaced this centrally managed list and has allowed the Internet to grow gracefully.

up to look closer at the full-color VGA monitor, their dark eyes laughing, smiles, and half of them standing up for the rest of the hour-long session. When it was over, a crowd around the machine, picking up copies of the *Online Access Magazine* and *Boardwatch Magazine* I brought, and more questions. And from their obvious tribal knowledge, they were saying 'That's Crow, that's Sioux!' from the colors and symbols in the various pieces of art.

"A heart-warming session with 40 Indian kids who seemed to get a glimpse of a future even they could participate in. And if I am right, by reaching these youth, starting with their own 'images of their inner selves' as Indians produced by such technologies, they may be better able to move on into the world of science, math, and the cold regions of technological and white man's society, while still not losing their identity or associations with each other. Perhaps even doing their life's work as professionals, from the reservation, thanks to these little devices."

Source: Adapted from a posting by Dave Hughes to the Consortium for School Networking Discussion Forum List (COSNDISC@BITNIC) on July 10, 1992.

Internet Resources

While a list of computer names would not be very helpful, a list of online resources is. **Resources** on the Internet are all of the useful things that you can access: hardware such as super-computers, graphics labs, computer centers, or printers, and online information, like the wealth of databases, documents, software, archives, pictures, and sounds available. Resources can also be people. If you can talk to a group of people to figure out the answer to a question or problem, they are a resource; so are mailing lists and conferencing systems. An online forum on school networking or a work group on molecular biology are both Internet resources. Your understanding of the astonishing array of Internet resources, and how to get at them, will grow as you learn your way around the Internet.

Internet or Outernet?

To better understand what the Internet is, you also need to understand what the Internet is *not* and what networks are *not on* the Internet. A number of worldwide networks use protocols other than TCP/IP and provide their own sets of services. Some don't allow remote login, while some employ different file transfer methods; many have a special connection to the Internet. These connections are not, however, the seamless web that was mentioned earlier, where the participating networks interoperate to allow the same services. Instead, these are connections of convenience, that—like marriages of the same sort—have their purposes but not a lot of other interaction.

Networks on the outside are called **outernets**, but understanding the distinction between outernets and the Internet can be difficult. Because of the differing governments and languages involved in the Internet and the outernets, there's only one basic service—electronic mail—that currently can move between them. Electronic mail moves from the Internet to the outernets through **email gateways**, the connecting points that translate the different email protocols of each network. Most academic and commercial outernets have established email gateways to the Internet. This worldwide system of networks and gateways is sometimes called the **Matrix**. Some network cartographers apply this term to the electronic regions discovered during their virtual journeys all over the world via electronic undergrounds and mazes; it's meant to encompass all the possible email passageways.

The Matrix is also sometimes called **the Net** by citizens of all networks. This term is ambiguous because it doesn't refer to any one network, but it works well in referring to the overall worldwide situation. If you hear someone say that he's "on the Net," it probably means that he can be contacted by email.

It's interesting to note that many computers on outernets these days have DNS names, so it may only *look* as though they're connected to the Internet. There's a neat feature in the DNS that allows for **Mail Exchange** (MX) computers. An MX computer is a gateway that's connected to the Internet and that

Email gateways allow Internet users to send electronic mail to people on other networks.

is willing—meaning that an arrangement has been made—to transfer email to an outernet computer. Instead of finding an IP address for the outernet computer in the database, the DNS obtains an **MX record**, or the name of the Internet computer that will deliver the email to the outernet computer. All of this should be transparent to the user, making it easier to send and receive electronic mail between the Internet and outernet networks. Which outernets have email gateways to the Internet? More every day, but some of the well-known international networks are FidoNet, a cooperative network made up mostly of microcomputers linked via telephone lines; BITNET (Because It's Time Network), an academic and research network; and UUCP, a network of computers that talk to one another over dial-up connections using UUCP (Unix-to-Unix Copy Protocol). Commercial networks, including CompuServe, MCImail, and Genie, have made connections too. As time goes on, more and more commercial networks are connecting directly to the Internet and are offering full Internet services to their customers. America Online and Delphi are two such services.

Network News

Another service available on many of these networks is called
network news. "News" in this context doesn't refer to current
events from the news wires but to discussions; it usually means
interest groups and conferences. There are thousands and thousands of different discussion groups on topics ranging from artifi-
cial intelligence to recipes, from politics to sex, from ornithology
to skydiving—some collectively generating the equivalent of a
book about the size of this one each day. News is transmitted on
the USENET network, which has special relationships and connections with some of the networks previously mentioned. For
example, USENET news can be transmitted across and between
the Internet and UUCP networks, allowing citizens of both cultures to participate. The protocol that is used to transport news
over the Internet is called Network News Transfer Protocol
(NNTP). USENET is "on its own," however, and no one person or
organization controls it. It's a huge cooperative anarchy, with
several million people participating worldwide.

Even though USENET is closely related to the Internet, and a
lot of its traffic travels over the Internet, USENET is *not* the
Internet. Many people who have access to USENET news don't
have Internet connections; similarly, Internet connectivity
doesn't always provide access to USENET news. Also, note that
USENET is a conferencing system, and is not considered an email
network.

Now that you know what the Internet is and what it's not,
it's time to get on with learning to use it. Conferencing, email,
and interactive online conversations are the most exciting new
developments in communications since the advent of the telephone. If you think the fax machine is great, wait until you try
the Internet! With just your fingers on the keyboard, you can
reach around the world.

Chapter 3

COMMUNICATING WITH PEOPLE

A network neophyte, faced with a cryptic computer prompt, may find it hard to picture the Internet as a friendly, peopled place. But every day, hundreds of thousands of people are communicating through the Internet—conversing, collaborating, working, playing, and letting off steam. Friendships—even marriages—are made and broken on the Internet. Clubs are formed. Problems are solved. Books like this one are written. Jobs are found. Handicaps and disabilities make no difference. Through email and the other methods of online communication, people have become best friends without ever seeing or talking to each other. It is not uncommon for people to turn to the Net for answers; a question posted to online communities—mailing lists and conferences—can yield dozens of invaluable tales of experiences and testimonials within hours.

Online communication, perhaps the ultimate in democratic exchange of information, eliminates barriers. You can't make judgments about whom you're "talking" to based on appearance, or even on voice. People can be whomever they want to be. Shy people become bold. Children give their views to adults, and the adults listen. Accounting clerks communicate on the same level as CEOs.

On the Internet, people can communicate asynchronously and in real time. Translation? **Asynchronous** (Greek for "not at the same time") communication means that someone can type in a message and send it off, but the recipient doesn't have to be around to receive it. This type of communication has some real benefits. You can send messages whenever you want to, they reach their destination quickly, and the recipients can read and respond when *they* want to. Answering machines and voice mail are everyday examples of asynchronous communication. **Real-time**, interactive communication (such as the Internet Relay Chat facility described later in this chapter), in contrast, means that as someone is "talking"—that is, typing—you see it on your screen as it is typed. Real-time audio and video conferencing is starting to become more prevalent on the Internet too. Both types of communication, asynchronous and real-time, are covered in this chapter.

ALL (OR ALMOST ALL) ABOUT ELECTRONIC MAIL

Electronic mail is the most popular application on the Internet today. It's a very powerful tool that's simple to use and easy to understand. Using email can give you a real feeling for the energy and reach of the Net. It's hard to imagine any other form of communication that can be so intimate and yet so wide-reaching, so focused, or so expansive. You can communicate as easily with someone across twelve time zones as with someone in the same building. Your message can be limited to just one person, or it can reach hundreds of kindred souls.

Email is sometimes compared to fax, but there are some fundamental differences. A fax is a graphic image that is digitized and sent over regular telephone lines using modems. Electronic mail on the Internet is, for the most part, text that can be sent over a variety of network links—everything from dial-up to fiber-optic lines. It usually costs the same to send email to one person as it does to send it to a group of people, while it would cost more (in time and maybe paper) to send a fax to those same people, especially if they're a long-distance call away. Both are asynchronous forms of communication, eliminating "telephone tag"—that is, it's not required for the recipient to be present to receive either electronic mail or a fax. Interestingly enough, there are some projects on the Internet that combine the capabilities of both fax and email, and while interest is growing, the ubiquitous ability to fax over the Internet is not available just yet. Even so, these technologies will continue to collide, and someday you won't be able to tell the difference. One such project is a worldwide experiment in remote printing involving several countries. For example, a librarian using this experimental system in Canberra, Australia, could send a fax from his Internet-connected workstation to a remote printer (fax machine) in Riverside, California. (To obtain an article that explains this experiment, send email to *tpc-faq@town.hall.org*.)

Historically, Internet email has been text-based without some of the frills that many local-area, network-based email systems have. Text-based means that the message is only words— just like what you're reading right now—and can't include graphics, forms, and so on. Internet email is starting to branch out with some implementations, including the ability to query distributed directory databases (an online directory service for people's email addresses), encode/decode messages for privacy purposes (see the "Security Issues" section in Chapter 5), and send formats other than just text, such as graphic images, sounds, and different character sets (Asian language text, for example) using Multi-purpose Internet Mail Extensions, commonly referred to as MIME.

The reason you need something like MIME is that the current Internet email system cannot transfer a non-text file (such as a picture) without doing something special to it—there are funny characters in these files that can mess up their transfer. If you have a need to transfer non-text documents via email, be sure to inquire whether or not your provider's email application offers MIME support. If it does, you can "attach" sounds, word-processed files, or software, and send them off. The only catch is that the recipient of your message must have MIME capability to receive your attachments. And unfortunately, it's still not available everywhere.

There are other ways of sending software and graphics within a message if you don't have MIME support. Many email applications (some are mentioned below) support automatic con-

Normal Heroes Always Make a Detour

In 1990, after 15 years as editor, journalist, translator, and head of the Moscow News Computer Department, Anatoly Voronov started exchanging email with Dave Caulkins, an American setting up GlasNet in Russia. Their offices were three blocks apart, but their messages went through the Moscow Teleport host in San Francisco, which had a connection to the Internet. Voronov ascribed the roundabout routing to the famous principle expounded in the Russian movie classic *Atbolit-66*, "Normal'niye geroi vsegda idut v obkhod" (Normal heroes always make a detour).

GlasNet became fully operational in 1991, with Voronov

(Continued)

version of non-text files into ASCII format; that way, those funny codes in the binary file are converted to something the mail system can handle (plain text) without burping. One such program that's sensitive to the Internet's email digestive system and can convert binary files to text is called BinHex, and it's available for both Macs and PCs. To you, BinHex files will look like a bunch of nonsense—random characters—on the screen (they begin with the line, "This file must be converted with BinHex . . ."). If you receive one of these in your email or through other means (and it's not automatically converted for you), you'll need the BinHex utility to transform the file to its original format, a binary file. (See the Appendix for information on obtaining BinHex.)

Sending Email

Email is really fast—it is sent and received in seconds, minutes at the most. Postal mail is often called **snail mail** in comparison. Sending email is easy, too. All you need is access to the Internet,

on staff. This time the San Francisco connection went
through PeaceNet, a "detour" that proved very helpful during
the August coup d'état. "Our traffic grew tenfold," Voronov
remembers. "We got hundreds of 'get-well messages' from all
over the world. I remember a posting from a Chinese student
in America, a participant in the Tiananmen Square events in
Beijing, offering to share his personal experiences of how to
beat tanks in the heart of the city.

"People wondered why the KGB didn't cut our connection. I wonder too. I think they simply didn't know that we
existed. And we had a trick: the UUCP connection was
originated in San Francisco, because at that time a non-
authorized person or organization could not call abroad from
Moscow. And it was impossible even for KGB to cut the
phone link of the whole of Moscow."

an email program, and the email address of the person with
whom you wish to communicate.

Access to the Internet. Chapter 2 discussed the differences
between being directly connected to the Internet and being on
an outernet network such as UUCP or BITNET, or a commercial
service like America Online or CompuServe. If you have access
on any of these networks, then you can exchange email on the
Internet.

Email Programs. You'll need an email program that will run
on your own microcomputer or on whatever computer you're
using. Most large systems and public-access computers offer several email programs (sometimes called email readers or user
agents). Some commercial Internet service providers will supply
programs to load on your PC or Mac. A common characteristic of
email programs is that they let you compose and send email, and
then read and organize the email you receive. There are many

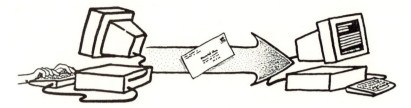

Internet email is usually sent to its destination in seconds.

different email programs; some of the more popular ones are listed below. Your choice of a program will depend on how you're accessing the Internet. If you aren't sure what's available, ask your system gurus for assistance.

Post Office Email Programs

If you're accessing the Internet using a PC or Macintosh, there are several different ways you can read and send email. Some of the more popular applications use the Post Office Protocol (POP). In a nutshell, the POP system allows your personal workstation to get its email from a big computer that serves as a post office, delivering the mail when you (or your computer) ask for it. This eliminates the need for your computer to be on all the time, constantly available to receive email. In order to use a POP-based email application, you need Internet access (via dial-up or full-time connectivity) and a POP mail account on a post office computer (ask your Internet provider). All of these applications provide intuitive editors. See the Appendix for information on obtaining POP service.

Email Addresses. The next big step on your agenda is to learn about email addresses. In order to send someone email, you need to know the person's address. An email address, like a postal mail address, contains all the necessary information needed to deliver a message to someone.

Internet email addresses are, in fact, very simple. They consist of a *local part* and a *host part*. The **username** refers to the mailbox, login name, or userid of the recipient on that computer. For example, if your friend Dave logs in on his computer as *letterman*, then that's his username. The host part of the address should be recognizable to you—a series of words separated by dots, as discussed in the domain name section of Chapter 2. The local part and host part of an email address are separated by an "@" sign:

```
username@hostname
```

Suppose that you know that Dave's computer name is *sullivan-theater.cbs.com.* You could send email to him using this address: *letterman@sullivan-theater.cbs.com.* (This and the following David Letterman examples are fictitious.)

Sending It Off. Once you have an email program and know the recipient's email address, you're ready to send a message. Each email program is different, so if you're not familiar with yours, you may have to fumble around a bit or actually read the manual or online documentation. You will need to specify that you want to *send* a message, either by typing **send**, clicking a *send* button, or by performing some other wonderful computer incantation. The email program will prompt you for information, asking for the recipient's email address, the key piece of information the program needs to send the message to the recipient. It will also ask for the subject of your message—usually a summary, title, or brief description. The subject is optional, but you should get into the practice of including it. A good subject description makes the person to whom you're sending aware of the nature of your message, whether it's important or whimsical. The program may give you the option of sending a "carbon copy" (cc) message. If there's someone else you think would be interested in the message, here's a chance to include his or her address. (You can send carbon copies to more than one recipient.) If you have the disk space, it's a good idea to send a copy to yourself so you'll have a record of your outgoing messages. (Or your email program may automatically save outgoing messages for you.)

Trading Places: New Dimensions to Interlibrary Loans

Paula Garrett of Batavia, Illinois, and Katie Wilson of Sydney, Australia, in an effort to see how the other half lives, traded homes and jobs for six months. Both are librarians, so no career changes were involved. However, taking over someone else's work habits is indeed a learning experience. About the only thing the women didn't trade were salaries or mortgage payments!

The venture was a complete success because of the Internet and the Australia Academic and Research Network (AARNet), according to Katie. "Such exchanges can take place without the Internet, but not as successfully as ours! We found it made a huge difference to be able to keep up with our jobs and keep things flowing smoothly. Six months was not a very long time in which to learn the jobs, and they are senior with a lot of responsibility, so the constant email communication helped us hold it all together! Plus we used the Internet to plan the whole thing." There's no question that the Internet has helped end the cloistered image of librarians.

There may come a day when you'll need to know exactly what you said to someone!

After you've answered all the email program prompts, you can compose your message, using your email program's editor, which may or may not be similar to the word processor with which you're familiar. It's important to make your message easy to read and understand; some hints for effective communication are discussed in detail in the "Netiquette" section of this chapter.

Anatomy of an Email Message

An email message has two basic parts, the "header" information and the body of the message. These pieces are separated by a blank line. In most cases, you'll be interested only in the body, or

the actual text, of the message. The headers contain items such
as "Date:", "cc:", "From:", and "Subject:". Sometimes there are
seemingly arcane lines such as "Received:" and "Message-Id."
These normally don't concern you, but they are necessary for the
email programs and for debugging purposes. Following is a
sample message:

```
From letterman@sullivan-theater.cbs.com Fri Feb 4 11:51:36
EST 1994
Received: by sullivan-theater.cbs.com id AA06414 (5.65+/
IDA-1.3.5.for melman); Fri Feb 4 94 11:51:35 -0500
From: David Letterman <letterman@sullivan-theater.cbs.com>
Message-Id: <9402041651.AA06414@sullivan-theater.cbs.com>
Subject: Tonight's Show
To: melman@sullivan-theater.cbs.com
Cc: letterman@sullivan-theater.cbs.com
Date: Fri, 4 Feb 94 11:51:34 EST
Status: OR

Larry "Bud",

For tonight's show, we'd like you to stand on your head
and sing the theme song to The Jetsons. And this time,
please try to be a good sport and don't scare the
children.

Thanks,

Dave
```

In this made-up example, David Letterman has sent email to
Larry Bud, asking him for a favor. Dave sent this message on Friday, February 4, at 11:51 in the morning, with the subject
Tonight's Show. He cc'd himself (so he has a record of his correspondence with Larry "Bud").

Receiving and Keeping Up with the Mail

Receiving email requires less effort than sending it. Incoming
messages are stored in your **inbox**. When you fire up your email

program, it fetches your mail from an online mailbox (if there's anything in it), and then usually displays a one-line summary for each message in there. This summary will include information such as the message number, the date the message was sent, the sender, and the subject. You can select which message you want to read by typing the corresponding number, or by selecting it with your mouse.

Here's an example of a message summary line:

```
1   Feb 4   David Letterman   (20)   Tonight's Show
```

This is message number 1 in Larry "Bud's" email box. It was sent February 4 by David Letterman. In this example, the number in parentheses indicates the number of lines in the message (20), but it could refer to the number of characters too. And the last column is the subject of David's message, "Tonight's Show."

If you think you can't keep up with the junk mail that flows into your snail-mailbox each day, then just wait until you collect dozens of "keypals" and you're busily exchanging messages every day. Most everyone *loves* to get email—it will probably give you a tiny thrill to see the message, "You have new mail," when you check your electronic mailbox. But because it's so easy to send and receive email, you may find that you can't keep up with all the messages you receive! You should set up a good routine for sorting your mail, deleting trivial messages, and filing the rest by saving them in separate electronic **folders** sorted by people or topics. If you don't keep up with your email efficiently, your messages will stack up in the inbox as they proliferate, and your email program may slow to a crawl. Your email program may allow you to sort incoming messages by date, sender, subject, size, or in other ways, and these functions can help you dispense of messages quickly.

Replying to Email

Email programs usually have some kind of "reply" feature to make responding quick and easy. For your part, this involves typing **reply**, or clicking a *reply* button with your mouse. The reply feature takes care of filling in the address and subject fields (using information in the original message's header), and puts you in the email message composer. A very common convention when replying to messages is to include the original message within your reply message, with each line prefaced by a ">" character (or just three spaces). Your email program may automatically do this for you or provide a command that does it. That way, people can distinguish between their original comments and your response. It may not seem important to provide explicit reference to parts of the original message, but some people receive so many messages that they may not remember your conversation without some background material.

The header lines will alert you to reply messages. For example, "Re:" will precede the original subject line, and there may also be an "In-Reply-to" line.

Sometimes you can carry on entire conversations, keeping track of who said what by how many ">" signs are in front of comments. You may want to edit out irrelevant parts of the conversation to eliminate some of the resulting confusion.

Bounced Email and Other Errors

Sometimes an email message may not actually reach its destination because of an incorrect address or some other error. Just as postal mail may come back to you stamped "Returned to Sender," you may get a **bounced message** back wrapped in an error message that gives you some clues as to what went wrong. Most often the problem is something you've mistyped in the address. One common error message is *User unknown*: the message is received by the computer specified in the address, but the local part, or username, doesn't match any username or mailbox on the computer. Most often, the cause is a typo or a misspelling, but if you think you typed it correctly, then you should contact the person you're trying to reach by other means to find out the correct username.

Another common error is *Host unknown*; in this case, the hostname is wrong. Again, check for typos first. Sometimes parts of the name are missing—for example, perhaps you forgot to include part of the domain name.

Other bounced messages—such as *Network unreachable,* (the computer) *Can't send for several days, Connection timed out* or *Connection refused,* and *Bad file number*—usually have something to do with problems on the network or at the destination computer. These problems are usually beyond your control, so you should contact your system consultants for assistance.

Most of the time, if you type something wrong or have an incorrect address, you will get a bounced message. Sometimes, however, your email will simply disappear into the elusive **black hole**, the place where lost messages go and where they'll never be heard from again—or at least that's what it feels like. There are several possible causes of this phenomenon. The message may arrive at the intended destination, where an error is detected, but because your own return address is incorrect, the bounced message can't be sent to you. Or, the message may arrive safe and sound, but your friend never reads it or decides not to respond to it. Usually, trying again, using another addressing method, or contacting your friend by other means to find out if the message was received will help you figure out what went wrong.

Finding Email Addresses

Probably the most frequent burning question from new users is how to find out someone's email address. Unfortunately, there's no comprehensive Internet-wide directory assistance available at this time, as there is for finding out telephone numbers in many countries. There are ways, though, to find email addresses, and the more proficient you become in using the Internet, the more tricks you'll be able to use. There's no law, of course, that prevents you from just calling someone and asking. In fact, if you are clueless, this is probably the first thing you should do to save yourself some time!

A new trend these days is to include email addresses on business cards, so when trying to reach a business associate, check there first. Or just guess—a frequently used and often successful method, believe it or not! For example, if you know where someone works, you can guess at the domain name (like *kodak.com*). Many organizations now allow email to be delivered to *person-name@domain-name,* where *person-name* is either the person's last name or the first and last name separated by a dot (as in *paul.shaffer*). As in the company mailroom, an email "hub" at the *domain-name* may distribute all the email to the correct computers internally. This is not standard, though, so don't count on it working every time.

Online directory service databases are springing up around the Internet. Many organizations have their own online "white pages," named after the white pages in phone books, but they are by no means universal. Some of these are mentioned in Chapter 5.

Sending Email to Other Networks

As was mentioned in Chapter 2, electronic mail is the one application that can be sent between the Internet and outernets. Most networks offer an electronic mail service, and many are connecting to the Internet by email gateways. (Remember, email gateways are computers that have connections to both networks and know how to translate the different email languages between those networks.) For example, if you have a friend or client who has an account on CompuServe, and you're on the Internet, you can send electronic mail to him or her, and vice versa.

Sometimes, sending email between networks is a bit tricky because you might have to specify a little bit more information in the email address, such as the actual name of the email gateway. If you have to do that, your email address might look like this:

```
username%hostname@gateway-hostname
```

Here, the email will be sent to *gateway-hostname,* which will then deliver it to the *username* at the *hostname.* For example:

```
daves-mom%olympics.bitnet@norway.olympics.org
```

This would send the message to *daves-mom* at the *olympics* node (which is part of the BITNET network) through the *norway. olympics.org* gateway.

FROM THE INTERNET TO THE OUTERNETS

Internet to:	Syntax
America Online	user@**aol.com**
Applelink	user@**applelink.apple.com**
ATTMail	user@**attmail.com**
BITNET	user@host.**bitnet**
	user%host.**bitnet**@gateway
	May need to specify an email
	gateway, such as **cunyvm.cuny.edu**
CompuServe	userid@**compuserve.com**
	Convert the "," in the CompuServe
	userid to a "."
	Example, **12345,678** becomes
	12345.678@compuserve.com
MCIMail	userid@**mcimail.com**
	Eliminate the hyphen in the userid.
	Example MCI address:
	123-4567 becomes
	1234567@mcimail.com
Prodigy	user@**prodigy.com**
UUCP	user@host.**uucp**
	user%host.**uucp**@gateway
	user@domain-name
	(if UUCP node has a DNS name)

In the preceding table, words in **bold** should be copied literally when
constructing an email address. Words in *italics* should be replaced
with the appropriate host, username, or gateway name. This table
lists the most common syntaxes for sending email from the Internet to
another network. If these don't work for you, contact your system
consultants. Note that some commercial services charge a small fee
for incoming and outgoing Internet messages. Many, many more
networks have connections to the Internet. For more information and
references, see the Appendix.

The MX records that were mentioned in Chapter 2 may come into play and bail you out. If the outernet computer to which you're sending email has a Domain Name System (DNS) name, then you can just use that. You don't need to specify a gateway explicitly; the DNS database will figure it out for you. In fact, you probably won't have to address email this way because nearly everyone has changed over to DNS. But it doesn't hurt to know about it in case someday you have to specify an email gateway.

CONFERENCING: GROUP SPEAK

You can limit your email use to swapping "letters"—just like your regular snail mail, only faster—but its electronic nature allows another dimension entirely. Imagine a newsletter focused on your interests, where every subscriber is also a writer, and the articles and information all flow around in hours or days instead of weeks or months. Imagine being able to send a question to a group and receive responses from twelve different people from all over the world in a matter of hours. Online conferencing can do just that. Some discussions and conferences are more opinion-centered than work-centered, like a newspaper's editorial page, except that the opinions, commentary, and letters are all online and are sent to every member of the list or newsgroup, not just to the editor. There are interest groups for everyone, centered on business, academia, research, games, humor, or hobbies—you name it. The possibilities for information sharing, problem solving, and—let's admit it—recreation are staggering.

Email Lists

Once you start using the Internet, you'll notice people talking about joining **lists** and participating in discussions on various subjects. They're referring to **electronic mailing lists**, which are group discussions or interest groups. Email lists can involve as few as two people or as many as tens of thousands. There are

Send one message to many people on an Internet email list.

literally thousands of different mailing lists on subjects ranging from cooking to etymology, from music to genealogy. And if there's not a list on a subject you are interested in, then you might be able to create one yourself. (Creating an Internet email list requires that you have the resources—a multi-user, directly connected computer, and knowledge of email system administration—to do so, or know someone else who does. Directions for doing this are beyond the scope of this book. Just ask around. Many times someone will volunteer to help you.)

A mailing list is simply a list of email addresses of people interested in a certain subject. Each list has its own distribution address, which looks just like the email addresses described above. All you have to do to get involved in an interest group is to request to be added or "subscribed" to it by sending email to the list administrator, which is either a regular human being or an automated list maintenance program. Your email address will be added to the list, and you'll start receiving discussion contributions from other list members. You may reply to these messages or send new thought-provoking topics at any time. Any message you send to the email list address will be distributed to every member of that list. You don't *have* to participate actively by sending messages all the time; you can just "listen" to the discussion. Such listeners are often called **lurkers** (with no derogatory connotation).

```
The Eggplant Lovers Electronic Mail List
List name:        Eggplant Lovers
Description:      An interest group for people who
                  love eggplants.
List address:     eggplant@vegetable.org
List members:     melman@sullivan-theater.cbs.com
                  Stephen_Cavrak@uvm.edu
                  sestrada@aldea.com
    ¡             pparker@oak.zilker.net
                  annie@hiney.com
```

How to Subscribe. To subscribe to an email list on the Internet, generally speaking, you send a subscription request to the list's administrative address, which is different and separate from the actual list address. In most cases, the administrative address name is the list address name with-*request* added to the end of it. Let's use our Eggplant Lovers list example above. If this list really existed and you wanted to subscribe to it, you would send email to the administrative address:

eggplant-request@vegetable.org

and then state your request in the body of the message. (For example: "I'd like to subscribe to the eggplant list, please. My email address is . . .") The list administrator will add you to the list and you'll start receiving any messages sent from fellow eggplant lovers. (You can also *un*subscribe with a similar request sent to the same address.) A common new-user mistake is to send subscription requests to the regular list address—a quick way to annoy the other list members, because it adds unnecessary mail to their already burgeoning inboxes. So don't forget about the administrative address.

The bottom line is to remember to read carefully any instructions or associated descriptions of email lists. Some may tell you to subscribe (and unsubscribe) by sending a sequence of commands to an automated list program (with a name like the below-mentioned LISTSERV, or Majordomo and Listproc); other lists are handled by humans.

LISTSERV

A cousin to the Internet email list is the BITNET LISTSERV. You will hear LISTSERV mentioned a lot because there are hundreds and hundreds of interesting LISTSERV groups. You may want to join one, so it's important to know what they are. Remember that BITNET is an outernet-type network, and the only application that can be sent between it and the Internet is electronic mail.

LISTSERV, which gets its name from "list server," is an automatic discussion list service. It's a program that runs on a BITNET computer (or BITNET node) and handles all the list administrative functions, such as subscribing and unsubscribing people to and from interest groups. There isn't such a powerful automatic list maintainer in widespread use on the Internet yet, where most subscription requests are still processed by an actual person, a maintainer of each list.

A LISTSERV accepts commands requesting different actions, such as subscribing to a list or listing members of a group. On BITNET these commands can be sent to the LISTSERV using an interactive message facility. If you're coming from the Internet, however, you have to send commands within an email message to the LISTSERV address. After the LISTSERV performs the requested functions, it will send you a status report via email so that you will know what happened.

Now, here's the tricky part. The actual BITNET interest group will also have a different email address from that of the LISTSERV. What this means is that discussion messages are sent to the list address, while commands are sent to the *LISTSERV* address. Many people get these two confused and end up sending LISTSERV commands to the actual list, where everyone gets a copy of your command message. Here's an example so you'll understand the difference. You want to join the Late Night Infomercial Reviews discussion group (fabricated for the purposes of this book, but it does have possibilities!). The list address for this example is *INFOMERCIAL@CABLETV*. The LISTSERV address is *LISTSERV@CABLETV*.

Note that BITNET addresses are different from Internet addresses. A BITNET computer name is easy to recognize because it's usually one word (no dots), and sometimes is cryptic-looking. When you're sending email from the Internet *to* BITNET, you will need to alert your computer to that fact. Usually you can just append *.bitnet* to the end of the BITNET node name and your system will know how to deal with it. In some cases, however, you may need to specify the actual email gateway, as mentioned above.

Since you want to subscribe to this list, you should send an email message to the LISTSERV address:

`LISTSERV@CABLETV.bitnet`

Remember, you always send list *commands* to the LISTSERV address, *not* the actual mailing list address. It's the LISTSERV program that takes care of these administrative functions. Within the body of the message (you don't have to put anything in the subject field), you have to type the following command:

SUBSCRIBE INFOMERCIAL Susan Powter

(This is assuming your name is Susan Powter. If it isn't, then substitute your own name.) As you can see in this example, the *LISTSERV SUBSCRIBE* command is easy:

SUBSCRIBE *List-Name Your-Name*

Your-Name should be your name as you usually write it, *not* your userid or email address. (The LISTSERV gets your email address from the message header, not the body.)

Once you've put this command in the body of the message, you can send it. You should receive a welcome message saying that you are subscribed and giving you some important information about the list. You'll then get messages reviewing the latest in get-rich schemes and weight loss programs. Now, if you want to participate in the discussion—that is, send messages to this list—you should send email to the list address, *not* the LISTSERV address. So in this example you would send your contribution to *INFOMERCIAL@CABLETV.bitnet*. If you want to unsubscribe, repeat the steps above, sending email to the LISTSERV address, but instead of the *SUBSCRIBE* command, you type *SIGNOFF INFOMERCIAL*. That's it.

There are many other LISTSERV commands besides *SUB-SCRIBE* and *SIGNOFF*. If you're interested in learning more about these commands, send email to *LISTSERV@BITNIC.bitnet,* with the command **INFO REFCARD** in the body of the message. You'll receive an email message containing a list of general user commands from the LISTSERV at the BITNET Network Information Center (BITNIC).

List Caveats

If you join an Internet email or LISTSERV list, how much traffic will you receive? That depends. Some lists aren't very active at all, so you might see only a few messages a week. Other lists can become very animated, however, so you'll receive dozens of messages a day. Many people get really excited about joining lists and subscribe to a whole lot of them. Then they get more email than they can handle. It's a good idea to keep track of the lists to which you've subscribed. That way, if you go on vacation for an extended period and don't want to deal with hundreds (or thousands) of email messages when you return, you can unsubscribe to all of the groups on your list (LISTSERV gives you the ability to temporarily turn off or postpone receipt of messages while you're away).

The amount of traffic an interest group generates can be reduced considerably if members avoid sending unnecessary messages to the whole list—for example, subscription requests and "I agree" or "Me too" responses. Don't get "reply happy" and feel that you need to respond publicly to every question that someone sends.

Often people use the reply feature in their mail program to offer a contribution to or continue a discussion, or to send a private message to the originator of the message. A word of warning here. You should *always* check to see to *whom* you're replying: is it the message sender or the entire list? Each email program is different, so you should familiarize yourself with your particular reply feature.

Picture this Maalox moment: You see a message from your best friend on an email list. She has made a contribution to a discussion. You want to reply to her personally and tell her about your bad day and how much you can't stand your boss, so you hit the *reply* button. You use words you shouldn't. You get descriptive in places. You finish the message and away it goes—to every single person on the list, including your boss! As unbelievable as it sounds, it happens all the time. The moral of the story is that you should always double-check to be sure your reply message is going to the right recipients. Either that, or stock up on the antacid pills.

Finding Lists

There are a lot of lists out there, and they can change quickly. You can download some online "Lists of Lists" and peruse them to find out which groups are for you. Just browsing the A's in one such List-of-Lists, you can find interest groups on Addictions, Art, and Animal Rights. Quite a range. The Appendix tells you where to access some online email list catalogs.

Network News

USENET was mentioned briefly in Chapter 2. It's a worldwide conferencing system, encompassing all sorts of organizations (universities, commercial enterprises, government agencies, even home computers) and supporting one service—news. USENET is a real community. People from all walks of life spend hours "together," reading, contributing ("posting"), and responding. Each group has its regulars, its "Norm Petersons." Others come and go. Some "lurk," while others seem to talk incessantly.

USENET is a breeding ground for free expression and thought. People are usually very frank on this network! It's a point of pride that USENET, for the most part, is an open and uncensored environment. As a result, some very explicit and candid discussions ensue, from political arguments, to religious

USENET newsgroups are forums for all kinds of interests and topics.

opinions and holy wars, to explicit stories with indecent themes. Be aware of this if you're easily offended, and simply avoid the groups that focus on subjects unpalatable to you.

USENET is divided into **newsgroups**. Devoted to a certain topic, each newsgroup is made up of **articles** or **postings** that look like email messages (each has a header and a message body). There are thousands of different newsgroups on USENET, but not every computer or site gets all of these in its USENET **feed**. Each site can pick which newsgroups it wants to "carry" or let its users participate in. Why wouldn't a site want to provide every single newsgroup? One reason is that volume of daily traffic is huge (over a 100 megabytes per day), and it takes up valuable disk space. Or the site may be paying long-distance charges to transmit and receive traffic, so it participates only in a small number of groups. Another very common reason is that some of the newsgroups deal with explicit subjects that may not be appropriate to carry.

USENET newsgroups are similar to email lists, but there are a few differences. With Internet email lists, every message is sent to each person who has explicitly requested to be a participant. On USENET, every newsgroup article is received and stored on *each* participating USENET *computer*, instead of being sent to each user. Even when you're not participating in a newsgroup, all of its articles are still stored on the computer, so you have easy access to any you want. It's difficult to know how many people participate or lurk in each newsgroup. Something you say might be read by as few as five people, or by as many as 100,000.

USENET Hierarchy and Newsgroup Names. Newsgroups are organized in a hierarchical structure; their names have dots in them, just like Internet domain names. The top-level (leftmost) word in the newsgroup name specifies the newsgroup's category. There are seven major USENET top-level categories, and a scattering of alternative categories, as shown below. Knowing what these categories mean can help you figure out what each newsgroup is about.

Access to USENET. As was noted at the end of Chapter 2, not everyone on the Internet has access to USENET. There's no one way to tell if you can participate, but with a little bit of sleuthing, you might have a better idea. Most universities and individual commercial Internet providers provide access to USENET newsgroups. Many businesses carry a subset (or all) of the groups. Remember, you can (and should) always call your provider's help desk and ask.

News Readers. In order to read or post news, you need to have a news reader program. There are thousands of newsgroups, and you don't want to have to sift through every one of them. A news reader will let you select which newsgroups you want to participate in by allowing you to "subscribe" to them (without having to send email to an administrator). The reader program will organize the newsgroups, display the articles for you to read, and allow you to post articles. Just as there are many email programs, there are many news readers. Some are user-friendly, while others use terse commands and are difficult to learn.

You'll have to get used to how your news reader works and how it displays newsgroups and articles. Some readers offer a "threaded" function that organizes articles within a newsgroup according to discussion threads—a helpful feature if you want to

MAJOR USENET HIERARCHY CATEGORIES

Category	Explanation
comp	Computer hardware, software, and protocol discussions.
misc	Topics that don't fit anywhere else, such as job hunting, investments, real estate, and fitness.
news	Groups that deal with USENET software, network administration, and informative documents and announcements.
rec	Recreational subjects and hobbies, such as aviation, games, music, and cooking.
sci	Topics in the established sciences, such as space research, logic, mathematics, and physics.
soc	Groups for socializing or discussing social issues or world culture.
talk	Lengthy debates and discussions on various current events and issues—politics, religion, the environment, and so forth.

SOME ALTERNATIVE HIERARCHIES

Category	Explanation
alt	Alternative group of discussions—not carried by all USENET sites. Some are controversial; others are "lite." Not considered a regular part of the USENET hierarchy. Alt newsgroups generate a lot of traffic.
bionet	Topics of interest to biologists.
biz	Business-related groups.
clari	Commercial news services gateway'ed to USENET by the ClariNet Communications Corporation.
k12	Conferences devoted to K-12 education.
relcom	Russian language newsgroups.

A SAMPLING OF NEWSGROUPS

rec.food.cooking	alt.internet.services
rec.humor.funny	soc.men comp.society
news.announce.newsgroups	biz.jobs.offered
alt.exotic-music	rec.motorcycles
soc.culture.french	sci.energy

follow a particular discussion within a newsgroup instead of hopping from one debate to another.

If you're not sure about your choices of news readers, check with your system administrator or news provider. If you're faced with a Unix command line prompt, try typing the name of some of the newsreaders mentioned in the "Unix Survival Guide" in Chapter 6 and see if that gets you anywhere.

PC and Mac owners should ask their Internet providers what user-friendly graphical applications are available to them. The Appendix also lists some pointers to PC and Mac newsreader applications.

Here's what a posting (or article) looks like in the *alt. fan.dave_barry* newsgroup. This one was posted by "The Man" himself:

```
Xref: world alt.fan.dave_barry:3296
Newsgroups: alt.fan.dave_barry
Path:world!news.kei.com!sol.ctr.columbia.edu!howland.
reston.ans.net!agate!dog.ee.lbl.gov!newshub.nosc.
mil!crash!pro-entropy!daveb
From: daveb@pro-entropy.cts.com (Dave Barry)
Subject: Re: Hey.
Organization: Pro-Entropy +1-305-265-9073 (DAR Sys-
tems Int'l--Miami, FL)
Date: Tue, 25 Jan 94 07:38:14 EST
Message-ID: <ap27604@pro-entropy.cts.com>
In-Reply-To: mwarner@uoft02.utoledo.edu
Lines: 9


I'd be SORELY ALARMED if people started posting
intelligent statements here. I think that stuff
should be posted in the alt.fan.williamF.BuckleyJr.
area, where it belongs. This area should be reserved
for the ISSUES, such as nasal humor.


-------------------------------------------------------------------
Pro-Entropy ©1993 by DAR Systems International.
Real Name: Dave Barry
```

Getting Started. Once you're able to access USENET news, the first thing you should do is read all the articles in the *news.announce.newusers* newsgroup. The many useful articles in this group are regularly updated and chronicle the history of USENET, explain concepts and common problems, provide a list of frequently asked questions along with the answers, give information on available news readers, explain USENET software and how to become a USENET site, and provide lists of USENET groups. This chapter cannot cover every detail you need to know, but these articles will get you up to speed. This newsgroup (*news.announce.newusers*) is not a discussion group—that is, you can't post questions or follow-up articles to it. If you have new-user questions, there is a newsgroup where you can post them, the *news.newusers.questions* group.

Posting Articles. When posting an article in a newsgroup, you're asked for some information. As when you send email, you're asked for a subject. Be descriptive, since there are many people participating and it's polite to give them a good idea of what your posting is about.

You also need to specify how far and wide you want your article distributed. Many times you'll want to make sure that everyone in the USENET world can read it, but sometimes your article may apply to a local geographic area. For example, if you post an article asking if anyone has any tickets to the Neil Diamond concert on Friday, you probably want to restrict it to your home town of Toronto rather than sending it to Tokyo and everywhere else. It's important that you exercise good judgment, not only by specifying geographic areas, but also by posting articles only to appropriate newsgroups. For example, it's probably not the best idea to post your resume to *rec.folk-dancing*.

If you write an article that is relevant for more than one newsgroup, you can **cross-post** that article. For example, you may decide that your article posted to *rec.cooking* about how you almost burned the house down cooking dinner should also be posted to the *rec.humor* newsgroup. Be careful when cross-posting, though. Sometimes it can anger the regulars in the cross-posted newsgroups because you're essentially "forcing" them into a conversation that originated somewhere else.

Moderators

The normal operation for most email lists and USENET newsgroups is to let everyone participate, sending or posting whatever they want. As you can imagine, this practice quite often results in what's called a low signal-to-noise ratio—lots of junk submissions that offer little or no quality to the discussion.

As a preventive measure, some email lists and newsgroups are moderated. Instead of being sent straight to the group, messages or articles are submitted to a moderator, who decides whether or not the submission has relevance to the topic at hand. The moderator may accept (or reject) each submission or may combine messages and articles to create a digest that gets posted periodically. Moderated lists and newsgroups usually contain a higher proportion of useful information, but many people don't like the idea of their postings being evaluated.

INTERACTIVE DISCUSSIONS

The types of communication that have been described so far are asynchronous—email, interest lists, and USENET newsgroups. The Internet also has interactive communication capabilities that allow one-on-one (just two people talking—typing—back and forth) or many-to-many (a bunch of people talking and listening) discussions. Since communication is happening in real time, you need an interactive connection to the Internet in order to use this feature. In other words, you can't participate in this type of communication if you're on an outernet network.

Interactive conversations aren't organized into email messages or postings; they are simply displayed on your terminal as they are received. Unless the communications program on your computer allows you to log your conversation, you won't have a permanent record of it.

Can We Talk?

One of the best-known interactive communication tools is *talk,* which allows you to set up a real-time dialogue with another person. Unlike electronic mail or news, both people must be present. Usually one person requests to *talk* to another person by using his email address. For example, if you wanted to chat with your friend Hal, who works with David Letterman, you would use the following command to set up a dialogue:

```
talk hal@sullivan-theater.cbs.com
```

A message will be displayed on Hal's screen, telling him that you wish to talk to him and giving him instructions on how to reach you. If he does indeed want to talk to you, he'll issue the command **talk** *your-email-address,* and a two-way interactive discussion can ensue. The talk program helps you keep "who's typing what" straight by splitting your terminal screen in two. Whatever you type is shown in the top half, while the other person's response is shown in the lower half.

This type of communication is fun, and it can be a very useful tool. It can, however, be somewhat frustrating if you aren't a great typist, for there's a tendency to feel pressure to type as fast as you can—which, of course, introduces all sorts of interesting and creative errors. There's also the "who talks now" problem, for which you have to resort to some radio communication techniques. For example, when you're done typing, you can type **o** for "over," meaning that you'll wait for the other person to type in his response.

The talk capability, unfortunately, is not universally available. Some implementations on certain types of computers don't work very well, so you may run into compatibility problems. Also, some system administrators turn this capability off. You may have to just grin and accept the fact that you can't "talk" with everyone.

Everyone Join In!

The Internet has a many-to-many interactive discussion capability called **Internet Relay Chat** (IRC). This type of communica-

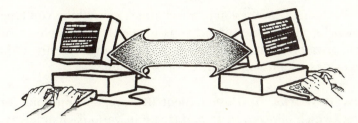

"Talk" or "Internet Chat Relay" gives you interactive communication with other Internet users.

tion is similar to conference calls, where there are lots of people talking and listening at one time. Michael O'Brien—a.k.a. Mr. Protocol, the Miss Manners of the Internet—once said, "In general use, it resembles a bank of 900-number party chat lines." If you're a gregarious person who likes to stay up late at night typing in your thoughts and dreams to people from all over the world, this interactive capability will definitely appeal to you (participants claim it's very addicting). In spite of its "frivolous" appearance, IRC has proven to be a useful tool for business and education conferencing and information access, as evidenced by its ability to disseminate live reports quickly during major events, such as the Persian Gulf War, the failed Soviet coup of 1991, and natural disasters.

The newsgroups on IRC, however, are called "channels," and they are not permanently established—they are created and available only as long as people are participating in them. Anyone can create a channel and, having done so, is known as the "operator" of that channel. Operators have special privileges; they can deny access, as well as change the mode of the channel. For example, some channels are private and deny access to curious outsiders, some are moderated (all communication goes through the operator first), while others are public and open to anyone—it's all up to the operator. Two public channels that always seem to be populated are *#Hottub* (a virtual hot tub community) and *#initgame* (a game involving initials). Channel names are prefixed by "#" or "&" characters and are not guaranteed to be very descriptive; the original purpose for a discussion may last a few minutes before shifting into a whole different topic.

Remember, when you join a channel, everything you type is shown for all channel participants to see. It is possible to converse privately with people by sending a message directly to their nicknames, identifiers that IRC users register.

How It Works. You use a client IRC program on your computer, which allows you to participate in various channels (you can communicate in more than one channel at a time). Your client controls your screen—status messages, commands, and your own messages are typed in the bottom two lines of the screen. The channel conversation goes on above those lines. Your client program communicates with an IRC server, which takes care of managing all the individual clients and distributing channel traffic between it and other servers. It is recommended that you use a server that's geographically close to you, but in most situations your server enables you to speak to people who are connected to other servers.

Access to IRC. Not everyone has access to IRC. To see if you do, first ask your Internet provider. If you get access through a Unix computer system, try typing **irc** and see what happens. The very first thing you should do after firing up IRC is read the help and intro files. (Start by typing **/help intro**). Keep in mind that all IRC commands are prefaced by a slash, **"/"**. To get help, type **/ help**. To get a list of channels, type **/list**.

For More Information. If you're interested in diving into the raging IRC waters, be sure to read all the IRC documentation you can find and to make liberal use of the IRC help command. There are IRC client programs for many systems, including PCs and Macs. (See the Appendix for pointers to IRC documentation and software.)

Seeing and Hearing Is Believing

In addition to interactive text-based talking, there are interactive audio and video applications being used on the Internet. Unfortunately, these are not available to the average user dialing in from home, but with advances in network connectivity and application development, this capability may extend to everyone before long.

The MBONE. The most powerful audio and video applications are being run on the Multicast Backbone, or MBONE, for short. The MBONE is a "virtual network" that supports the exchange of video and audio material. Right now, the type of people who are able to participate in MBONE audio and video conferences are "lucky ducks" with high-powered workstations (such as a Sun Microsystems or DEC workstation), high-speed connections, and quite a bit of technical prowess. This is not a general-public application, so more than likely you won't have immediate access to it—yet. Many of the participants are members of the Internet Engineering Task Force (the IETF mentioned in Chapter 2), who use it to meet online with members of various technical working groups.

The MBONE is being used to do all sorts of things. When President Clinton spoke at the University of North Carolina at Chapel Hill in honor of its 200th anniversary, he was seen by more than just North Carolinians watching local TV and cable channels. The video and audio from this event was also transmitted live over the MBONE to Internet users all over the world. Dave Hayes, a budding Internet disc jockey who also happens to work for NASA's Jet Propulsion Laboratory, broadcasts his own hundred-minute radio program called *Ecclecticity* over the Internet to MBONE participants. The program airs on Mondays and Fridays at 1:30 Pacific time, on the "Radio Free Vat" channel.

CU-SeeMe. Those who don't have access to the high-powered equipment and fast networks that are required for MBONE participation may be able to join another type of video conferencing. Cornell University is currently developing software for low-end workstations called CU-SeeMe. With just a Macintosh or PC, video capabilities (a video card and camera), and a moderately

The Live Connection

A particularly interesting use of the broadcast audio capability over the MBONE, according to Steve Casner, one of the MBONE developers, is a "lurkers" audio channel to which people from all over the world (an average of 50 at a time) are continuously plugged into. Most of the time this channel is silent, but every now and then someone will ask a question and anyone who is listening can pipe up with a response. Steve found this channel particularly useful one day when setting up some equipment by himself in an auditorium located in Washington, D.C. Since no one was around, he turned on the audio channel and asked if anyone could hear him. An answer immediately came back from someone in Australia.

fast link (a direct link of at least 56kbps) to the Internet, you can tap into video "reflectors" and participate in interactive video conferences. CU-SeeMe is the enabling technology for the Global Schoolhouse, a project bringing together schoolchildren from all over the world to participate in joint learning activities. (For more information on both the MBONE and CU-SeeME, see the Appendix.)

NETIQUETTE, ETHICS, AND DIGITAL TRICKS OF THE TRADE

It's easy enough to use email and news, but there's an art to communicating effectively online. Here are some general guidelines and some advice, gentle reader, on how to behave.

Listen to Me!

If you want to make sure people "listen" to what you have to say, don't bore and confuse them with rambling messages or postings, which tend to be skipped in favor of shorter messages that concentrate on one subject. If you've got several widely different things to say, it's probably better to organize a bit and send a message on each topic separately. Some people get hundreds of messages a day, so you can't expect them to remember what was said in a previous message. Remember to include background or pertinent material that will help your audience understand the intent of your message.

Some advice on how your message or article should look: There's no hard-and-fast rule, but a good message size is a screen or two. Neatness *does* count, and spelling and correct grammar are important. Even though online conversations are informal, sloppy messages that are full of errors really stick out. Take advantage of the asynchronous nature of email and news, and spend some time making your message or posting readable. Limit each line length to 70 characters or less. If you're creating messages or postings using your word processor, make sure the document is converted to "text with line breaks," meaning that a carriage return is introduced at the end of each line. If you don't do that, your message is going to end up looking funny on the screen, and will be very difficult to read.

Try to avoid using acronyms. If you can't resist, here are some that are well known: FYI (for your information), IMHO (in my humble opinion), BTW (by the way), and RTFM (read the friendly manual).

Signing On and Off

There are accepted methods by which to begin and end messages. You almost never begin a message or posting with a salutation such as "Dear Sir." You do, however, initially address the person to whom you're writing ("Dave, I'm looking forward to your show"). Instead of signing off messages and postings with a "Sincerely," or "Love," many people end with their **signature**, which is a kind of digital identifier. Signatures should be short—preferably four lines or less—and should include information such as your full name, your organization, and how to reach you. You'll see all sorts of signatures—including very fancy ones,

The Global Schoolhouse

Don't you wish you were a kid sometimes? The Internet is stretching its tentacles to the classroom, and children are finding that their playground is the whole world, not just the monkey bars and jungle gym in the field behind the school. One project, called The Global Schoolhouse, is not only promoting the Internet for education but also giving it eyes! Participating Global Schoolhouse classes are holding video conferences over the Internet using low-cost equipment and CU-SeeMe. The first pilot, in the spring of 1993, involved four classes in California, Virginia, Tennessee, and London. After reading *Earth in the Balance* by Al Gore, the children performed watershed pollution studies in their own cities. They used email to collaborate on results, and at the end of the project they held a video conference over the Internet to present their findings.

complete with pictures or cute quotes. Your signature may be included automatically by your newsreader or email program, so be careful that it doesn't appear twice. It's good to include a signature in case the addressing information in your message or article header is incorrect or not complete. This might be Paul Shafer's signature:

```
Paul Shaffer          shafer@sullivan-theater.cbs.com
Director of the CBS Orchestra          1-800-MRMUSIC
          "The David Letterman Show"
```

Beginning Behavior on Newsgroups and Email Lists

You want to be heard, but you don't want to be misunderstood. In addition to making your online communication readable, you need to be considerate of the folks on the other side. Here are a few tips on how to act when you begin participating in newsgroups and email lists on the Internet.

Remember that you're entering a world where there are a lot of experienced folks (including technical gurus and wizards) who have been around a long time. You should treat mailing lists and newsgroups as you do any other club you join for the first time. In other words, don't get on and start blabbing without checking out the territory first. Spend some time lurking to get a feel for the nature of the group and the types of discussions. This background will help you realize what topics have already been discussed in detail and beaten into the ground. It also gives you time to observe the experienced list veterans in action; imitating the experts is definitely recommended (but you don't have to *think* like they do). And while you're silently getting up to speed, there's bound to be some other "clueless newbie" who asks the very questions you're itching to send.

New users can't be expected to know everything about discussions that have gone on—sometimes for years. So the "in" thing is for the "regulars" on mailing lists and newsgroups to compile new-user questions and the answers to them in documents called **Frequently Asked Questions**, or **FAQs**. The purpose of these informative articles is to reduce the number of "noise" postings—common questions that everyone has seen a zillion times. Not every group or list has a FAQ, but the ones that do publish them regularly (usually once a month). There are now hundreds of FAQs available, on a variety of subjects, from junk mail to supermodels to crossword puzzles. These documents detail resources, facts, and opinions from people all over the world and can make very interesting reading. (See the Appendix for information on how to obtain some useful FAQs.)

Your Invisible Audience

Online communication is informal. It's much less intimidating to type your thoughts and fire them off to thousands of people than it is to stand up and say something, live, in front of the same group. But because you can't see all these people, it's easy to become careless, forgetting to include necessary background information or not thinking about your intended audience. It's also

easy to think that because email doesn't use the formal conventions we're all used to in letters on paper or in face-to-face meetings, it is an unrestrained free-for-all. To deal with this, the Net
has acquired its own conventions and etiquette.

One problem is that electronic conversations are missing
body language and voice intonation, crucial components of effective communication. Take these elements away and people are
forced to fill in the blanks when a typed online message doesn't
come across quite right. For some reason, people become much
more sensitive when they're online, and they tend to blow things
entirely out of proportion—for example, taking a couple of sentences originally meant to be humorous or sarcastic entirely the
wrong way. It's even worse if you've had a bad day and you've
decided that "no one likes you" (we've all had those moments);
you're much more susceptible to misunderstanding messages.
Once that happens, everything can go downhill quickly. Instead
of asking for clarification ("You were kidding, weren't you?") or
just ignoring it, many people—forgetting that they're dealing
with another human being on the other end—decide to defend
themselves and tell the originator of the offending message exactly what they think of him or her. This outcome is what's
known in the business as a **flame**. If both sides begin insulting
each other, it's called a **flame war** (kind of like fighting fire with
fire). These digital battles often erupt in "public" and can sometimes be very entertaining to the lurkers.

Friendly Advice

To avoid being involved in a flame war with someone in an electronic public square or a misunderstanding in regular one-on-
one communication, follow this advice.

Showing Emotion. First and foremost, always be polite and
considerate of the folks on the other side. Because you're missing
the important visual and aural cues that add nuance to direct conversation, you need to learn how to show emotion online—not an

easy task. Probably the most common trick to show emotion is :-). That's a sideways smiley face (tilt your head 90 degrees to the left) used to indicate humor or sarcasm. Since there's no smiley face on the keyboard, you have to "roll your own," using a colon, a hyphen, and a right-end parenthesis. You'll also see variations on the smiley. Sometimes people use a semicolon to indicate winking: ;-). Or a sad face will look like this: :-(. There's quite an art to the smiley face, and there are hundreds of variations.

Upper case is used for shouting, so don't use it unless you want to make a point. For example, if someone wanted to indicate that she was excited or mad, SHE'D SURE AS HECK LET YOU KNOW THAT!!!! Or, she could let you know what she was REALLY thinking by using caps in appropriate places. You can also introduce some online intonation by the use of asterisks in certain places. For example, "This *is* what I meant!" places emphasis on *is*.

Terse Responses. Terse responses can sound rude. For example, responding to someone's question with only a single sentence—"No, you can't do that!"—might make him feel as if he's inconvenienced you, that you can't be bothered to explain why he can't do something. If he asked you "live," in person, you'd probably explain. You don't have to be verbose, but a few extra sentences will go a long way to ensure that you don't hurt someone's feelings.

On the other end, if you receive a short message that leaves you wondering, "What did I do to deserve this?" don't lose too much sleep over it. Perhaps the sender was in a big hurry and didn't have time to explain everything fully.

What may be worse than a terse response is no response at all. Don't expect an immediate response to your email or news queries. People tend to get bogged down in unread and unanswered electronic correspondence. You might get an answer in five minutes—but it also might take five days, or *weeks*. Just because you don't hear from someone immediately does not mean she or he thinks your message was unimportant.

Always Point a Loaded Mailer or Newsreader at the Ground. Just as you shouldn't drive when you're angry or upset, you shouldn't send responses to email and news articles when you're mad at someone. If someone has "ticked you off" and you're bound and determined to respond to a message or posting, go ahead and type your response—but don't mail it for at least a day. A delay may seem frustrating, but chances are that when you come back later to read your response, you'll be glad you didn't send it. And you should realize that many times people will say things just to yank your chain. The thing these folks want most to see is an emotional, tear-stained response from you. Don't give them that pleasure!

You should also watch what you say in everyday situations. A good rule is never to send anything that you wouldn't mind seeing on the front page of a major newspaper. Online correspondence can be easily archived, retrieved at a later date, and sent out to a large number of people. Avoid saying anything insulting about someone or disclosing confidential information. Private, sensitive email messages, or even public flames, could come back to haunt you someday; in fact, they may "follow you around" for the rest of your life.

The security and privacy, or lack thereof, of corporate—and even private—email has caused quite a stir lately, and you've probably got a few concerns about the security of *your* mail. It's best to resign yourself to the fact that email is not very secure. Once you transmit an email message, its privacy depends on the security of the destination system, over which you basically have no control. Chapter 5 discusses computer and network security further.

Internet Ethics

As noted, you can't depend on email being secure. About the only thing you can hope for is that people will behave themselves and not snoop around in others' accounts, reading private correspondence. You should be careful not to violate copyrights by transmitting another person's work verbatim without permission. Additionally, everyone is under a moral and ethical obligation to respect other people's property and wishes. A common courtesy is to refrain from forwarding private electronic mail to anyone without the permission of the author. For example, you should be careful when you reply to a message sent to you personally—you may want to "cc" other people in your reply. Keep in mind, however, that the sender of the original message may not want his or her words forwarded to other people.

Because it is so easy to transmit information, you may be tempted, on occasion, to broadcast your message to the world. You should realize, however, that even though you are free for the most part to post and email anything, you are expected not to abuse this privilege by being inconsiderate. In other words, be selective in choosing newsgroups and email lists to receive your submissions. There are many recorded cases where a zealous Inter-prophet has broadcast his "end of the world" (or related) message to every newsgroup and email list he could find. While it may appear that little damage is done when this happens—it's only electronic information, right?—there are many people and organizations located on the "outskirts" (rural areas and foreign countries) who end up footing the bill for the extra traffic or on-line time such a message may incur. This consideration also applies to your one-on-one correspondence. It's worth finding out what the recipient's local connectivity situation is before you blast him or her with a large email message or file.

Advertising. In reality space, we're constantly being bombarded with advertisements, subtle or obnoxious, everywhere we go. We're used to it, and we don't think anything about TV and radio programs being interrupted with a "word from our sponsor." On the Internet, however, direct advertising is considered by most to be rude and invasive. There are several reasons for this. The original users of the Internet community, the researchers and academics, disdain self-promotional activity, preferring to review and promote products and information in a scholarly fashion. The second reason has to do with the National

Science Foundation's Acceptable Use Policy for the NSFNET, which once forbid blatant advertising and commercial activity on U.S. government-funded networks. The AUP in many cases doesn't apply anymore since the proliferation of commercial Internet networks, but its legacy lives on.

There are still lots of ways to get your company's message across through more passive channels (such as providing a public information service). Just be aware that you're playing with fire if you initiate a direct email campaign; you'll probably be flamed for quite a while, and you're likely to do more harm than good for your reputation.

This section cannot cover every aspect of ethical behavior on the Internet. In general, you should rely on common sense and good judgment.

Now that you know how to use the Internet to communicate, you'll soon be adept at email and conferencing, LISTSERVs and chat. And no doubt you're ready to move on to explore some of the wondrous realms of information resources now at your fingertips. Stay tuned. The very next chapter looks at the information resources on the Internet, and shows you how to use Internet tools to tap into the world's online library of libraries.

Chapter 4

FINDING INFORMATION

et ready to switch gears on the infobahn! Instead of communicating with people, we're going digging for information. What is available on the Internet is as varied as life itself. Almost anything you can think of is there for the taking—graphics, software, books, library catalogs, bulletin boards, data, sounds, movies, journals, newsletters, newspapers, and magazines. There are many thousands of independent databases, archives, and online services available via the Internet, making it one huge virtual library.

Unfortunately, this electronic library is not as well organized as a real library. There isn't just *one* card catalog where you can check to find what's available or where things are located. However, graphical interfaces and user-friendly tools have entered the scene, and can help you chart a course through what at first may appear to be a vast and unnavigable info-jungle.

Of course, not everything is online yet, but the amount and diversity of information available online is increasing so rapidly that today you *can* find quite a bit of what you are looking for. The Internet landscape is constantly changing, and enumerating its resources is next to impossible. The first edition of this book reported an impressive number of free public offerings, most of which were found in the academic and research domains. Since then, an increasing number of commercial organizations have begun offering free online catalogs, manuals, brochures, services, and software. Additionally, more and more commercial providers

"Libraries are the last democratic educational institution . . .
the most important and democratic source of information . . .
and the last refuge of those without modems."

—Gloria Steinem, speech at the American Library Association in July 1992.

of info-goods are popping up all over the Net. For example, Dialog Information Services, Inc., provides online newspaper and professional articles, the *Official Airline Guide*, financial services, and pharmaceutical directories—all accessible to subscribers. The Lexis (for legal research) and Nexis (for business, financial, and general news) databases from Mead Data Central are also accessible. A company called ClariNet Communications Corporation transmits Associated Press (AP) and Reuters news feeds. The Online BookStore (OBS) sells books, and many virtual malls have recently opened their doors.

There are too many useful information resources to list. This chapter will help you take advantage of the Internet by engaging it as an external brain, a vast storehouse of information resources. Already there are applications that utilize distributed hypertext; they link related resources together, allowing users to travel a never-ending web of information.

What are the implications of having such widespread, ready access to timely information? Businesses and governments have been built and destroyed based on the information they had available to them. The U.S. government is working to ensure universal—affordable and accessible—services for Americans on its National Information Infrastructure. The world is on its way to becoming everyone's information oyster and, therefore, the ways we learn and do business will probably change. People who will succeed in tomorrow's world will be those who can learn, discern, and deal with issues rapidly and intelligently using information tools. This requires a fundamental change in the way we operate our business and schools.

Everything You Know About Intellectual Property Is Wrong

Thus, the rights of invention and authorship adhered to activities in the physical world. One didn't get paid for ideas, but for the ability to deliver them into reality. For all practical purposes, the value was in the conveyance and not in the thought conveyed.

In other words, the bottle was protected, not the wine.

Now, as information enters cyberspace, the native home of Mind, these bottles are vanishing. With the advent of digitization, it is now possible to replace all previous information storage forms with one metabottle: complex and highly liquid patterns of ones and zeros.

Source: John Perry Barlow, "The Economy of Ideas: A Framework for Rethinking Patents and Copyrights in the Digital Age (Everything you know about intellectual property is wrong)," *Wired* magazine, March 1994.

There are some things to keep in mind while accessing information over the Internet. In reality space, there's no guarantee that what you're hearing or reading is one hundred percent correct. It's the same on the Internet. However, on the Internet you can obtain information from a variety of sources to cross-check and form your own opinions. As for the validity and accuracy of documents, keep in mind the plausible situation in which a document has been archived, downloaded, annotated, edited, and saved by a friend before being emailed to you. Unless the document contains complete attribution, checking its source and authenticity might very well be a nightmare.

The following pages will walk you through the most basic Internet information access and retrieval tools: remote login and file transfer. It's useful to know about these applications and how they work, but with the proliferation of graphical and menued front ends, you may not need to pull them out of your info-

CAN YOU GET THERE FROM HERE?

Reading this chapter may tantalize and frustrate those who have only
limited access to the Internet. You may be able to reach all of these
resources, or only some of them. If you're on an outernet network,
you're limited to using email servers—where they exist—to retrieve
files and access services. Technical, economic, and political barriers
are factors that can limit Internet access, but—fortunately for us—
nothing in life today changes faster! Your system or provider may
add Internet services or connections tomorrow or next month. So
experiment and find out what you can and can't get at. If you *really*
need access to a particular resource, your system gurus or provider
may be able to offer you another path. Once you know what's
available, you may find that you need better access. If so, shop
around for a connection that offers what you need. Chapter 7 tells
you about Internet connection options.

toolbox. The new applications on the block are painting the
Internet neighborhood in bright colors, essentially giving it a
face-lift. The latter half of this chapter explains how to get started
with information discovery and retrieval applications such as
archie, Gopher, WAIS, WWW, and Mosaic.

USING ONLINE RESOURCES AND SERVICES

There are several classes of info-tools described in this chapter.
All of these tools require that you have a direct connection to the
Internet—meaning, you're not on an outernet. Also—and this is
part of the Internet standard disclaimer—the tools may operate
differently on your system, so be sure to read local documentation and any instructions shown on the screen. In some cases,
you have to type the commands; in others, you may use a
straightforward menu system; in others, you may be clicking
icons. The examples used in this chapter will, for the most part,
be from a command-level perspective, showing the commands
(most of them in lowercase) as you would type them on many

computers. If you understand these basics, it shouldn't be hard to use an icon-based system.

The first info-tool class includes the very basic, low-level, devices you can use to access just about anything. They're called remote login and file transfer. The second class consists of information discovery and retrieval tools. These present archives and databases in a user-friendly format, and let you search or peruse them. These tools are archie, Gopher, WAIS, and WorldWide-Web. The third class can be considered not as a tool, really, but as a tool shop. These are interfaces, applications that present the Net as a graphical environment, using icons, which when selected will call up appropriate tools and select the right resources. One such application is Mosaic, and it's explained at the end of this chapter.

Keep in mind that the services explained in this chapter will most likely not be located on your own computer. You're not transmitting and receiving communication as you were in the last chapter; you (or your applications) are going out and actively getting information from other places all over the globe. The explanations here refer to the location of a desired service as the remote computer. A remote computer isn't necessarily thousands of miles away. It could be in the same room; it could be four countries away. The point is, on the Internet, it doesn't matter where it is, nor do you need to *know* in many cases where it is.

Let Me In!

Despite system differences, you will usually need to know a few specific pieces of information, such as the name of the computer or host that you want to connect to, perhaps a login id, and a password. Some computer systems require that you know the magic word to "be let in" to an account, and usually "please" won't work. What's an **account**? It's like your own room in a hotel. You have a key that lets you into your room (the account), where all your treasured possessions (files) are stored. On a computer, the key is most often a combination of a unique id and a secret password. The id (also known as a username or userid) lets the computer know who you are, and the password (which only you should know) proves it's really you.

If you live in Amsterdam, it's unlikely that you're going to have an account on a computer in Tokyo, unless you have some type of special arrangement with an organization there. But many people do have accounts on remote systems, for various reasons.

Public Services

If you don't have any accounts on other systems, you may be wondering what you can use these tools for. You will have occasion to use them—more than you may realize at first. Lots of organizations are providing services, such as public information archives and databases. To use them, you don't need a personal account on the computers where they reside. (If you do need an account, you're usually given an opportunity to apply for one.) All you need to know is the login id or name of the service, and that's usually easily available or very well known. Most of these services don't require passwords or, if they do, they either publish them, accept anything as a password, or request that you type in your email address or some other information that lets them track who's using their resources.

A word on the hospitality of people and organizations providing publicly accessible services, file transfer sites, databases, and other resources. Many of these services are made available by volunteers, so act politely and try not to hog resources. Sometimes it's requested that you use a service after working hours; if so you should respect that rule, keeping in mind the time zone as well.

Different Environments

When you are accessing remote services, you are connecting to another environment that may look very different from what you're used to using on your own system. It should be obvious by now, but there isn't just one way to do things in the Internet world. Different organizations, different computers, and different operating systems all provide different services. Each remote system and service is going to have its particular look and feel.

Bienvenidos a Mexico!

Sometimes the benefits of networking come in subtle packages. The Bush School in Seattle, Washington, is one of the first schools in the world to give Internet accounts to all the students, not just the teachers. Fred Dust, the school's Headmaster, relates how the Internet plays a very important role in learning, professional development, and parental involvement at his school. "All the teachers, students, and parents are encouraged to participate," he says. "The results have been tremendously positive." For example, two ninth graders were experimenting one day with online library access. Not content with the local libraries, they connected to a catalog in Mexico. To their surprise, the interface greeted them in Spanish. "That floored them," said Dust. "They'd lived their lives in English-speaking Washington State, had taken classes in Spanish, but hadn't realized it was actually used somewhere. They also realized their entrance into other countries wouldn't be blocked by the technology, but by language barriers. It was a very powerful discovery that they made on their own. This experience couldn't have been duplicated in a traditional classroom setting."

The interface—the face that the other computer presents to you—will probably be different from the one you're familiar with. The words may even be in a foreign language. Don't worry; the public interfaces to these systems are pretty robust, so you won't harm anything if you make a few mistakes. Keep in mind that things change on computers, too. Information is added and deleted. Interfaces change. Most of these online services don't come with manuals, so you'll need to read the instructions and use the help screens that are shown when you sign on. It doesn't hurt to make a few notes. A contact name is sometimes listed with the description of the service or on one of the initial login screens; if you have problems, you can email or call. Remember that you're accessing another computer, so your own system gurus may not be able to assist you.

Error Messages

Occasionally you'll get an error message or just not be able to get to that computer. One or more things may be wrong. First—and most likely—is that you misspelled or mistyped the name of the computer, in which case you'll get a message such as *unknown host*. If that happens, check to be sure you have the right hostname. If you're sure you have the right name, then it's possible that this computer simply doesn't exist anymore.

If you know that the computer exists and that you have the correct name, and you still get an error message, you can try something else. Remember from Chapter 2 that the Domain Name System (DNS) allows you to use computer names instead of IP addresses. It could be that your computer is having a hard time figuring out what the remote computer's IP address is. If this is the case, and you do know the IP address, you can always try substituting it for the computer name.

If you have the right computer name, and the remote computer doesn't respond after you initiate a connection using an information tool, there may be problems with the network or the remote computer may be "down"—that is, not working or available. Just try again later. If the problem persists, contact your network provider or system administrator for more clues.

ACCESSING INTERACTIVE SERVICES

Remote login is a basic tool that lets you "fly" electronically all over the world, reaching your destination in a fraction of a second. This section will tell you how to connect to other computers and services using remote login.

How It Works

Remote login on the Internet is a lot like using your modem to dial into another computer, but it's usually much faster and you don't actually have to dial a phone number. The name of the protocol that enables remote login is **Telnet**, which is also the name of the command on many systems to allow you to login to other computers. (Don't confuse "Telnet" with "Telenet," a public data network that was around for a long time.)

When using Telnet to login to a computer, just issue the *telnet* command followed by a space and the name of the computer. (You can also issue the *telnet* command without the computer name, at which point you'll be in command mode. When you see a `telnet>` prompt, you can type commands or **help** for more information.) For example, if you want to check out an online book order service called Book Stacks Unlimited, Inc., type the following:

```
telnet books.com
```

The Telnet program will make a connection to the *books.com* system. In this particular example, you'll be asked to type in your full name, pick a password, and specify your contact information (email and address). You can then use the menu system to search and order books (over 240,000 titles are offered), and participate in a book discussion group.

Now, when you telnet to most other systems, you are usually greeted by a computerized "Who goes there?" routine. The typical prompt is `Login:` or `Username:`, at which time you type your login id or username followed by the <RETURN> key. If you already have a username, type it in; you'll then be prompted for your password. When you supply the password, don't worry that it doesn't appear on the screen. It is not shown because your password is supposed to be secret, and you don't want any folks kibitzing behind you to see what it is.

In some cases when you connect to a resource, you'll have to specify an additional identifier called a **port number**. There can be many services running on a single computer; the port identifier serves to keep them separate. When a port number is required, you usually don't have to type in a username or password. Let's test-drive this command:

```
telnet madlab.sprl.umich.edu 3000
```

Here it was necessary to specify the port number, *3000*, because it identifies a specific program. Resource guides always include the port numbers with the instructions for accessing resources, so if you don't see one, don't worry about it. In this case, you're connecting to the "Weather Underground," a service provided by the University of Michigan's College of Engineering. The Weather Underground has a menu system that's almost easier to use than your automatic teller machine. There's something for everyone, such as local weather reports, snow ski reports for some parts of the country, earthquake reports for other parts, and hurricane reports.

Sometimes when you login to another system, you'll be asked about your terminal type. In most cases, you can say you're emulating a "VT100" (or something similar) terminal, and you'll do just fine. Some resources, such as online library catalogs, are running on IBM mainframes, however, so you might have to use a different version of Telnet called tn3270 (if it exists on your system) in order to emulate an IBM 3270 terminal. It works similarly, though the keys may not correspond exactly to what you're used to; just substitute *tn3270* for *telnet*.

Let Me Outta Here!

Why is it so hard to say good-bye? Sometimes the biggest problem new users have using publicly available services is getting out of them without shutting down the computer or turning off the modem. When you're remotely logged in to another computer, everything you type is being sent to the remote system for execution. There are two ways to exit a system. One way is simply to logout of the service. Unfortunately, there's no standard "let me go" command. The best advice is to read with care any instructions that show up when you login to a system. If the screen doesn't tell you anything, try one of these commands: *exit, quit, logout, leave, bye, goodbye, ciao, disconnect, CTRL-D, CTRL-Z*.

If you still can't exit, then you can terminate the session by signaling your *local* telnet program that you wish to quit. Using a special "escape" character or command allows you to suspend your telnet session temporarily, and you're brought back to a telnet prompt (usually `telnet>`) on your home system. The escape character can vary, but on many systems it's a *CTRL-]*. (Hold down the control key and at the same time press the "*]*" key.) On some systems, *CTRL-^* is used. You can then quit the telnet session by typing **quit** at the telnet prompt.

ONLINE RESOURCES

The Weather Service is neat, but it's just the tip of the tornado! There's much, much more. Here's an idea of the types of resources that are accessible via remote login and how to try some of them out.

Online Library Catalogs

Some of the most common and most often mentioned Internet resources are the online library catalogs. At least 500 catalogs are accessible via the Internet, mostly at academic organizations all over the world. Most don't allow you to look at or transfer entire online books; they just let you review bibliographic records. You can peruse a certain library's collection, verify a citation or reference, or see if a book is checked out or if it's available through the interlibrary loan system. Online library catalogs, by the way, are usually open all day and all night!

Some online catalogs offer more than just bibliographic records. For example, to explore the UHCARL Library System at the University of Hawaii, Manoa, type:

```
telnet starmaster.uhcc.hawaii.edu
```

At the `enter class` prompt, type **lib**. Select **5** for VT100 emulation. Wander through the menus. (See if *this* book is in the database!) Items of interest include an index of Hawaiian sheet music and the 1993 edition of the Hawaii Data Book. Some online library catalogs even offer access to online encyclopedias. Not every service offered in the menus may be available to out-

plokta /plok'ta/ (Acronym for 'Press Lots Of Keys To Abort')
v. To press random keys in an attempt to get some response
from the system. One might plokta when the abort procedure
for a program is not known, or when trying to figure out if
the system is just sluggish or really hung. Plokta can also be
used while trying to figure out any unknown key sequence
for a particular operation. Someone going into *plokta mode*
usually places both hands flat on the keyboard and presses
down, hoping for some useful response.

Source: *The New Hacker's Dictionary*, edited by Eric S. Raymond, with assistance
and illustrations by Guy L. Steele, Jr. © 1991 Eric S. Raymond. Published by The
MIT Press, Cambridge and London, 1991. Reprinted with permission.

side users. For example, most online encyclopedias may be limited to registered users because of licensing restrictions.

Other Sites Accessible via Remote Login

In addition to online library catalogs and commercial services,
there are many other types of services you can access via remote
login.

Bulletin Board Systems. Bulletin board systems (BBSs) on
the Internet are a lot like the electronic bulletin boards that you
can dial into using a modem. Most BBSs offer a menu of services.
Some supply conferencing capabilities, while others provide
"read-only" information, similar to regular bulletin boards at a library, where information is tacked up for everyone to read and
taken down when it's no longer relevant.

FreeNets. FreeNets are community-based bulletin board systems
with email, information services, interactive communications, and
conferencing. Funded and operated by individuals and volunteers—
in one sense, like public television—they're part of the National
Public Telecommunication Network (NPTN), an organization based

in Cleveland, Ohio, that is devoted to making computer telecommunication and networking services as freely available as public libraries. The FreeNet concept—promoting community networking—is catching on, and they're opening up in more and more cities. Access is usually by a local phone call using a modem, and a good number have connections to the Internet.

A popular FreeNet is the Tallahassee FreeNet, which is organized like a small city. Thousands of people access this system each day, chatting with each other and visiting the Government Complex, the Library, the Science and Technology Center, or the Home and Garden Center. Want to try it? Here's the command to visit the Tallahassee FreeNet:

```
telnet freenet.fsu.edu
```

If you're a first-time user and don't have an account, you can demo the system by selecting the *visitor* login choice. From there you can apply for an account free of charge, if you wish, or you can just explore the system.

SPACE SCIENCE HOMEWORK HELPER

SpaceMet Internet	telnet spacemet.phast.umass.edu
NASA Spacelink	telnet spacelink.msfc.nasa.gov (New users login with the **newuser** id and **newuser** password.)
Center for Advanced Space Studies	telnet cass.jsc.nasa.gov Login as **cass**; password: **online**
NASA/IPAC Extragalactic Database (NED)	telnet ned.ipac.caltech.edu Login as **ned**.

TRANSFERRING INFORMATION

Imagine that you're creating an important report at your personal workstation. You want to print it out, but you don't have a printer nearby. So you copy the document onto a floppy, put on your Keds, and run down the hall to load the floppy at the nearest workstation-printer site. This process is known as **file transfer**, because the report is being transferred to another computer. If both computers were on the Internet, you could have transferred this file in a matter of seconds using the file transfer capability. Instead of sending the file through the slower "SneakerNet," you could have sent it over the electronic highway. In short, the file transfer capability gives you the ability to copy files from one computer to another.

What Is a File?

A file can be anything. It can be a document you create in your PC's word processor. It can be a spreadsheet or a software program. It can be a picture, or even music. Or it can be ASCII (American Standard Code for Information Interchange) text, which is plain text with no formatting codes, such as boldface or underlining.

Many of the documents are just text, readable no matter what computer or software you're using. You should be aware, however, that some of the files you transfer won't mean anything to the computer system you're using. A word processor document—one that was prepared by Microsoft Word, for example—has special typesetting codes within the document. Obviously, this file won't be useful if you don't own the Microsoft Word application. Similarly, a file can be a software application. Not all software will "run" or work on every computer. In fact, it's safe to say that there isn't one piece of software that will work on every type of computer.

File Transfer Clarified

Many people get file transfer and remote login confused because both applications allow you to connect to other computers and obtain information. File transfer is a more specific and straightforward tool. Its main mission is to transfer files between computers. You're not actually interactively querying another computer's database or using a service to find out any information.

There are also similarities and differences between file transfer and electronic mail. Email is used for transferring personal messages, although you can send and receive information in the form of files, too. You wouldn't use file transfer to deliver personal messages, but if you and another person need to transfer a file, such as a text document, back and forth, electronic mail will work just fine. Indeed, in most cases it is probably preferable, because you don't want to give another person your username and password. Two warnings, however. Some computers cannot handle extremely long email messages. If your file is very large, you may need to send it in smaller sections. Some email systems can also throw extra characters into your text, but file transfer guarantees integrity.

If the file is a non-text file, such as a software program, then it's almost always better to transfer it by using the Internet file transfer tool. As mentioned in Chapter 3, you can send non-text files, such as software and graphics, if your email application (and the receiving end) supports MIME, or if you have the necessary tools like BinHex to encode for transmission and decode upon reception. Since the latter process requires several extra steps, it may just be simpler to use file transfer rather than email.

How File Transfer Works

Using the file transfer capability on the Internet is fairly straightforward. The protocol is called File Transfer Protocol (FTP). On many systems, the actual program that you will use is called *ftp,* which stands for "file transfer program." FTP allows you to connect to another computer and perform certain actions, such as listing the files in a directory and copying files back and forth between both systems.

To start a session, type **ftp** *host-name.* (Or you can also use the **ftp** command by itself, at which time you'll be put into the command interpreter, which waits for more instructions from you. The **open** *host-name* command will establish, or open, a transfer connection.) You should be prompted for your username and password on the remote system, just as in the telnet

File transfer (above) lets you move files between computers. Remote login (below)
lets you interact with another computer's services.

process. Once you've identified yourself to the remote system,
you'll most likely see a prompt that looks like this: ftp>.

When you use FTP, be sure to check local system documentation for more information. It will tell you about the many other
commands you can use and things you can do, as well as any
system-specific characteristics you should know about. Keep in
mind that most of the following commands will tell you information about and perform actions on the *remote* system. For example, you can find out what files are in the remote directory
using the command **dir** (for "directory") or **ls** (for "list"). You
can change to another directory where other files are stored using the command **cd** *directory-name* ("change directory"). To go
back up the directory ladder to the parent directory, use the
cdup command. If you don't know which directory you're in,
the **pwd** ("print working directory") command will tell you.

If the changing directories part of this confuses you, then you need to understand that directories in computers are organized similarly to folders in a filing cabinet. A directory is basically an electronic folder with files and perhaps other folders in it, and when you change directories, you're just opening up a new folder. Once you're "in" the right directory on the remote system, you can do several things, two of which are *getting* a file (or files) and *putting* a file (or files). To download or transfer a file from the remote system to your local computer, use the **get** *filename* command. To upload or put a local file on the remote system, use the **put** *filename* command. You can always get help by typing **help** (for a list of commands), or **help** *command*. In fact, you should probably check out the help screens on any system when you are using it for the first time. When you finish transferring files, you can close the connection and exit by typing either **bye** or **quit**.

Many of the public archive sites run the Unix operating system, so if you're familiar with that, then the listing **dir** produces will make sense. If you're not, it may help to know that the Unix file system is a hierarchical directory structure similar to that of a DOS or Macintosh computer. (Hierarchical means that you start at the top, also known as the root, and work your way down through various directories.) Also, Unix is case-sensitive, so if a filename is shown in lowercase, then you must type it in lowercase. (A good rule is to *always* type the instructions or filename exactly as shown.) Chapter 6 ("Unix on the Internet: A Survival Guide") tells a bit about Unix commands and applications. Following is a sample listing of a directory on an anonymous FTP host that runs Unix:

```
-rw-r—r—    1 tracy   ftp      198 Apr 10 13:16 README
dr-xr-xr-x  2 root    bin      512 Apr  1  1991 bin
dr-xr-xr-x  2 root    bin      512 Apr  1  1991 etc
-rw-r—r—    1 tracy   ftp    88349 Aug  2 15:26 glossary
dr-xrwxr-x 14 ftp     ftp      512 Jul 23 09:10 pub
```

In this example, the filenames are on the far right. On the far left are the permission and file type specifications. The letter *d* in the first column indicates that the entry is a directory, so *bin, etc,* and *pub* are directories. The file creation date and time are easy to spot: *README* was created or modified on April 10 at 1:16 p.m. Another thing you should notice is the number immediately to the left of the date—the size of the file in bytes. The glossary file is 88,349 bytes, which is fairly large. Because it's so easy to transfer files, you may find that you can fill up your disk space quickly, so you'll need to implement a good file management system. Remember to delete the files you don't need and to compress the ones you want to keep. (A list of file formats and compression tools is included below.)

Publicly Accessible Files

The transfer of publicly available information is one of the most widespread uses of the file transfer capability on the Internet. Many of the organizations connected to the Internet provide openly accessible file transfer sites with information that anyone can obtain (or *get*). Files are stored in "open" or public areas of computers, and you can access them by using the file transfer program to connect to those systems. A file that is "available via anonymous FTP" is publicly available, and you can connect to a public archive computer and use the file transfer program to copy it to your own system.

Remember that you need a login name and password to be allowed into a computer. For publicly accessible files, the login name is **anonymous** and the password can be anything, although it's a good idea to type your email address. (Sometimes **guest** is the specific password required.) Once you master spelling the login name *anonymous,* you can roam around the public storage areas on computers on the Internet just as you explore public libraries.

Not every computer on the Internet makes public file storage areas available, but there are thousands of systems that offer gigabytes and gigabytes of "published" information. (One recent count put the number of publicly available files at well over 2.2 million.) These sites are making available electronic books, public domain software, and graphic images—lots of amusing, useful, and interesting stuff. (Check the Appendix for instructions on obtaining a list of anonymous FTP sites.)

Navigating around different computer public storage areas takes some practice. As was mentioned before, there are different kinds of computers out there, and some present their electronic folders a bit differently. Many systems provide README files that explain what files are available or anything you might need to know about the collection of files. You simply transfer the README file: **get README**. (There's no standard name for an information file; they may be called *00README*, or *readme*, *READ.me, INFO, INDEX,* or something similar. You can usually tell what file will provide information when you get a directory listing.)

Let's transfer a file called *Special Internet Connections* by Scott Yanoff. He has compiled a sort of travel guide of interesting places to visit on the Internet. (Of course, you should read the rest of this chapter first to understand how to access many of the sites listed.) *Special Internet Connections* is available via anonymous FTP on the computer *csd4.csd.uwm.edu,* in the directory *pub,* with the filename *inet.services.txt.* Also, take note that this is a text file (the extension ".txt" gives this away). This bit of information will come in handy, as you'll see in a moment. Not all filenames have an extension that specifies file type, but many do. See the "Common File Formats on the Internet" table for a listing of the more common ones.

The example on the next page will not walk you through executing a directory listing (using the *dir* command), but remember that you can use that command to see what other files are available. The steps we will take in this example include connecting to the remote computer, *csd4.csd.uwm.edu,* specifying an "ascii" transfer, changing to the *pub* directory, getting the file (*inet.services.txt*), and then disconnecting. If you wish to rename the file as you're transferring it to your system, the command is **get** *remote-file new-file-name.* Here's what you'd see on your screen (the commands you would type on many systems are shown in bold):

```
sport>ftp csd4.csd.uwm.edu
Connected to csd4.csd.uwm.edu.
220 csd4.csd.uwm.edu FTP server (Version wu-2.1c(3)
   Fri Oct 29 13:50:21 CDT199.
Name (csd4.csd.uwm.edu:tparker): anonymous
331 Guest login ok, send your complete e-mail address
as password.
Password:
230-
230-University of Wisconsin-Milwaukee FTP server
230-Local time is Sun Jun 5 14:05:27 1994
230-If have any unusual problems, please report them
230-via e-mail to help@uwm.edu.
230-If you do have problems, please try using a dash
230-(-) as the first character of your password -- this
230-will turn off the continuation messages that may be
230-confusing your ftp client.
230-Please read the file Policy
230- it was last modified on Mon Dec  6 08:06:40
230-1993 - 181 days ago
230 Guest login ok, access restrictions apply.
230-
Remote system type is UNIX.
Using binary mode to transfer files.
ftp> ascii
200 Type set to A.
ftp> cd pub
250-This directory contains public files for anonymous
250-users. Files may be read, but not written (use
250-"/incoming" for writing new files).
250 CWD command successful.
ftp> get inet.services.txt
200 PORT command successful.
150 Opening ASCII mode data connection for
inet.services.txt (48244 bytes).
226 Transfer complete.
local: inet.services.txt remote: inet.services.txt
49151 bytes received in 0.81 seconds (59 Kbytes/s)
ftp> quit
221 Goodbye.
sport>
```

After connecting to this computer, one of the first messages you get before the `ftp>` prompt is "Using binary mode to transfer files." This means that the system is assuming you are transferring non-text files—images, software, or compressed files, for example. If you know you're transferring a text file, then immediately set the transfer type to "ascii" by typing the command **ascii**. If you don't do this, your file may appear funky because the line terminators might not transfer correctly.

Non-text Information

If you're planning on transferring non-text, then you need to do a **binary transfer**. Files that have been **compressed** are binary files, as are software programs. A compressed file is basically "dehydrated"—or squeezed—to conserve disk space and also to make the transfer time faster. As was noted above, some systems automatically assume you're doing a binary transfer, but if not, you can set this mode easily by typing **binary** <RETURN> before you type **get** or **put** to transfer a file. This tells the system that you're moving a compressed, or non-text, file. Typing **ascii** will put you back in text mode.

Obtaining Software

Software archives are all over the Internet. The Washington University Public Domain Archives is a great place to start, with a boatload of public domain and shareware software for the Amiga, Apple II, Atari, CP/M, DOS, GNU, Macintosh, Sun, TeX, Unix, VMS, and X Windows systems. There's so much on this system that it's advisable to obtain any README files in each directory to learn about what's available when you're exploring. If you want to check out this system, type **ftp wuarchive. wustl.edu** and login as **anonymous**, and use your email address as a password. (Don't forget to specify *binary* transfer for software!) Before you stock up on software, read the section on security in Chapter 5. And check the Appendix for some other places to find software.

guiltware /gilt'weir/ n. 1. A piece of freeware decorated with a message telling one how long and hard the author worked on it and intimating that one is a no-good freeloader if one does not immediately send the poor suffering martyr gobs of money. 2. Shareware that works.

Source: *The New Hacker's Dictionary*, edited by Eric S. Raymond, with assistance and illustrations by Guy L. Steele, Jr. © 1991 Eric S. Raymond. Published by The MIT Press, Cambridge & London, 1991. Reprinted with permission.

File Formats

As was mentioned earlier, certain files work only on certain computers, so it's good to have a little knowledge of the types of files, how to know which is which, and what programs, if any, you'll need to use the files.

Macintosh programs are sometimes in the BinHex (ASCII) format. Once downloaded and un-BinHexed, the files will most likely have to be uncompressed. Because PC files and programs are usually in compressed format, they will almost always have to be uncompressed with a utility like PKZIP or StuffIt after being downloaded.

The chart opposite shows some of the more common file types you'll see—sounds, graphics, and compressed—the programs they work with, and how you should transfer (ASCII or binary mode) each of them. A document available via anonymous FTP explains most file compression, archiving, and text-binary formats, and tells where you can get software to convert these various formats. This regularly updated document is maintained by David Lemson, and can be obtained via anonymous FTP from *ftp.cso.uiuc.edu*, in the directory *doc/pcnet* (type **cd doc/pcnet**), filename *compression*.

Obtaining Information via Electronic Mail

If you don't have direct access to the Internet, are you forever cut off from publicly available files? No—there are other ways to

Common File Formats on the Internet

Ext	File Program Name	File Type	Computer	Transfer Method
.bin	MacBinary	binary	Mac	binary
.cpt	Compact Pro	compressed	Mac	binary
.sit	StuffIt	compressed	Mac	binary
.hqx	BinHex 4.0	encoded	Mac	ASCII
.hqx	BinHex 5.0	encoded	Mac	binary
.sea	self-extracting	binary	Mac	binary
.qt	Quicktime	video	Mac/PC	binary
.arc	ARC, PKPAK	compressed	PC	binary
.arj	ARJ	compressed	PC	binary
.lzh	LHArc	compressed	PC	binary
.pak	PAK	compression	PC	binary
.voc	Soundblaster	sound	PC	binary
.wav	WAVE	sound	PC	binary
.zip	PKZIP/InfoZIP	compressed	PC	binary
.zoo	zoo	compressed	PC	binary
.snd	NeXT audio file	sound	Unix	binary
.Z	compress & uncompress	compressed	Unix	binary
.gz	GNU Zip Archiver	compressed	Unix	binary
.tar	tar	archive	Unix	binary
.xbm	X-Bitmap	image	Unix (X)	binary
.au	Sun Ulaw	audio	Unix/any	binary
.rs	Sun raster	file image	Unix (X)	binary
.ps	PostScript	page description	Any	ASCII or binary
.gif	GIF	graphics	Any	binary
.txt	text	text	Any	ASCII
.uu/uue	uuencode & uudecode	encoded	Any	ASCII
.jpg/.jpeg	JPEG	image compression	Any	binary
.tif	TIFF	image	Any	binary
.mpg/.mpeg	MPEG	video compression	Any	binary

get files. If you are in a situation in which you can't interactively use FTP, you might want to check out the alternatives explained in this section.

Using what's called an *info-server*, or an *email-server*, you can get publicly accessible files by just sending an email message with a command (such as **send info**). One command that should always work is **help**. The message is sent to a server that processes the order and emails the requested files back to you within a few minutes or, usually, by the next day. That's all there is to it.

Many anonymous FTP sites also provide an email service for access to their own files. Some computers, however, will act as general purpose email/FTP translation servers. This means that the files don't have to exist on those computers—you can send orders for *any* publicly available files, no matter what computer they're on. These are known as FTP-by-email servers; they transfer the files from the computers they reside on, and then email them to you.

One FTP-by-email server is *ftpmail@pa.dec.com*. Send an email message to that address, with a one-line message in the body: **help**. (Don't worry about the Subject—anything will do.) You will be sent a help file telling you what commands to use to obtain files. Another server is BITFTP, named because it processes file requests from BITNET users. If you're on BITNET, send email (command **help**, initially) to *BITFTP@PUCC* or *bitftp@pucc.princeton.edu*. You should receive a help file explaining how to use BITFTP. (The Appendix lists some other FTP-by-email servers.)

FINDING RESOURCES AND FILES

So many resources and public archives are available that it's impossible to cover everything, and people all over the world are constantly cooking up interesting new offerings. There are *lots* of resource directories, guides, lists of public FTP sites, and lists of online library catalogs that can help show you the way to important resources. Usually they're maintained by volunteers and made available without cost via anonymous FTP, posted regularly to certain mailing lists and newsgroups, or in hardcopy form

Faster Than Braille Mail

Like a lot of undergraduates these days, Tina Ektermanis roams the Internet for research and recreation. From the terminal in her dorm room at Northwest Missouri State University, she uses all the standard tools and utilities—email, FTP, Gopher, news, and IRC. The Internet doesn't know that she's blind.

Ektermanis, a computer science major, uses voice-synthesizing hardware to read the output from her screen. The ASCII text she brings home from the Net is easier to scan and search than the braille and cassette sources she uses offline in her studies, and the USENET news is far more timely. Logging in to GENIE's forum for disability issues allows her to communicate seamlessly with other handicapped Internauts, particularly the deaf, whose signing she can't interpret in real-life.

She bumps against the limits of her system only when she crosses a language barrier—a MUD game in Stuttgart made her voice synthesizer crazy—or encounters ASCII art. A rose is not a rose on her terminal—it's a maze of audible punctuation marks. Otherwise, she sails along like any other student on the Net. "When I'm home on vacation," she says, "I really miss it!"

for a nominal price. The Appendix lists the more popular guides. You can also learn about new resources through mailing lists and USENET postings, or by word of mouth.

Uniform Resource Locators

As our lives seem to become increasingly complex, finding key pieces of information, both in your office file cabinet and on your computer's hard drive, can be difficult, especially around tax time. You've probably been heard to mutter more than once, "I need a new system."

As the Internet has matured, the different applications and resources have grown up too, and the need for a new resource naming system has become apparent. Pick up any documentation or guide describing the great Internet resources you can access, and chances are you'll see a lot of different ways of describing *how* to find that information. A new naming methodology for locating information has surfaced recently and, as of the writing of this updated edition, is currently still in development. The chances it will be adopted universally are very good.

The naming system is called Uniform Resource Locators (URL), and it applies not only to "stuff" that can be accessed via current information retrieval and discovery tools, but to any applications that are developed in the future. The URL naming system can be used by people when referring to a particular resource (in an email message, resource guide, or book), and by computers when giving directions to an application on how and where to access a resource. As with anything in the computer and networking industry, the URL system can get quite complicated. This section explains some of the more common ways you'll see it used. The *basic* anatomy of a URL is as follows.

First Part. The first identifier you see refers to the type of application used to access the information, for example, FTP, Gopher, and so on. This identifier is always followed by a colon.

Second Part. For Internet applications, the URL designation begins with a double slash, "//", and then specifies information needed to find and access the host where the resource resides. This includes a user login name and password (if needed), the domain name of the host, and a port number (if needed). Usually, what follows the double slashes is just the hostname. You'll know if a port number is referenced because following the hostname there will be a colon and then a number. That number is the port number. If you don't see one, you don't have to worry about it.

Third Part. Once you've accessed the host, the resource needs to be located on that host. This part describes the "path" of the information.

Here's an example URL:

```
ftp://nysernet.org/pub/resources/guides/
                              surfing.2.0.3.txt
```

This describes an FTP site, *nysernet.org*, and the directory path */pub/resources/surfing.2.0.3.txt.* (The file listed above is an article called "Surfing the Net.") To retrieve this file, use ftp to connect to the host:

ftp nysernet.org

Then change directories:

cd /pub/resources/guides

And then get the file:

get surfing.2.0.3.txt

Here's another URL:

```
gopher://rugcis.rug.nl:70/
```

This is the URL describing a Gopher server for the Netherlands (Gopher is described below). In this example, a port number is specified: *70.* In this case, 70 happens to be the default port number for the Gopher application, so you usually don't have to type it in. But if you did, here's how you could access this resource:

gopher rugcis.rug.nl 70

URLs can also describe USENET newsgroups. Here's a USENET URL:

```
news://rec.arts.marching.drumcorps
```

Keep in mind that the preceding description is only meant to get you started in learning how to understand a URL. The URL system is very flexible, so there are many ways to use it. See the Appendix for pointers to the URL standards documentation.

Information Discovery and Retrieval Tools

Online lists and guides are useful for reading about interesting online services, but there are so many resources and information archives available that it's hard to keep these guides up-to-date.

They can also be difficult to search if you've got something particular in mind that you want to know about. If you subscribe to a resource announcement email list, like *net-happenings@is. internic.net* (staffed by a very famous dedicated volunteer, "Mr. Re-Post Man" himself, Gleason Sackman—see the Appendix for more information), you may start scribbling names and numbers all over the place. Most people starting out use the "Post-It Database System," sticking those little yellow memos all over their computer monitors. Save yourself the effort, because there's no way you can keep up with all the new and great stuff that's made available every day. There is a better way.

What you should spend your time on is learning about the electronic tools (the second class of info-tools mentioned earlier) that are available to you, tools that help you search and browse documents, retrieve information on certain subjects, and locate interesting resources. In 1993 there was an explosion of access and interest in powerful tools such as archie, WAIS, Gopher, Veronica, and WorldWideWeb. Most of them are responsible for generating the phenomenal growth rates in network traffic; for example, as was pointed out in Chapter 1, the traffic for the WorldWideWeb in 1993 increased by 341,634 percent. (So if you get caught in an Internet traffic jam, you know whom to blame.)

Each of these applications provides a single interface into the hundreds of disparate services and databases on the Internet, offering easier ways to search or browse them. In other words, you don't have to remember computer names, port numbers, or directory structures, or learn lots of new interfaces to hundreds of different computers. These applications can even establish links and relationships between themselves and other services, cross-referencing and helping you find information more easily. Unfortunately, though, you'll still be forced to play confusion roulette every now and then to figure out which application is needed to find a resource.

Clients and Servers

To comprehend how these advanced applications work, you need to understand a fundamental networking concept—the

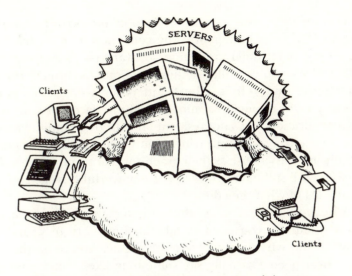

Client programs hide network details from you. Server programs find most Internet
resources and deliver them to your computer.

client/server model. This is a very powerful networking concept, and it's used all over the Internet for more than these applications. In general, **clients** are applications that run on your own computer, taking advantage of its special features. A graphical client, for instance, will allow you to use your mouse instead of typing in commands. A client program hides many of the network details from you, including computer names, ports, and commands, and it obtains its information from servers. **Servers** are programs running on computers that are reachable via the network. They know where the data and documents are, and they take care of servicing client queries.

Unfortunately, the client/server model requires a *direct* network connection to the Internet. If you're sitting at home with just a microcomputer, modem, and terminal emulation software, you probably won't be able to partake of these powerful applications right away. However, there are ways to turn your PC or Mac into a *directly* connected computer even though you're dialed-in, simply by using some special software. This type of connection (described in Chapter 7) uses protocols called SLIP and PPP that must be supported by your Internet provider. If all you've got is terminal emulation software (such as Kermit or PROCOMM), you can still use these applications through **terminal clients** and **telnet clients**; in other words, you either remotely login to public terminal-based interfaces, or you use a client application that's not resident on your own computer (perhaps on the computer into which you've dialed). They're not as friendly and easy to use as their graphical client counterparts, but at least you'll still have access to these powerful servers, and can get an idea of what they do.

One more thing: Because there are so many different ways to access resources, you need to take an inventory of your local situation and what is available to you. Once you're on the net, you'll hear people casually say something like, "Point your gopher client at *sunsite.unc.edu.*" You should first take note of the method of access (in this case, Gopher), and the destination (in this case, *sunsite.unc.edu*). Most of the time, people will not give you explicit instructions when telling you about a great resource (that is, type **gopher sunsite.unc.edu**, or select "Another Gopher" from the file menu and type **sunsite.unc.edu** in response to the prompt), because there are just too many ways to get there. Once you understand how to use the applications on your own system, an instruction like the one quoted above should be enough to get you going. The following explanations will help you understand what's available for your situation; you need to follow up and read suggested help files to learn the specifics.

Gopher

By far the easiest tool for novices is **Gopher**. You're just going to love Gopher, because it's simple, it's fun, you don't have to get dressed up to use it, and it gets you places fast. Just one Gopher session will fly you to a hospital in Melbourne, the Minnesota State Legislature, the Exploratorium in San Francisco, the Wellington City Council, and Chulalongkorn University in Bangkok.

And if you're not up to it, you don't have to go places. You can browse and download magazines, such as *Wired, The Economist, Inc.,* and *Financial World Magazine.*

The name *gopher* can mean several things. In the traditional sense, it is a "gopher" for information. You can also think of it as a furry animal that runs out and sniffs around "Gopherspace" for you. The name actually came from its birthplace, the University of Minnesota, whose mascot is the gopher.

So get ready, 'cause you're about to go gophering! Gopher organizes access to Internet resources using a menu system. It provides smooth passage into other Gopher servers, allowing you to browse and search documents, and links you to resources and databases, such as USENET news, online library catalogs, and campus-wide information servers (explained below). You may not know it, but while you're "sniffing" around Gopherspace, you're actually doing things like transferring files, changing directories, telnetting to computers, and querying servers all over the world.

Organizations can easily bring up their own Gopher servers and menus, and make available any information they want. When this book was first written in the summer of 1992, there were around 100 Gophers. As of today, there are as many as 25,000 Gophers poking their heads out of the ground. The estimated growth rate for Gopher traffic in 1993 was 997 percent! Most of the participating Gopher servers are tied together by Gopher links in their menus, so by connecting to one organization's Gopher, you can usually "break away" and burrow into other gopher holes across the world.

How to Use It. Gopher is a hierarchical menuing system. When you initiate a Gopher session (with a client program), you can either connect to a default Gopher server or specify a particular server. Either way, you'll be accessing some organization's top-level menu. You travel Gopherspace by either typing the corresponding menu item number, using your arrow keys to position a menu arrow, or clicking on an icon. This will lead you to another menu, another computer (via Telnet), the document you seek (which may be text, an image, or a sound file, for example), or a searchable database. Once you figure out your local Gopher situation, you should familiarize yourself with all the commands and options available to you; be sure to read all the help messages on your screen. For example, when a Gopher menu item leads you to a Telnet session, it will warn you that you're "leaving Gopher." At this point, the instructions on your screen (if there are any) should explain how to login and how to use the system. During a Gopher session, you may burrow down very deep into menu after menu before you find what you're looking for. At this point, you can either quit or work your way back up through the menus until you get back to where you started.

Accessing Gopher. There are lots of different ways to access Gopher. One is by using a public Telnet Gopher client. To do this, you simply telnet to one of the public Gopher computers and login. This is not the best way to use Gopher, because these public clients are often maxed to the limit; but if you do use this method, choose a host that's geographically close to you. Below is a list of computers you can telnet to, login as **gopher** (usually), and then use their menu system.

The second way to get access is by using a Gopher client on your own computer. If you're on a Unix system, for example, try typing **gopher** at the Unix prompt and see what happens. There are easy-to-use graphical clients available for most computer systems, PCs, Macs, Unix (X Window, Emacs), and so on, but they need to be directly connected to the Internet in order to work. The Appendix lists places where you can download free gopher client programs for your computer.

Terminal Gopher Systems. If you're accessing Gopher via a terminal client (not a graphical client), here are some useful instructions. First take a look at the sample Gopher menu below. As you can see, each item has a "/" following it. That means each

Some Public Gopher Sites Accessible via Telnet

Geographical Area	Hostname	Login Id
North America	consultant.micro.umn.edu	gopher
North America	ux1.cso.uiuc.edu	gopher
North America	gopher.msu.edu	gopher
North America	panda.uiowa.edu	panda
Europe	gopher.ebone.net	gopher
Sweden	gopher.sunet.se	gopher
Australia	info.anu.edu.au	info
South America	tolten.puc.cl	gopher
Ecuador	ecnet.ec	gopher
Japan	gan.ncc.go.jp	gopher

All these gophers are accessible by Telnet. For example, type **telnet gopher. sunet.se** and login as **gopher** to access the Swedish gopher.

of those selections will actually take you to another menu. Other symbols you'll see on gopher menus:

<TEL>   Telnet session
/   Another directory
<?>   A keyword search

Terminal Gopher Navigating. By using your arrow keys, you can navigate Gopher quite well. The up and down arrows position your cursor arrow; the right arrow selects the item; the left arrow takes you back up to the previous menu. (You can also go back up a level by typing **u** for "up".) You can skip forward and backward through the screens using the following commands:

Next Screen: >, +, Pgdwn, space
Previous Screen: <, -, Pgup, b

Other commands include **h** for help and = to display technical and location information about the entry (useful for when you use Veronica—discussed below). You can also save files to your hard disk by typing **s**. For a list of other commands, type **?**.
    Here's a sample Gopher menu for the Internet Wiretap (*wiretap.spies.com*):

```
      Internet Gopher Information Client v1.11

               Internet Wiretap

—>   1. About the Internet Wiretap/
     2. Clinton Press Releases/
     3. Electronic Books at Wiretap/
     4. GAO Transition Reports/
     5. Government Docs (US & World)/
     6. North American Free Trade Agreement/
     7. Usenet alt.etext Archives/
     8. Usenet ba.internet Archives/
     9. Various ETEXT Resources on the Internet/
    10. Video Game Archive/
    11. Waffle BBS Software/
    12. Wiretap Online Library/
    13. Worldwide Gopher and WAIS Servers/

Press ? for Help, q to Quit, u to go up a menu    Page: 1/1
```

Where to Start. To get an idea of the extent of Gopherspace, select "Other Gopher and Information Servers" (or something close to that) if it's available on your top menu. You should see a menu item called "All the Gopher Servers in the World." Choosing this will give you an alphabetical list of every registered Gopher server in the world.

In the above Wiretap example, to get to "All the Gopher Servers in the World," you would select number 13, "Worldwide Gopher and WAIS Servers." Choosing that will give you another menu, with the top selection "All." This is the selection that shows you the alphabetical list of all Gopher servers. So you see, the street signs are not standardized, but by carefully reading each menu for clues, it's easy to cruise Gopherspace.

If you browse this list of every Gopher server, you'll see a lot of university entries. Gophers are native to the university environment; the system was invented as a way to provide campus-wide information systems (CWIS). Today Gopher CWISs are serving as digital kiosks that provide campus-specific information, such as event calendars, phone and email directories, newsletters, restaurant guides, local weather, available jobs, athletic and cultural events, and course catalogs. While much of the information may not be of interest to outsiders, some of the services do provide links to useful databases and online library catalogs. Also, these systems may be a good place to look for email addresses. Try visiting the Earlham College Gopher, based in Richmond, Indiana (*gopher.earlham.edu*). Or Gothenburg University in Gothenburg, Sweden (*gopher.gu.se*). Or Griffith University in the Brisbane-Gold Coast corridor of Australia (*griffin.itc.gu.edu.au*).

Even though there are a lot of university Gophers, more and more companies are realizing the advantages of providing online access to information about their products and services. For example, many publishers are making their book catalogs available online. And you can even make purchases online using Gopher! All you need, of course, is a credit card. Just think, no waiting in long lines at the mall or suffering through high-pressure pitches on infomercials!

If the long list of "All the Gopher Servers in the World" overwhelms you, check out the other menus that organize Gophers geographically (by continent, country, state, or city) or by subject. If you've been following the examples in this book, you've probably seen these menu items.

Navigation Paths. Many resource guides list ways to find a document hidden deep down in Gopher menus. A common way to represent this is to list all menu items separated by slashes, "/". Using the Wiretap example above, let's say a friend found an article she wanted you to see. She might send you email telling you how to find it using this notation:

```
Wiretap Online Library/Music/Various Top 100 Lists/
Worst 100 Singles of Last 25 Years
```

She could just tell you the menu item numbers (12, 11, 4, 7), which would be shorter, but Gopher menus can change easily, and some client applications don't list items numerically. So it's better to just list out the complete path.

Bookmarks. Once you've gone gophering and gotten lost in Gopherspace a few times, you'll appreciate this next feature. Gopher allows you to tag places of interest to you and assemble all of them in one easy-access menu. To do this, you simply mark an entry with a **bookmark** and it gets added to your bookmark list. So instead of bumbling around and looking lost, use the bookmark feature!

Here's how you tag entries using a terminal gopher client. Suppose you are browsing the MTV Gopher (*mtv.com*), and you decide to bookmark the "reviews" menu. Position the arrow on the "reviews" entry and type **a** (for add). The "reviews" menu item will be added to your bookmark list. To access your bookmark list (a Gopher menu), just type **v**. (To leave the bookmark list, type **u** or the left arrow.)

You can also add entire menus to your bookmark list by typing an **A** (an uppercase "A"). If you typed **A** in this example, the entire MTV Gopher menu would be added to the list.

It's easy to delete bookmarks. First, call up your bookmark menu by typing **v**. Then position the arrow on the item you wish to delete and type **d**.

Veronica

Going gophering can become an addictive hobby, and it's an engaging way to find out all sorts of interesting things you don't really need to know. But what if you need to find an idea for a game to play at your next family reunion, and you don't have time to go burrowing through every Gopher site in the world? You can rest easy because there's a device nestled within reach of most Gopher menus called Veronica. **Veronica** was developed by the University of Nevada, and stands for Very Easy Rodent-Oriented Net-wide Index to Computerized Archives.

Veronica lets you search for an item from every Gopher menu in the world. You supply it with a keyword (or several words), and it will compile a single Gopher menu of items containing that word (or words). This is quite handy, because now you have everything available to you at once, instead of having to sift through mountains of menus. From your results, item 1 may be from a Gopher server in Chile, while item 2 might be found in Hong Kong. You can find out where selections were obtained by positioning the arrow to the desired item and typing = if you're using a terminal gopher client.

Accessing Veronica. Veronica is "built into" Gopher, so at this time, you don't need a special client program to access it. It's usually available as a menu item on most Gophers. There's no standard name for it, but try selecting the following items to find it: at the top-level Gopher menu, select "Other Gopher and Information Servers." That should produce a menu listing choices of other Gophers indexed by geographical region. There should be a selection called "Search Titles in Gopherspace Using Veronica." When you select that, you should have several selections to choose from. (Be sure to select the items that begin with "Search gopherspace at"). In the Wiretap example, Veronica can be found via this path: *Worldwide Gopher and WAIS Servers/Veronica.*

Veronica is a very popular tool, and during peak times you may get a "busy signal" from the Veronica servers. If this happens, just try again later, perhaps in the evening or early in the morning. Rush hours on the Internet are usually during work hours. Since people are always working somewhere in the world, that doesn't help much. But remember, even though you may be playing around on the Internet during your lunch break, you may be accessing a Veronica server in some part of the world when it's 3 a.m.! Also, a Veronica search may return a menu of 213 items, 50 of which are exactly the same. That's because many sites "mirror" Gopher menus. Veronica doesn't care—it dutifully tells you about each one. There's also no indication (on the menu) if they're all the same or, if not, which is more up-to-date. So you'll just have to gut it out and either check them all or act on faith.

For More Information. For general searches, using Veronica is pretty straightforward. If you want to learn more about the inner workings or how to compose more involved search queries, read the "Veronica Frequently Asked Questions" document and "How to Compose Veronica Queries" selections available on the Veronica menu.

Jughead

Veronica is great when you want to do a survey of all of Gopherspace, but Veronica servers are frequently too busy to help you. Here's where Jughead comes in. **Jughead**, or "Jonzy's Universal Gopher Hierarchy Excavation and Display" (isn't that amazing!), searches only a *local part* of Gopherspace, rather than all of it. Many organizations provide Jughead menu items for their own Gopher servers, so if you want to confine your searching to a local area, use Jughead (if it exists on that Gopher). Jughead can be found and used in the same way as Veronica on a Gopher menu. There's no standard place or name for a Jughead menu item, but you can spot most of them because they contain the word "Jughead". Here's a sample Jughead menu item for the University of Texas at Austin Gopherspace:

```
Jughead: Search menus in University of Texas at
                        Austin gopherspace <?>
```

Selecting this item will allow you to search for a keyword from the menu items of the University of Texas at Austin gopherspace.

Archie

Archie (derived from the word, *archive*) is an online file-finding utility originally developed at the McGill University School of Computer Science in Montreal. If you've ever looked high and low for a file on your microcomputer's hard disk, you'll understand the usefulness of this tool. About 1,500 (and growing) known public sites are providing access to files via anonymous FTP. Trying to figure out where a particular document or archive is located on the Internet is like looking for the proverbial needle in a digital haystack.

The archie system maintains a database of all the names of files stored at known public archive sites. A user can search this database by using a client program, by remotely logging in to an archie server computer using Telnet, or by sending email (with commands) to the server. Quite a few server computers are scattered throughout the world; you are requested to pick the closest one. If you don't have an archie client program, you can login (using telnet) to a public archie server. Be aware that, as with Gopher, this is not the recommended way to use archie.

Here's an example using a Unix client archie. Suppose that you're giving a big speech, and you're looking for a good opening joke to break the ice. A great starting point is to search archie for any files with the word "jokes" in their titles. All you have to do is type **archie -s jokes**. (The **-s** option tells archie to return filenames that contain the substring you've specified—in this case, "jokes.") Your client will search a default server and return the results to you. If you want to specify another server, you can do that with the **-h** option (server host). For example, to switch to the Canadian server, type **archie -h archie.uqam.ca -s jokes**.

If your Internet access is limited and you can't telnet to an archie server, you can access archie via email. Basically, you send commands in an email message to an archie server, and the results are emailed back to you. To test this out, send a message to *archie@nearest-archie-server* (see accompanying table for a list of archie servers), with the command **help** in the body of the message. A description of the basic commands will be sent to you. You can then use the "FTP-by-Email Servers" described earlier to obtain the files you want.

Wide Area Information Servers

Archie will tell you *where* a file is, based on a name that you give it, but it can't help you search for information based on what's *in* the file. That's a job for an application called **Wide Area Information Servers** (**WAIS**, pronounced "ways"). WAIS was conceived by Brewster Kahle in the late 1980s, and was developed by Dow Jones, Thinking Machines, Apple Computer, and KPMC Peat Marwick as a joint project. Since then, Brewster has formed a company called WAIS, Inc., which is now developing WAIS as an information tool for corporations. But many WAIS databases and applications are still freely available on the Internet.

WAIS allows you to search for information in databases located on server computers. Think of WAIS as a sort of electronic reference librarian. When you ask it where you can get information on a certain subject, it searches databases and returns documents it thinks will help you. Now, the servers don't actually *understand* your question; they simply look for documents that contain the words and phrases you used. The documents can be pictures and sound as well as text. The neat thing about WAIS is that once you find some articles that fit the bill, you can ask WAIS to find more documents with those characteristics. WAIS tries to "listen" to the feedback you give it before continuing its search. If you're using a WAIS client, you can save your questions and ask WAIS to continue searching at regular intervals for updates to it, or only when you specifically ask for something.

The WAIS system is very powerful and covers a lot of territory. At least 600 databases (more being made available all the time) are on server computers all over the world. Here's just a small sampling of the information you have access to: poetry, sheet music indexes, science fiction reviews, journalism periodicals, and organic gardening. There are also archives of many mailing lists and USENET newsgroups searchable by WAIS.

Accessing WAIS. As is the case for archie and Gopher applications, you can access WAIS either by using a client program running on your system or by remotely logging into a public client. There are client applications available for Unix systems, called **swais** and **waisearch** (**xwais** for X Windows systems).

You can try out a simple WAIS terminal interface by remotely logging in to *sunsite.unc.edu*; login as **swais**. When you login, it will ask for your terminal type; in most cases, you'll be emulating a VT100 terminal. Although this interface is very

PUBLIC ARCHIE SERVERS

You can query these servers several ways. The best way is to use an archie client program and specify the nearest server. For example, if you live in Sweden, use the archie.luth.se server. (See previous Archie section for instructions.)

If you don't have an archie client, you can telnet into most of these, and login as **archie** to use the service. Again, use the one closest to you. Once you're on, type **help** to get a list of commands. If you want to start searching for a file, type **set search sub** <return> and then type **find** *filename,* where *filename* is the name of the file you're searching for. Archie will "think" for a while, and then produce a list of every place that has a file by that name. You can then have this list sent to you via email by typing **mail** *your-email-address.* When you're done searching, just type **exit** to get back to home base.

Location	Archie Server Name
ANS server, NY, USA	*archie.ans.net*
Rutgers, NJ, USA	*archie.rutgers.edu*
AT&T, NY, USA	*archie.internic.net*
SURAnet, MD, USA	*archie.sura.net*
U. of Nebraska, NE, USA	*archie.unl.edu*
Australia	*archie.au*
Austria	*archie.edvz.uni-linz.ac.at*
Austria	*archie.univie.ac.at*
Canada	*archie.uqam.ca*
Finland	*archie.funet.fi*
Germany	*archie.th-darmstadt.de*
Italy	*archie.unipi.it*
Japan	*archie.wide.ad.jp*
Korea	*archie.sogang.ac.kr*
New Zealand	*archie.nz*
Spain	*archie.rediris.es*
Sweden	*archie.luth.se*
Switzerland	*archie.switch.ch*
Taiwan	*archie.ncu.edu.tw*
United Kingdom	*archie.doc.ic.ac.uk*

powerful, it's not very user-friendly. There are other options—
graphical clients are available for PCs and Macs. The Appendix
lists where to obtain them and details how to get started in becoming a WAIS expert. In the meantime, you may have an occasion or two to search WAIS databases accessible via a Gopher or
the WorldWideWeb interface (explained below).

WorldWideWeb

WorldWideWeb (**WWW** or **W³**) is a browsing and searching
system originally developed by the European Laboratory for Par-
ticle Physics (also known as CERN). It allows you to explore a
seemingly unlimited worldwide digital "web" of information.
The WorldWideWeb is built upon the concept of hypertext and
hypermedia, which links independent interrelated documents
and pictures into a three-dimensional cyberspacious world. Almost every piece of information you look at provides you with
pointers, or hooks, into other documents on related subjects.
And these documents aren't just text—they can also be sound
and images—so the WorldWideWeb is really a hypermedia information retrieval system.

The Web is a continuous distributed-information construc-
tion project; tens of thousands of people are adding knowledge to
it daily by bringing up their own **web servers**, which provide
content and links, or bridges, between documents. Servers are
also referred to as **pages** or **home pages**; for example, you may
hear someone say, "Visit the Dr. Fun home page located at
SunSITE." Think of home page as a front door to the WWW. At
the time of this writing, there were 4,000 web servers, and that
number is growing every day.

The Web lets you embark on digital journeys, traveling information links by simply clicking (or selecting) highlighted words
or phrases. Once you make a selection, a hyperlink is followed to
the destination, a related document, which may also contain
links to other documents (and so on, and so on). WWW does
more than just let you browse—it also allows you to search for
key words in certain documents.

This hypertext Web environment in a way mimics your thought processes. We don't think or learn in a linear fashion; most of our thought processes can be pretty random at times. For example, while you're driving to work, the song on the radio reminds you of a party you were at several months ago, and then you start thinking of Joe, who you saw at that party. You haven't seen Joe in a long time, and you decide to give him a call. A simple song on the radio led you to Joe's doorstep. So who knows what the Web will lead you to?

The WWW uses some special protocols. One of these is **HTTP**, which stands for **HyperText Transfer Protocol**. This protocol simply allows very quick network file transfer, and it's used in WWW browsers as a faster alternative to FTP. **HTML**, or **HyperText Markup Language**, is a very simple language used for basic formatting and presentation of hypermedia documents. You can use HTML to specify the format of the document, where the hypertext links go, where images and sounds go, and so on.

Getting Access to the WWW. There are a number of ways to plunge into the WorldWideWeb. The programs that provide an interface to the WWW are also known as **browsers**, which come in two flavors: terminal (text-based) and graphical. Your options depend on how you're connected to the Internet. If you're dialing in and using a slow modem, you're limited to the terminal clients; two well-known ones are the CERN LineMode Browser and Lynx. If you've got a high-speed dedicated connection, you can probably use powerful graphical client applications, such as Mosaic, Cello, and TKWWW. The CERN browser, Lynx, and Mosaic are explained in this chapter. If you're interested in learning more about other browsers and servers, explore the Web for information about the Web (here's a URL to start: *http://info.cern.ch/hypertext/WWW/status.html*), or obtain the WWW FAQ (see the Appendix).

Public Telnet Clients. If you don't have a WWW client program installed on your computer, there are public browsers you

Publishing Redefined

My wake-up call to online publishing came back in the spring of 1989, when I first received a forwarded posting from dissident students in Tiananmen Square. Their first-person accounts represented my initiation to the instantaneous, unmediated communication the Internet makes possible. Used as a global publishing machine, this medium presents us with a fundamentally different, reader-driven and boundless means of reciprocal recorded communication that promises to redefine the one-way street we used to call "publishing."

Laura Fillmore, President, Online BookStore (OBS).

can access via Telnet. You can try connecting to the granddaddy of them all, the WWW server located at CERN in Geneva, Switzerland. Just type **telnet info.cern.ch** (this is a really popular site, so you may have problems getting through). Another one that's publicly available is located at the University of Kansas. Type **telnet ukanaix.cc.ukans.edu**, and login as **kufacts**. Or you can try one located at the Hebrew University of Jerusalem in Israel: **telnet vms.huji.ac.il**, login as **www**. (The WWW FAQ lists some other public sites.)

The public telnet clients are good for evaluating the WWW, but they're heavily visited sites, so it's better to use a local client browser instead. To find out what's available on your system, ask your Internet provider.

CERN's LineMode Browser. This application is a very basic interface to the WWW for those users without graphical client capabilities. If it's available on your system, you simply type **www** and a start-up (home) document will be shown on your screen. You'll see numbers scattered throughout the document; these specify the links. To select a link, type the corresponding number.

At the bottom of the screen is a status line that tells you what type of document you're looking at—if there's a number range (for example, 1-15 equals 15 links), it means a hypertext document with links to other documents. If there are a lot of links in the document, you'll have to page through each screen to see all of them (since they can't all fit on the same screen). If you press <RETURN> (perhaps several times, if there are several screens), you'll see the rest of them. A **help** command lists all of the commands and a brief explanation. The last command option allows you to **quit**.

The very first thing you should do, of course, is type **help** to get a list of commands. There are some keywords that will help you navigate; for example, you can type **home** to return to the home (startup) screen, and **back** will put your browser in reverse, navigating backward on your Web path. If you follow a lot of links (by typing their corresponding numbers), and get yourself deeper into the Web, you can then back up to each link you referenced by typing **back**.

The other commands, **top, up**, and **bottom** help you navigate when you're looking at a document with a large number of links (150, for instance). At any time you can type **up** to look at the previous screen, <RETURN> to look at the next screen, **top** to return to the beginning of the document, and **bottom** to jump to the end.

You will definitely want to learn how to jump to other Web servers when you hear about them. The command to do that is **go** *URL*, where URL specifies the desired server. For example, if you wanted to peruse *Wired* magazine's web server, type: **go http://wired.com**.

Lynx. Lynx is available on Unix and VMS systems. Lynx differs from the CERN Browser in that it's a full screen-oriented application—you can use your arrow keys to position your "pointer" on the different links in the document. If Lynx is available on your system, you can start it up by typing **lynx** at the command prompt. You'll see a screen with text, a "home page," containing words and phrases that stand out (bolded or highlighted) from the rest of the text. Each of these phrases provides a hyperlink to another document, which may contain more links, and so on.

The three lines at the bottom of the screen contain helpful instructions. Here's a summary of some of the commands:

H)	Help	G)	Go to URL
O)	Options	M)	Go to Main (Initial) Screen
P)	Print	Q)	Quit

You can navigate the WorldWideWeb Lynx application by using your arrow keys—the up and down arrows position your cursor on a link, and the right arrow (or return key) selects that link. To return to previous links (backing up your Web path), simply use the left arrow key.

If you find a URL for a great Web server that you'd like to test-drive, you can jump directly to that also. Using the *Wired* magazine example above, you would type **g http://wired.com**.

Mosaic

The terminal client browsers will give you an idea of what's available in the Web, but keep in mind when you're using these that you don't have access to sounds, images, and movies, only to text-based documents. There are other ways to access the WWW besides a text-based terminal browser. Weighing in on the Client Mega Scale is the Mosaic hypermedia distributed information discovery and retrieval browser, developed by the National Center for Supercomputing Applications (NCSA) in Champaign, Illinois. The Mosaic client is a graphical interface to the WorldWideWeb of information, and is one of the neatest applications to make the Internet scene. An Internet jack-of-all-trades, Mosaic also has hooks and gateways into Gopher, USENET, WAIS, archie, and other front ends. It does just what its name implies—that is, show the Internet as a world made up of colorful, varied, and interesting pieces of information, including text, images, sound, and movies. Taking a Mosaic journey is a real trip—you can indulge all sorts of online whims and curiosities.

Many people confuse Mosaic with the WWW and vice versa. They are two separate but related entities; just remember that the WWW is a global hypertext world of information, whereas Mosaic provides an *interface* into this world (as well as into the other applications mentioned above).

When you fire up Mosaic, it presents you with a start-up screen, also known as a home page. As is the case for LineMode Browser and Lynx, this home page is actually downloaded from a server that is located somewhere on the Internet. If this is your first time, your home page may be downloaded from NCSA. Be sure to select the *Demo Document* to check out recommended must-see items. Keep in mind that your Mosaic client program is customizable; you can change your front door to open anywhere on the Internet. To begin your search, all you have to do is point and click on underlined (or highlighted) words and phrases. Every time you do this, a related document (which can be text, sound, or pictures) is downloaded and presented to you. Mosaic provides a "bread crumbs" feature, known as a **hotlist** (similar to Gopher bookmarks), that you can use to find the places you're interested in quickly without having to go searching through layers and layers of the Web every time you fire up the application. Mosaic will also let you specify a URL to visit directly—a useful feature when someone announces the availability of a new resource (look for a menu item that lets you "Open URL").

During a Web session, it's likely that you will jump around quite a bit from one home page to another. Mosaic keeps track of where you've been in a particular session, so you can easily navigate backward and forward. Look for arrow buttons on your screen that, when selected, will help you retrace your steps. There's also a menu that lists all the places you've been. To go back home, simply click on the "home" icon or select "home" from the menu. When you quit a session, all of these history features will be lost, so be sure to add the most interesting places to your hotlist.

What's New, Mosaic? Groping your way around the WorldWideWeb can be akin to getting dropped off in a strange city with no directions or maps. There are several resources that can help you find what you want in Webspace. A popular one is the *What's New with NCSA Mosaic* page, a regularly updated source of announcements of new Web servers and the latest World-WideWeb developments at NCSA. This server is available via the NCSA Home Page (the default home page for many Mosaic applications), or by jumping directly to *http://www.ncsa.uiuc.edu/SDG/Software/Mosaic/Docs/whats-new.html.*

If you need to find a specific resource, you should check out the Internet Resource Meta-Index page, accessible via the NCSA home page, or by jumping directly to *http://www.ncsa.uiuc.edu/SDG/Software/Mosaic/MetaIndex.html.* Included in this page are pointers to subject catalogs (for WWW, Gopher, WAIS, and Telnet) and searchable indexes of WorldWideWeb servers.

Unfortunately, Mosaic is one of those "power user" applications. In other words, if your Internet access is obtained by a PC or Mac and a dial-up line, you may not have the patience to sit around while it inhales the huge image, sound, and movie files off the net for your viewing and listening enjoyment. If you've got a really fast modem (14.4Kbps), and you're using SLIP or PPP (see Chapter 7 for more information), you can participate, but it's pretty slow, and it's easy to start imagining the application huffing and puffing while it's lifting large documents off the net. Your Mosaic application has an option that lets you turn off automatic image-download feature—in this case, you'll just download text without any graphics, which is much faster, especially for dial-up SLIP/PPP links. In order to hear and see everything, Mosaic requires a lot of "pieces/parts"—meaning, you need "external" (to Mosaic) viewer and player applications installed on your workstation to see and hear what's out there. And if that isn't enough, your workstation needs a pretty big engine, ample disk space, and a lot of memory. Assembling and installing all these parts, if they're not already available on your workstation, will take a while and might cause you some frustration.

Mosaic has been hailed as the "killer app" (killer, or way-cool, application), a portent of Internet interfaces to come. Many businesses are considering using it to provide easy access to their company product information and services, or for providing commercial information services. They won't have to convince people! Mosaic is so popular right now that it's being blamed for traffic jams and bottlenecks on the Internet.

Mosaic Clients and Web Servers. If you do have all the right stuff and want to test-drive Mosaic, you can download the client applications via anonymous FTP from the *ftp.ncsa.uiuc.edu* host in the *Mosaic* directory. Clients are available for Unix workstations running the X Window system, Apple Macintoshes, and PCs running Microsoft Windows.

If you're interested in publishing (serving) information that other people can access, there are introductory documents available on this very subject via the WWW. To get started, check out the WorldWideWeb Initiative Page: *http://info.cern.ch/hypertext/ WWW/TheProject.html*. To learn more about publishing your own info, start with the WWW and HTML Developer's JumpStation: *http://oneworld.wa.com/htmldev/devpage/dev-page.html*.

As you roam the Internet, you'll definitely get the sense that there's a culture and a shared history—things that people just "know." So that you don't feel left out, Chapter 5 will give the flavor of Internet culture, review some of what's gone on before you made the scene, share some "insider" information about security, and tell you where in the network world you can go to get help.

Chapter 5

INTERNET IN-THE-KNOW GUIDE

*N*ow that you've learned what you can do on the Internet and a bit about how it works, it's time to cover a few "advanced Internet topics." The Internet is more than just how-to. It has its own culture, its own myths and legends. There are fantasy games on the Internet that become a world unto themselves for many of the players. You should know, too, about the organizations dedicated to the Internet and to network users. And there are some niceties—such as directory services and advanced methods for finding email addresses—that you can master if you're willing. Technical necessities, like computer security, are a must-read. A "Finding More Help" section of this chapter gives some direction for times when you need additional information or help with an Internet problem.

Put a few million people together anywhere, even in electronic cyberspace, and they'll develop some kind of culture—a fabric of shared experiences, shared recreation, shared fears, shared rules of behavior—that makes them all feel part of a community. The Internet's formal and informal codes of conduct were discussed in Chapter 3. Now it's time to learn about some of the less tangible aspects of the Internet culture, the Net legends, and the notable—and notorious—subculture of network games.

LEGENDS ON THE INTERNET

Probably everyone knows at least one story that qualifies as an "urban legend"—a story that, while it may have started with a grain of truth, has been embroidered and retold until it has passed into the realm of myth. It's an interesting phenomenon that these stories get spread so far and so fast—and so often. Urban legends never die—they all just seem to end up on the Internet! You won't be on the Internet long before you start seeing references to these legends. Experienced Internet users have seen some of these old chestnuts come around regularly for years.

The following stories document the most well known of the bunch. You will probably be exposed to these, or variations of the theme. Be "street smart" and wary of any posting promising fame and fortune, or asking you to forward a message far and wide. Check the source before you act.

The Infamous Modem Tax

The FCC Modem Tax Scare is a classic example of an Internet legend that refuses to die. Several years ago, a proposal surfaced in Washington to put a telecommunications tax on modems. The tax was quickly squashed in a congressional committee, and it was not—repeat *not*—under reconsideration at the time this book was published. But you wouldn't know that from some users of the Internet. The scare resurfaces continually on the networks, just like Jason from the *Friday the 13th* movie series, riling new users at the prospect that their new-found electronic freedom is about to be taxed. Even since the first edition of this book was published (November 1992), people still report modem tax sightings.

The FCC story is essentially innocuous, although its constant recycling through the Internet wastes people's time, as well as network resources. It has also created a "cry wolf" situation, and if another modem tax ever *is* proposed, it will certainly be harder to mobilize the opposition. Imagine the damage, though, of a malicious rumor or flat-out lie, broadcast around the world again and again. After you imagine it, promise you'll think twice before you forward anything, and check the facts before you do.

A Catchy Title Should Appear Here

Dave Barry, noted author and nationally syndicated humor columnist for the *Miami Herald,* is an Internet regular. His column, released worldwide on the Internet through the ClariNet UPI news service (called *clari.feature.dave_barry*), has been keeping users entertained on a weekly basis for several years. Wanting to understand the erudition and sensitivity of his articles, thousands of jacked-in Dave followers formed a USENET newsgroup called *alt.fan.dave_barry.* There, fans from Waterloo to Waxahachie discuss his articles and books, recent Dave sightings, those witty postcard replies to his fans, and his thriving presidential campaign in 1992 (his catchword was "A Catchy Slogan Should Appear Here"). When asked what he thought of his electronic devotees, the Internet, and this book, Barry had this to say: "I think it is truly a wonderful thing that, through the Miracle of Computers, millions of people can read my column instead of leading productive lives." Humor abounds on the Internet, and even researchers and educators have been known to search out a laugh.

Get-Well Cards Gone Amok

Back in the mid-eighties, a British seven-year-old named Craig Shergold was diagnosed as having an inoperable brain tumor. Craig wanted to set the Guinness record for receiving the most get-well cards, and his efforts got worldwide publicity, from mimeographed sheets to email pleas.

Shergold is in his late teens now, and he's doing just fine; his brain tumor was successfully treated. He did set the Guinness record for get-well cards in 1989, and has gotten more than thirty million cards to date. That's the good news.

Incredibly, however, the Craig Shergold story keeps circulating on the Internet, as fresh as the day it started. Sometimes it mutates into requests for postcards or business cards, but otherwise the story is the same. The hospital where Craig was treated is still being buried with cards. The Shergolds (Craig's parents), the hospital—even Ann Landers—have sent out pleas to stop the flow, but the story has taken on a life of its own, and the cards keep rolling in. In short, the situation has taken on a nightmarish quality for all involved. The hospital and post office, which have to cope with all the mail, sell some of it to stamp collectors and paper recyclers. Guinness has discontinued the category to prevent anything like this from happening again.

So, if you see a plea on the network for cards for a little boy who's dying with a brain tumor, pass it up. And pass the word that Craig Shergold is doing just fine. No more cards, *please*!

How to Win Enemies and Influence People Against You

The promise of easy and fast money is one that few people can resist. Combine some ambitious entrepreneurs with the broadcast capability of the Internet, and there's bound to be trouble. Enter the latest class of chain letters, the "Make Money Fast" genre. This type is basically a digital pyramid scheme on fast forward. If you don't want to "Lose Your Friends" or "Lose Your Internet Access," just say no to chain letters and pyramid messages in general. Chain letters violate every known acceptable policy. So don't send them.

Speaking of things not to send—everyone hates junk mail, but Internet users hate it even more. In fact, they're fighting back with a vengeance. You may be tempted to take advantage of the Internet for your business marketing programs, but consider the consequences before broadcasting commercial product and service advertisements: literally thousands of angry people will bombard your email box and tie up your phone to tell you how much they don't appreciate your doing that. A recent widely publicized case involved a lawyer in Arizona who sent a description of his services to more than 9,000 USENET newsgroups. He received over 30,000 email messages, and it's probably safe to say that none of them are fit to print in this book.

Following the Internet to the Letter

Jayne Levin is an independent businesswoman who has successfully substituted Internet know-how for start-up capital to fund her own newsletter.

She uses the Internet for interviews, production, reviews, marketing, and sales. After one year, her newsletter has been very successful, and she expects it to be profitable after the first year of publication.

"I decided to launch *The Internet Letter* after exploring and writing about the Internet for a year, feeding my intellectual curiosity and seeing its power to help companies cut communications costs, gather corporate intelligence, and leverage scant resources.

"As a start-up company, I didn't have much money . . . and no staff. I knew I had to conserve funds to make this venture work. The Internet offered invaluable resources, including desktop publishing software that was much less expensive than similar software sold at a computer store.

(Continued)

Just because the current models of advertising and direct mail don't work doesn't mean that you can't use the Internet to promote your products. It's perfectly acceptable to provide a database or archive with details of your offerings that people can peruse when *they* want to. Some recommended books and journals that explain this new fine art of doing business in cyberspace are listed in the Appendix.

GAMES

Just about every computer user has at least one game tucked away somewhere—the kind you play surreptitiously when the boss isn't watching or when you've got a bad case of writer's block. The Internet is no exception. There are shareware and freeware games you can download for your own computer, as

"With an Internet account that cost only $15 a month, I greatly reduced long-distance phone bills, conducting interviews online. I also cut my research costs by accessing CARL (Colorado Association of Research Libraries) through the Internet. CARL, a free database service, provides abstracts (sometimes full text) on articles that have appeared in national dailies and other publications.

"The Internet also provided a vehicle to distribute and sell my newsletter. I announced the availability of the premiere issue, including subscription information, on several Internet mailing lists. Within hours, information about my newsletter was forwarded to other mailing lists and people around the world. I was contacted, via email, by a person in the former Soviet Union who asked for permission to translate the newsletter into Russian. I received requests for trial subscriptions from people in Turkey, India, Brazil, Cuba, Singapore, and Israel, and others used the electronic subscription coupon to sign up as charter subscribers."

Source: Jayne Levin, Editor and Publisher, *Net Week, Inc.*

well as game newsgroup discussions and email lists. Games are played on the Internet, too. There's the Trivia USENET Newsgroup, whose participants have gotten past naming all the seven dwarfs and have now moved on to higher-order thinking—naming all the characters in sitcoms from long ago (*Gilligan's Island, the Brady Bunch, Laverne & Shirley*). Try the Weekly Trivia Contest on the USENET newsgroup *rec.games.trivia*.

As you might imagine, the "big" games on the Internet tend to match the network itself in scale and complexity, and they are a world and culture unto themselves. Generally, the games—with names like Galactic Bloodshed, Empire, Multi-User Dungeons (MUDs), and MUD-Object-Oriented (MOOs)—are adventure, role-playing games or simulations. Devotees call them "text-based virtual reality adventures." The games can feature fantasy combat, booby traps, and magic. Players interact in real time, and can change the "world" in the game as they play it by creating environments, rules, and characters.

All the games demand an intense learning process to figure out all the characters and game idiosyncrasies, not to mention the rules. They can be extremely addictive—small-time players may spend no less than an hour or so a day. Some people literally spend all of their waking hours in the game. Many of the game players seem to feel the need to leave their mark on the game, and generations of game variations have evolved. Empire, for example, a military simulation written by Peter Langston, has five or six multi-player spinoffs and a single-player version. According to *The New Hacker's Dictionary,* all of the Empire games "are notoriously addictive."

In most games, new players take on a persona and then participate in the game. To quote from the Frequently Asked Questions document for Multi-User Dungeons, "You can walk around, chat with other characters, explore dangerous monster-infested areas, solve puzzles, and even create your very own rooms, descriptions, and items. You can also get lost or confused if you jump right in." If these games sound interesting, check out the USENET newsgroups under the hierarchy *rec.games.muds* or *alt.mud.* Read the postings there and then study the Frequently Asked Questions (FAQs) documents for "your" games.

SECURITY ISSUES

Computer security is a major issue no matter where you go, what type of computer you use, or whether or not your computer is connected to a network. No doubt you've heard stories about break-ins on the Internet and would like to know what should concern you. You might be wondering, "Can people read my email? Can they login to my computer? Will my computer get a virus?" This section will provide some insight into security on the Internet and the answers to those questions.

First of all, you should realize that despite its military origins, the Internet is not a classified network. The ARPANET was a network research experiment, so there was a lot of collaboration, with information being transferred between machines and researchers. Collaboration is difficult if computers are locked up tight. Besides, the ARPANET was a small community, and users left their doors unlocked, just as trusting folks in small towns do. Today, the Internet is a massive cooperative with tens of thousands of networks—several orders of magnitude larger than the ARPANET—all "tied" together. And because there's still a lot of research being conducted, it's still considered an open, "sharing" network. That doesn't mean, however, that security is not an issue. Sensitive information is stored on computers on the Internet and is therefore vulnerable to attack from intruders. To further complicate matters, the Internet has spread its tentacles worldwide. Any computer directly connected to any network is potentially at risk if proper precautions are not taken.

What's not so secure about the Internet? Basically, the computers—different computers running different operating systems, each with its own characteristics, bugs, misconfigured software, and so forth. The security of each computer is the responsibility of a system administrator. When a new computer arrives at an organization, all the factory-set passwords and network configurations need to be changed; if they're not, the host will be an easy target for break-ins and outside attacks. Surprisingly, many system administrators don't bother to seal well-known security holes, or they may not know about them. Since all parts must work together to make the entire Internet secure, it's probably best to assume that things just aren't and act accordingly. If you follow a few simple rules, you'll probably be okay. Well-publicized compromises in security have happened and will continue to happen. Fortunately, when they do, lessons are learned, "holes" or weaknesses get fixed, problems are highlighted, and the Internet takes another step toward becoming more secure.

Breaking Down Account Doors

The press regularly reports on hackers breaking into computers and causing damage. The term *hacker* seems now to describe any denizen of the night or fourteen-year-old out on an electronic

The Food Is Better in the Virtual Dorm, or, Finding the Quad on a Penta Chip

A simple multi-user role playing game in cyberspace called Multi User Dungeons (MUDs) may turn out to be the key to an entirely new approach to education. Recent Internet explorers playing MUDs saw new applications for these interactive, virtual worlds that were far from the Dungeons and Dragons and Star Trek realms of the early MUDs and their derivatives.

In an attempt to incorporate education and distance learning into the virtual environment, MIT's MicroMUSE (Multi User Simulated Environment) University laid the foundation for educational uses of a technology once viewed cynically as a time-wasting and resource-gobbling game.

Over the last two years, virtual colleges have begun to appear. Unlike traditional online, email-based distance learning classes, virtual colleges provide micro-worlds that enhance the subject matter being presented and provide environments in which students and faculty interact in real time. Typical of these new environments are DeanzaMUSE at De Anza College in Cupertino, California, and MariMUSE at Phoenix Community College in Phoenix, Arizona.

DeanzaMUSE is a precise replication of the "real" De Anza college. Students and faculty easily navigate this virtual

(Continued)

joyride. Actually, a more accurate term for these computer hooligans is **cracker**. **Hacker** in the computer world is a term of respect—hackers are basically nuts about computers and like to learn systems inside and out. Real hackers aren't angels, but they don't get their kicks from breaking into other systems to exploit holes and snooping in someone else's information. Most break-ins are accomplished by incredible patience and brute force. There isn't anything magical about those who do it. "Cookbook" environment based on their familiarity with the actual college. At the same time, the VR (virtual reality) campus serves as a metaphor for navigating the information resources of the Internet. For example, the DeanzaMUSE campus planetarium has specialized links to astronomical resources around the world, the Euphrat Gallery features exhibits of JPEG images drawn from a variety of sources, and the Bio-Sciences classrooms access data from similar programs at major universities and research centers. DeanzaMUSE has recently expanded to include links with local high schools, Cupertino City Hall, corporate neighbors, and several local businesses.

Phoenix College offers a credit course through its Language Arts division taught entirely on MariMUSE. Students and faculty log on to the Internet from their homes, offices, or classrooms and attend regularly scheduled classes. Depending upon the course being offered, class might be held on the deck of a Viking ship, at a street corner in New York City, or in a quiet study in sixteenth-century England. With nearly two years of experience in the newly emerging field of virtual instruction, MariMUSE instructors are doing pioneering work in the development of instructional tools and techniques.

Virtual colleges may provide an entirely new and highly cost-effective environment in which to explore education in the twenty-first century.

Source: Stan Lim

recipes, giving step-by-step instructions on how to break into certain systems, have even been published over the network.

What Can You Do?

As a user of the Internet, you can't do much about fixing security problems if the computer you're using to access the Net is not your own. There is, however, something very important that you

mudhead n. Commonly used to refer to a MUD player who sleeps, breathes, and eats MUD. Mudheads have been known to fail their degrees, drop out, etc., with the consolation, however, that they made wizard level. When encountered in person, all a mudhead will talk about is two topics: the tactic, character, or wizard that is supposedly always unfairly stopping him/her from becoming a wizard or beating a favorite MUD, and the MUD he or she is writing or going to write because all existing MUDs are so dreadful!

Source: *The New Hacker's Dictionary,* edited by Eric S. Raymond, with assistance and illustrations by Guy L. Steele, Jr. © 1991 Eric S. Raymond. Published by The MIT Press, Cambridge & London, 1991. Reprinted with permission.

can and must do. You can stop an intruder in his or her tracks simply by being responsible about the password(s) you use.

Most levels of service on the Internet require some type of authentication to prove it's really you accessing the service. Most of the time, this involves a user identification and a password to allow access. Your userid is usually well known (you give it out so people can send email, for example), so the only way you can protect yourself is with a secret password. Your password is the key to the locked door of your account or your electronic mail service. Most common security problems can be prevented by simply being careful with your password.

If an "undesirable" gets your password and uses it to enter your account uninvited, worse things can happen than just your files being looked at, modified, or deleted. Crackers have been known to post articles to newsgroups or mailing lists from accounts they shouldn't be using. You may find that, without your knowledge, "you" made an insulting, politically incorrect statement that infuriated everyone who read it. No matter how many follow-up apology messages you send to rectify the situation, damage will have been done. A lot of people may not get your real message, and many who do won't believe you.

Never give anyone your password without a valid reason. When you do give it to someone so that he or she can obtain necessary information or perform an action, change the password as soon as he or she is done. If you get an account on another system, such as a public database or bulletin board, do not use the same password that you use on your local system. You have no way of knowing where it is stored or how private passwords on other systems are. Don't write your password down and leave the paper in an obvious place, such as in the desk drawer next to your computer. Some computers tell you upon login when you were last seen on that account. You should check to make sure it agrees with when *you* were really last logged in to that computer. If there's a discrepancy, call your system administrator.

Copying the scams in which callers try to get your credit card number over the phone, some potential intruders call or send email claiming to be a system administrator. These con artists will tell you that, for various reasons, you need to change the password for your account to the one they provide you. Be careful of anyone claiming to be a system administrator. If you're not sure, get a telephone number and call back or try to see the individual in person.

How to Pick a Password

An easily guessed password is one of the most common causes of security problems. If you don't know how to change your password, put it at the top of your list of things to learn. Passwords should never be based on your own name—not even your name spelled backwards. They should also not be easily guessed, such as your husband's or wife's name, girlfriend's or boyfriend's name, the dog's name, your license plate, the street where you live, your birthday—you get the picture. Passwords also should not be dictionary words. Crackers often use online dictionaries and programs to guess words by "brute force."

So what *can* passwords be? There's nothing left to pick, right? Well, be creative. Take your favorite saying—"Take a long walk off a short pier"—and use the first letters from each word,

"Don't Try This at Home . . ."

You can't point-and-click on CompuServe to make toast in Cairo, but way out on the frontiers of Internet development, the cognoscenti are whipping up elegant hacks to do just that.

TGV, Inc., a networking software company in Santa Cruz, California, first got involved in networking home appliances at a chance meeting between then TGV Technical Support Manager Stuart Vance and Simon Hackett of the University of Adelaide. In December 1989, Stuart was in Adelaide for a networking conference, and discovered in conversation with Simon a mutual love of perverse (interesting) computer and networking applications. Simon had been developing control hardware and software for multimedia applications. They decided that it should be easy to extend control across a network, using the TCP/IP network management protocol SNMP (Simple Network Management Protocol).

Upon returning home, Stuart managed to persuade TGV management to fund Simon's development of a custom controller to interface to a Pioneer Stereo system. <geekspeak on> Pioneer components have a "remote in" jack in the back, allowing them to be controlled by TTL signaling. The custom controller Hackett developed included a 68000-based microprocessor, a chip to generate TTL signals, and a serial interface. Engineers at TGV wrote a small IP stack for the

(Continued)

"TalwoasP." (It's recommended that the word be at least six characters long.) This way the password is not a word, but it's easy to remember and hard to guess. You can also combine words, such as "baby-cakes." It's also recommended to mix some numbers with the letters and throw in some punctuation for pizzazz, but never make your password all numbers.

microprocessor, and Hackett and Vance ported the Epilogue Technology SNMP agent to run on the controller. Additionally, they developed (but never quite completed) a home electronics SNMP Management Information Base for selecting input (CD, tuner, cassette deck, phonograph), volume, tuner band and frequency, and other standard stereo features. <geekspeak off> The world's first network-manageable stereo system debuted at INTEROP 90.

The stereo system project led to further collaboration between TGV and Hackett, including:

- one of two independent implementations of an SNMP-manageable Sunbeam toaster;
- an SNMP-manageable Sony 60-disc CD jukebox;
- and the Interphone, a scheme for audio communication over TCP/IP.

Simon has since founded Internode Systems, a networking company in Australia, and continues to work with Stuart on connecting unconventional (and conventional) devices to the Internet.

Perhaps Hackett and Vance were influenced by Stephen Wright (a comedian), who several years ago told this story: "In my house, there's this light switch that doesn't do anything. Every so often, I would flick it on and off just to check. Yesterday, I got a call from a woman in Germany. She said, 'Cut it out.'"

Source: Stuart Vance

Can People Read My Email?

Can they read it? Yes, they can. That doesn't mean that there is always someone out there reading your email. With millions of people on the Internet, individual messages most likely get lost in the crowd. But you need to realize that once email leaves your system, it may sit on another computer hundreds or thousands of miles away, and you have no control over who has access to it. What if that computer has a liberal security policy, or is full of security holes? The best thing to do is to realize that your email is not going to be secure, and to avoid transmitting sensitive material, as already recommended in Chapter 3. Even if no one reads your email while it's in transit, the recipient could forward the message on to whomever he or she pleases.

It is physically possible to "tap" networks, just like tapping telephone lines. And if someone is able to do that, he or she can read anything going across those wires. But all hope is not lost—there are ways to make your email more secure. One way is to encrypt it before it leaves your computer. **Encrypt** means simply that it's encoded into something that no one else can read without the proper key (the digital equivalent of a Captain Marvel decoder ring). Upon receipt, the message must be decrypted on the recipient's machine. There are no *automatic* mechanisms available in the Internet right now to encrypt email, but if you have the necessary software on your computer, you can do it.

An increasing number of people are interested in the privacy of their correspondence, and a number of programs and solutions are popping up to assist them. An Internet standard called **Privacy Enhanced Mail** (PEM) will take some of the worry out of sending "naked" email. PEM provides for, among other things, encryption and authentication services. (Authentication ensures that it's really *you* who's sending the message.) PEM implementations are unfortunately not in widespread use yet, but they've begun to proliferate, and may be coming soon to an email application near you. Another encryption program in use on the Internet is called **Pretty Good Privacy** (PGP), and it's used a lot outside the United States. If you're interested in learning more about PEM and PGP, check the "Security" section in the Appendix.

Viruses

Should you lose much sleep over viruses on the Internet? Well, no, and yes. Your computer can't get a virus from using electronic mail or telnetting around to other computers. If you're just transferring text files, then you shouldn't worry; they're not going to reach out and "grab" your computer and do something to it. Well, actually, there have been cases where this has happened, but it's very rare. During the Christmas season several years ago, a seemingly innocuous text-art picture of a Christmas tree was mailed to unsuspecting users on an IBM network. When the picture, which contained special codes, was printed on the screen, it also took the opportunity to spread the cheer, duplicating and sending itself to the recipient's closest friends. (This type of activity can effectively grind a network to a halt.)

Even though it's happened in the past, you don't need to spend as much time worrying about viruses or worms in text files as you do in other types of files. In order to avoid catching "the gleep," a good general rule is to be wary of all public domain and shareware software (available via anonymous FTP, Gopher, and other tools). If you remember that you have to do a *binary* file transfer to get this software, then be aware that you're transferring something that could possibly carry a virus. To guard against problems, there are several things you should do. First, always keep backups (copies) of all your work. Second, to guard against viruses from the Internet and elsewhere, be sure that you have the best available virus-detection software installed on your computer. And keep it updated—new viruses appear all of the time.

Where there's a problem, a solution is usually near at hand, and security advice is readily available on the Internet. The Computer Emergency Response Team (CERT), now officially referred to as the CERT Coordination Center, focuses on the security needs of the research community. Based at Carnegie-Mellon University, CERT has an anonymous FTP archive of security advisories, tips, tools, articles, suggested references, and so on. The computer name is *cert.org.* Start by reading the CERT FAQ, available on the CERT archive as *pub/cert_faq.* There's also a LISTSERV called *VIRUS-L,* a moderated, digested mail forum for discussing computer virus issues. The USENET newsgroup *comp.virus* has the same postings as *VIRUS-L,* only in a slightly different, non-digested format. The VIRUS-L FAQ document answers questions on how to get the latest free/shareware antivirus programs. It's available on the CERT public archive in the directory *pub/virus-l,* filename *FAQ.virus-l.* See the "Security" section in the Appendix for the CERT contact information.

INTERNET ORGANIZATIONS

The Internet has spawned a number of organizations and interest groups over the years, with many different missions and purposes. Some are special interest groups; some are task groups responsible for certain aspects of the Internet. An organization that may be of interest, and that provides direction and information for the entire Internet, is the Electronic Frontier Foundation (EFF). The Electronic Frontier Foundation's concerns extend beyond the networks to cover all of the social and policy issues that arise as we integrate computers and networks into our culture.

The EFF was founded in 1990 to "help civilize the electronic frontier; to make it truly useful and beneficial to everyone, not just an elite; and to do this in a way that is in keeping with our society's highest traditions of the free and open flow of information and communication." The catalyst for EFF's founding was the heavy-handed investigation of supposed "computer crimes" by Secret Service agents who, as the stories go, hardly knew a disk drive from a discus. In addition to practically bankrupting a couple of innocent small businesses, the investigations rode roughshod over the free speech and privacy rights of electronic communications. EFF's most famous founder, Mitch Kapor, developer of Lotus 1-2-3 and current president of ON Technology, led the charge in finding funding and hiring lawyers to assist in defense. The EFF has continued to represent computer network users in debates on public policy covering privacy, law enforcement procedures for computer crime, network development, and more.

Local Groups

The latest trend is to establish local interest groups devoted to the Internet or to the WorldWideWeb. For starters, there are Internet User Groups in Austin, Texas, and in Baltimore, Maryland.

Many computer user groups associated with universities and community colleges are covering Internet topics and providing training. User groups are popping up all over the world; if there isn't one in your area, start one! If you're interested in finding out what's available near you, inquire on a local USENET newsgroup (for example, *ott.general*, if you're in Ottawa), or post a query on *alt.internet.services*, a newsgroup devoted to discussions about general Internet services.

HELP! GETTING MORE INFORMATION

As it was so well put in the FAQ on MUDs, "What if I'm completely confused and am casting about for a rope in a vast, churning wilderness of chaos and utter incomprehension?" If you're confused, have questions, and don't know where to turn, here are a few survival tips. First of all, realize that you're not alone, and that we all started off feeling dazed and bewildered. Everyone's digital digestive system is different; sometimes it takes a while to get the drift of all of this. Remember, even *net.veterans* don't know everything! (In fact, the bigger the Internet gets, the less we know.) There is no way you can ever know about or visit everything on the Internet, not even if you studied and gophered all day and night for the rest of your life. The Internet is bigger than you can imagine.

Knowing this, relax a bit and take a load off while reading this section. The biggest hurdle is figuring out exactly what your problem is. The kinds of things that stump people include figuring out what they can do from their system (what applications they can use, what levels of services are available to them, and so on); how to use the applications; how to diagnose problems once they do figure out the applications; and, after they've learned those ropes, finding the resources that will help them.

Think Globally, Ask "Locally"

If you've got a problem that needs solving or a question that needs answering, the very first thing you should do is start close to home when you look for help. Consultants who understand the applications running on your system or network will be able to give you the best assistance. The Internet's flexibility in being able to connect so many different types of computers has been one of the reasons why the Internet has been so successful. It's also a reason why the Internet is so "difficult." Each type of computer runs different TCP/IP implementations, graphical user interfaces, and client applications, and this makes documenting or providing answers for every situation next to impossible. There are an infinite number of combinations available to be used at any one time. So your best hope is your local help desk, which is more than likely accessible by email or phone. Now, realize that "local" refers to your own Internet provider's help facility, which may not be geographically near you. Be as specific as possible when you do ask for help. Write down error messages exactly as you see them on the screen (including all numbers and punctuation), and try to recall the chain of events that got you into trouble.

If you're getting network access through work or college, there most likely is a local consulting office or help desk in the computer center that can give you information about applications and available services, such as documentation, manuals, and online help. Many help desks offer their own online Gopher systems that provide easy-to-use interfaces to steer you in the right direction, help you learn about your local network and the Internet, and provide links into other systems.

If you are getting (or planning to get) your Internet access through a commercial provider, you'll need to look to the provider for help. Ask about support before you sign up. (Chapter 7 includes information about the types of connections and applications that are available.) Commercial providers should have telephone hotlines, make documentation about their services readily available, and offer an email address to contact for more information.

Network Information Centers (NICs). NICs offer information about the Internet and their networks and services. Your network provider isn't required to have a NIC, but if it does, check out what it has to offer. NICs are springing up all around the Internet; many nationwide backbones have them, as well as most of the mid-level and regional networks. These organizations vary in size and services. Many provide online guides, newsletters, and tutorials. Others offer seminars and classes. This may be more information than you'll ever need, but it's useful to familiarize yourself with what's available.

Another Source for Help

As the Internet continues to grow and evolve into the National Information Infrastructure, user and information services have become a more important part of network operation. Recognizing this, the U.S. National Science Foundation funds a NIC to serve Internet users around the world. It's known as the InterNIC, and it offers three different types of services: Information, Registration, and Directory and Database.

One Size Fits All. If you've got a question and you're a bit overwhelmed by the information below about all three services, just call the toll-free 800 InterNIC hotline (if you're inside the United States). It's a one-interface number into everything, and the person on the other end should be able to steer you to the right group. The best way to access all three services at once online is through their Gopher server. The InterNIC tries to be as flexible as possible to reach, but there are simply too many addresses and services for a new user to wade through his or her first time around.

INTERNIC CONTACT INFORMATION AND RESOURCES

InterNIC Toll-free Phone Number: 1-800-444-4345
InterNIC Direct Telephone Number: 619-455-4600
InterNIC Email Address: *info@internic.net*
InterNIC Archive: Gopher Client: *gopher.internic.net* or type **telnet gopher.internic.net** and login as **gopher**
Web Site: http://www.internic.net

asbestos longjohns n. Notional garments often donned by USENET posters just before emitting a remark they expect will elicit flamage. This is the most common of the asbestos coinages. Also asbestos underwear, asbestos overcoat, etc.

Source: *The New Hacker's Dictionary,* edited by Eric S. Raymond, with assistance and illustrations by Guy L. Steele, Jr. © 1991 Eric S. Raymond. Published by The MIT Press, Cambridge and London, 1991. Reprinted with permission.

All of these groups provide access to information via an email "hotline" (read by a human), Gopher, FTP, WAIS, and Telnet. If you're on an outernet, you can use the email server listed to access the files the InterNIC offers.

Information Services (IS). As a new user, this is the service you'll probably be most interested in. The Information Services Desk is run by General Atomics, and it provides assistance with new users' common questions, such as finding an Internet provider and locating online resources. Also offered are regular training seminars geared toward new and intermediate users, reference material available via the Internet, a newsletter called *NSF Network News,* and a CD-ROM of useful Internet information, called NICLink, which boasts an easy-to-use hypermedia interface.

Registration Services (RS). This service is run by Network Solutions, Inc., (NSI) and serves as the official Internet Registrar for IP network numbers and domain name registration, among other things. Unless you're a network administrator or Internet provider, you probably won't need to contact this group. (Chapter 7 refers you to the InterNIC Registration Services if you're connecting your organization's local-area network to the Internet.)

Directory and Database Services (DS). Run by AT&T, this resource will help you find users and online resources.

As you'll read later on, finding someone's email address is sometimes almost next to impossible on the Internet. One of the problems is the large number of separately maintained directories. The Directory and Database Services group tries to solve this problem with a front end into several different types of directory applications, but it's still very confusing and not very intuitive to new users. There are two ways to access the DS. First, and preferably, point your gopher client at *gopher.internic.net,* and select number 4, "InterNIC Directory and Database Services (AT&T)/".

You can also access similar services using Telnet. Type **telnet ds.internic.net**, and login as **guest**. In the Telnet main menu there's a user tutorial, which may shed some light on the various database offerings, but probably not much. Your best and easiest bet is to select the Gopher option ("Browse the InterNIC DS Server File Space") from the Telnet menu.

FINDING EMAIL ADDRESSES: THE SEQUEL

Finding email addresses was briefly mentioned in Chapter 3. Now that you know more about using Telnet, FTP, email, Gopher, and WAIS, here are a few more advanced methods for tracking down email addresses. Literally millions of people can be reached via electronic mail. And, as you've seen, the Internet is growing by leaps and bounds, with more computers and people being added every minute. People are getting "on," but are having a hard time locating the people with whom they wish to communicate.

Unfortunately, there is no *one* way to find email addresses. You simply need to be an electronic detective. There isn't a central database, nor is there a distributed database directory system for you to query. If you are willing and have some time, you can "feel" your way around the Internet, though, and you'll probably find someone's email address, or at least get close. Some of the more common methods are mentioned here.

Directory services on the Internet are classified as two basic types: **white pages** and **yellow pages**. White and yellow pages get their names from the corresponding pages in a printed phone book. In other words, white pages refer to directories of people, and yellow pages refer to directories of resources.

Providing comprehensive directory service information is difficult for several reasons. First, many people have more than one address, and those addresses can change often. For example, you may have a CompuServe address, an Internet address from a commercial Internet service, and a BITNET address from a local university. Each of these addresses has a slightly different format, and is part of a different organization's directory system. To compound matters, computer names can change; therefore, your email address may change. Privacy and security are other issues; you may wish for your CompuServe address to remain private, but be willing to publicize the others. Some organizations don't wish to release their entire directories of contact information. And others just don't have directory information compiled yet, due to lack of staff or other reasons.

Network Information Servers and Tools

Some well-known services and methods for finding email addresses are discussed below. Basically, you have to know a lot about the person you're trying to reach in order to query a database or service to reach him or her. It helps if you know where they're located, what organization they work for, what university they attend, or what network provider they're getting access from. If you have that information, try to find an online directory for that particular organization. Don't worry if these databases aren't always very intuitive or understandable. They may contain the answer you're looking for, but the bumping and tripping you'll go through just to search them will take you longer than calling (by phone) the person you're trying to reach. Most of these databases are provided by universities, but more and more companies are making their directories available online.

Directory Services Standards. The three most common directory standards in use right now at various organizations are

WHOIS (yes, that's *who is*!), X.500, and CSO. These databases can be accessed a number of ways, but they're all available via—you guessed it—Gopher.

The Gopher Directory Way. Look for a menu item on your local Gopher called "Phone Books" or "Directory Services." If you've got that, you can play around with each of the services through the menu system. If you don't see one on your own Gopher menu, the University of Minnesota has an extensive menu of all of these directory services. Point your gopher at *gopher.tc.umn.edu*, and select the "Phone Books" entry. You should see menu items for "Phone Books at Other Institutions" (another menu that includes CSO, X.500, and WHOIS), and for "Internet-wide Email Address Searches" (which is a menu for Netfind, explained below, and a USENET database of email addresses). You can also access many directory servers through the Internic Directory Servers. See page 155 for directions.

WHOIS. Many computers have a whois client program available on their systems. If you have this available, and you're on a Unix operating system, you can type **whois -h** *host-name person-name*. The whois client is available for other systems, and may require a slightly different command format. To find Adam Curry (who is registered at the InterNIC) if you're on a Unix system, type the following:

```
whois -h whois.internic.net "Curry, Adam"
```

You can also query the InterNIC's WHOIS database to find out the contact for a country. To find the contact for the Korea domain, you would type:

```
whois -h whois.internic.net "domain KR"
```

Here, KR is the two-letter country code for Korea. Since there are two entries that match KR, the WHOIS database returns a one-line summary of each:

```
Keith Rodwell (KR1-DOM)                        KR.COM
Korea (Republic of) top-level domain (KR-DOM)      KR
```

The second one is the entry we want. To find out more information, send another WHOIS query, this time specifying the **handle** or the string in parentheses:

```
whois -h whois.internic.net KR-DOM
```

This will return information on the Korea Network Information Center.

The InterNIC's server is considered the "official" WHOIS database, so someone who just mentions the WHOIS database is probably referring to the InterNIC's. However, the InterNIC probably won't have information on the person you are seeking. To access other WHOIS databases, just substitute the *whois. internet.net* part with other WHOIS servers. A list of WHOIS servers can be retrieved via anonymous FTP: *ftp://sipb.mit.edu/pub/ whois/whois-servers.list.*

An easy way to access all the WHOIS servers without FTP'ing the list is via Gopher. Point your gopher at *sipb.mit.edu.* At the top menu, select "Internet whois servers". You'll then get a menu of over 180 items. Use the Gopher menu searching feature to locate an organization. Instead of Adam Curry, let's look for the famous Sandra Johnson, who works at the University of Texas at Austin. Search for the organization (hint: at the Gopher menu of WHOIS servers, type **/University of Texas at Austin** <return>). When you get the "Words to search for box," type **Sandra Johnson**. At this point, you'll be given two choices—you should choose the "Commit to search for . . ." item. The results may show more than one Sandra Johnson, but not a lot of information for each person. To further define your search, look at the uid (userid) of each entry. You want the Sandra who works for the Office of Telecommunication Services, and her uid is "sjohnson." So, quit (type **q**) and then back up to the full WHOIS server page (you have to retype the query). Select the University of Texas entry again, and this time type **sjohnson**. Again, select "Commit to search for . . .", and you should see the full entry for Sandra Johnson. (Now that you have her email address, drop her a line and tell her about yourself!)

X.500. Committees, working groups, and standards bodies have wrestled with the directory problem, and they are working on a directory services standard called **X.500**. But don't hold your breath waiting for a complete worldwide X.500 directory system any time soon. It's true, however, that many organizations are making their internal directories available via the X.500 database format. There are a lot of different ways to access X.500 servers, but the easiest way to start is through Gopher (mentioned above).

CSO. CSO actually stands for Computing Services Organization, the group at the University of Illinois at Urbana-Champaign that developed this electronic directory service. Many other universities and organizations have set up CSO servers that contain information about employees, students, or faculty. If you're just beginning, check out all the CSO directories through Gopher (using the instructions above). There are also client and server applications, respectively known as "ph" (for phone) and "qi" (query interpreter). So you may be able to type **ph** on your own computer to look up people's names.

Netfind. Netfind is an intelligent directory "clearinghouse" service. It doesn't actually store names and addresses; rather, it tries to provide a "one-stop shop" service that knows which directory services, databases, or computers to contact, based on the keywords (login name, first and last name, organization) that you supply. You can query Netfind through Telnet: **telnet bruno.cs. colorado.edu**, login **netfind**. You can also access Netfind through many Gopher menus (look for "Netfind" in the directory menus).

Knowledge Information Service. KIS is based on the concept of a **knowbot**—a knowledge robot that knows how to navigate networks in search of information. KIS queries a number of directory services to help you find directory assistance information. You can access this service using Telnet: **telnet info.cnri. reston.va.us 185**. You'll be asked for your email address (for the guest book). The first thing you should do is type **help** to learn about the possible commands, but you can also get started by typing **query** *name*, where *name* is the person you're searching for. To find out which directory services KIS is searching, type **services**.

Other Methods

Finger. A program called **finger** is available on many computers directly connected to the Internet, and many people use it to find information about users on other computers. It's simple to use: type **finger** *name@hostname*. When you use finger, you have to know what computer the user is on. You do not, however, always have to know the exact login name of the user. You can usually use any part of the person's name, and finger will return essential data on all the users with that name on that computer. The type of information finger returns (depending on how much is available) includes their name, login name, office and location, phone number, and so on. Many organizations make their entire online directory available and searchable using finger. Usually these are located on "official" or well-known computers. You can also use finger to find out about all the users logged into a computer at any one time. To do this locally, just type **finger**. Or to check for all the users at a remote system, you can type **finger@** *remote-hostname*. Unfortunately, finger isn't available on all computers, or it may be disabled for security reasons, so you can't depend on it to provide all the answers. One of the more obvious security reasons is that many people don't want others to know where they are or when they were on the computer last.

As an aside, some organizations use finger to provide frequently updated information, such as the weather or daily headlines. These include *NASA Daily News*, which you can get by issuing the command **finger nasanews@space.mit.edu**, and up-to-date earthquake reports, available by issuing the command **finger quake@gldfs.cr.usgs.gov**.

USENET Addresses. USENET has an address database of all the people who have posted articles to USENET, which has

We'll Make You a Star!

Jean Armour Polly and Jane Dunlap Smith see each other every day. Jean works in Liverpool, New York, while Jane hangs her hat in Chapel Hill, North Carolina. How do they do that? They use CU-SeeMe, video-conferencing software developed by Cornell University, to keep their virtual friendship alive. Both keep video cameras rolling during working hours, beaming their images over the Internet to a "reflector" that retransmits incoming video streams to viewers who have "tapped" into it. They go about their day and, from time to time, other people, friends, and coworkers "pop in" to chat with them. Through it all, they've become quite famous; their faces have been shown coast-to-coast and overseas during demonstrations to large seminars and TV news broadcasts. Don't they get nervous having "big brothers" all over the world? "You get used to it," shrugged Jean. "After several days, you don't even notice the camera anymore."

This gives new meaning to "See you on the Internet."

proved very useful. To use this service, send email to *mail-server@ rtfm.mit.edu,* and type the command **send usenet-addresses/** *name* in the body of the message; *name* should be the name or names you're looking for. The search is "fuzzy"—meaning, you don't have to put the exact name, but can use several words you think might be in the address. For more information, send the command **send usenet-addresses/help**. This USENET database is also searchable via WAIS (Wide Area Information Servers); the WAIS database is called *usenet-addresses.*

Directory Projects. A number of enterprising individuals are taking it upon themselves to provide directory services for the world. Next time you're at the bookstore browsing in the Internet section (probably an entire wall of books by now), look for the humongous books that list people's email addresses.

While these books can be useful, you should be somewhat wary of **shovel-ware** compilations—huge databases of addresses scooped up from various sources around the Internet and printed out. It is nice sometimes to have all this information in one place, but you can save money by just learning how to query the regularly updated sources. See the Appendix for information on some good directory projects like NetPages and Sled.

You're making great progress—you're almost an official cyber-sleuth by now! The next challenge—ahem, opportunity—is learning the ups and downs of Unix, an operating system that's very prevalent on the Internet. It has been said, "In Unix, no one can hear you scream," but the next chapter will calm your fears somewhat and show you that Unix is not so bad. In fact, it's actually pretty easy to use once you know how to hold your mouth right. So stay put, get out your thinking cap, and get ready for Unix! As they say, it's not just for geeks anymore.

Chapter 6

UNIX ON THE INTERNET: A SURVIVAL GUIDE

*O*nce you're a regular on the Internet, you'll notice that a lot of computers out there run the Unix operating system. Unix was, and is, popular among researchers and computer science departments (which made up the early Internet), partly because some of the first versions of TCP/IP were distributed free with one version of Unix known as the Berkeley Software Distribution (BSD). Many computer companies sell their machines with Unix and TCP/IP bundled in, which makes it a more popular combination than some of the other computers and operating systems, for which TCP/IP support has to be ordered separately.

You don't have to be a Unix expert to use the Internet, but it doesn't hurt to know some of the basic commands. Unix—fairly or unfairly—has gotten a reputation for being unfriendly. If you're using the Internet, however, sooner or later you'll have to deal with Unix face-to-face, so included in this chapter are some explanations of the more common idiosyncrasies and applications you may encounter when using Unix on the Internet. Knowing how to navigate through directories and use some of the basic Unix commands will make you a more powerful Internet user.

Be aware that this chapter will give you only the barest of tools to get you started and help you accomplish what you need to do. There are many different ways to do things on a Unix operating system, and these instructions offer just one way. You should also know that there are different flavors of Unix. Most of the commands here will work for whatever version you're using. If they don't, you should use the help facility (explained below), or call your local help desk to find out what the proper command or sequence of commands is. If you're interested in going beyond what's discussed here, be sure to check out the Appendix for more Unix resources.

LOGGING IN

Let's start with the basics—getting access to your Unix account. You'll need a userid and password. Typically, the login looks like this:

```
login:
```

At this point, type your userid. The next prompt is for your password:

```
Passwd:
```

When you type your password, it will not (and should not) display on the screen.

Important! Be sure to type your userid and password *exactly* as they've been given to you, preserving upper- and lowercase. Unix differentiates between the two, so if you've got the caps lock key on, you'll probably have some problems. Later on, you'll see lots of commands and filenames, mostly written in lowercase. A good rule is always to type whatever you're told to *exactly* as shown.

GETTING HELP

Unix may not always offer a lot of help outright, but it does have a help facility called **man**, which stands for "manual pages." If you ever need help with a command, type **man** *command* where *command* is the name of the command. For example, to learn more about man, type **man man**.

More

The man command uses another Unix program called **more** that lets you page through files—meaning it shows you one screen at a time of the file instead of letting it fly off the screen. To advance to the next page, simply hit the space bar once (typing <return> will only advance the file by one line). If you want to quit looking at the file, type **q**. Finally, to get a summary of "more" commands, type **h** for help.

Other Things to Know

Many of the applications and commands mentioned below refer to **control commands**. This means that you need to use your control key in conjunction with a command letter. The control key is usually represented in documentation and helpfiles by CTRL or "^". When either of these precedes a letter, you should hold down the CTRL key, and at the same time, press the command letter. For example, if you see *^G, ^g,* or *CTRL-G* written in documentation, you should hold down the control key while pressing the "g" key (lowercase "g").

THE UNIX FILE SYSTEM

The Unix file system—the way files are organized on the computer's hard disk—is hierarchical, similar to the DOS file system. If you understand how the DOS file system works, then it shouldn't take you long to find your way around Unix systems. Since a good number of the public file archive sites are computers running the Unix operating system, learning your way up and down a Unix directory (as was discussed in Chapter 4) will come in pretty handy.

As a user on a Unix/Internet system, you have your own space on the file system. When you login, you're placed in your "home" directory, which is like your own personal file cabinet. Everyone on the Unix system gets his or her own home filing cabinet. You can organize this file cabinet any way you want—it can be very structured, neat, and tidy, or it can be extremely messy and unorganized. If you like some order to your life, then you'll be happy to know that you can create directories that house files or other directories. A directory can be compared to a manila folder, which you can use to organize and store papers (files) and other folders (directories). The ability to create subdirectories within directories makes Unix a hierarchical file system. If you looked at it from the top, it looks like a tree. (Again, the following diagram and David Letterman examples are fictitious.)

David Letterman's Home Directory

Miles of Files, Directories, and Commands

Once you start surfing the Internet, you'll be pulling down articles, books, and software, among other things, from all over the place. You'll also probably be creating quite a few files, using either the Unix editors mentioned below, or by uploading them from your own PC or Mac (if you're dialed-in to the Unix system). You'll also probably want to save the email messages you receive. Because there are so many different types of files and so many ways to create them, you should definitely have an organized system for storing them.

First of all, to see which files you have in your home directory, you can use the **ls** command to list them. If you type **ls** with no "options," it will list your current directory (which, if you've just logged in, is your home directory). To list your **Mail** directory, you would type **ls Mail**. You can add options to the **ls** command to show you more about the files and directories. There are lots of options, but a common one is **-l**, which triggers a "long" listing. When you type **ls -l**, you'll see several columns of information that specify permissions, links, owner, group, size in bytes, and the time of the last modification for each file.

Here's a sample listing of David Letterman's home directory after he types **ls -l** to get a long listing:

```
sullivan-theater> ls -l
total [16]
drwx------   4 letterman   cbs    1536   Feb 13  14:34  .
drwxr-xr-x   8 root        cbs   29184   Feb 10  19:34  ..
-rw-r--r--   1 letterman   cbs    9383   Jan 17  11:03  LightBulbJokes
drwx------   1 letterman   cbs    3449   Feb 13  10:49  Mail
drwxr-xr-x   2 letterman   cbs    1024   Feb 12  10:39  News
-rw-r--r--   1 letterman   cbs     792   Feb  6  17:51  guest-list
-rw-------   1 letterman   cbs    5097   Jan 29  13:59  tonights-jokes
-rw-r--r--   1 letterman   cbs    5039   Jan  1  10:59  top-ten-list
```

The top two files indicate directories: "." is the current directory, and ".." is the parent directory.

Your listing may not have as many columns as in this example. Here, the first column lists permissions. It also indicates whether the file is a regular file or a directory. If the first character is a "d", it's a directory. In this example, there are four directories: current (.), parent (..), Mail, and News. Skip to the third column, which indicates the owner of each file. Here, "letterman" owns most of the files. The column after that is the group ownership. Letterman belongs to the "cbs" group. The next column indicates size in bytes. Sometimes you need to know the size of a file, especially if you're running out of disk space on your account. The next columns specify the date and time of the last modifications of the file. And finally, you'll see the file name.

When you login, your current directory is your home directory. You can change your current (or default) directory with the **cd** command. Suppose that you want to change to the *News* directory. You would type **cd News**. Now every command you type that doesn't explicitly list a directory will, by default, be performed in the News directory.

Again, another warning about case sensitivity. (The reason this is mentioned so much here is because it's such a common

Sydney Is Burning

"As I flipped through my email messages one morning, I suddenly received a new one entitled 'The Sydney Bush Fires.' The mail was from my Australian keypal, and he was telling me and some of his other keypals what it was like to be experiencing the bush fires that were burning all round Sydney. Forgetting all about my other messages for the time being, I quickly wrote back and arranged to go with him to the KIDLINK IRC (Internet Relay Chat). On IRC, a place where, amazingly, people can talk back and forth, I was able to ask my friend all about the disaster. It turned out he was less than ten kilometers from the fires, he could see the flame-tinged sky and smell the smoke from his window, and he was able to tell me how far the fires were from the famous Opera House and the Taronga Park Zoo. During the next several days, I communicated through email several times more with my Sydney friend, and the fires got even closer to his house. Ultimately, he was safe. However, all week long the information about the Sydney fires that I brought to current events in my social studies class was more up-to-date than anything in the newspapers.

"That is only one of my amazing network experiences, but it is one that illustrates the way being on a computer network and having access to the Internet has changed my life in wonderful ways."

From a winning essay, "Networks: Where Have You Been All My Life?" by Rachel Weston, *rweston@cap.gwu.edu*, Grade 7, Georgetown Day School, Washington, D.C.

problem.) You need to type commands and names exactly as they appear in resource guides, email, and news. If the output of an **ls** command shows a file called **LightBulbJokes**, and you want to look at that file, you need to type the name *exactly* as shown; **lightbulbjokes** or **Lightbulbjokes** simply will not work. This may seem a little tedious, so you might want to use the copy and paste functions of your workstation, if they're available.

There are several commands to view files; one of the most common ones, already explained above, is **more**. To look at the file mentioned above, type:

```
more LightBulbJokes
```

This program lets you page through a file. To continue to the next page, simply hit the space bar. To stop looking at the file, type **q** for quit. For a list of more commands, type **h** for help.

If you decide you don't want to keep the *LightBulbJokes* file anymore, use the remove file command, **rm**. In this case, you would type:

```
rm LightBulbJokes
```

Or, if you want to rename the file, you can use the move command, **mv**. For example:

```
mv LightBulbJokes LBJ
```

This would rename the file "LBJ."

If you forget where you are—what directory you're in—type the "print working directory" command, **pwd**. It will show you the pathname of your current working directory. You'll see a string of words separated by slashes—for example, `/home/tracy/IC-files`. In this particular case, the username is tracy, and her current working directory is *IC-files*. When "tracy" logs in, her default home directory is */home/tracy*.

If tracy wants to go back to her home directory, she can issue one of two commands in this example. She can type **cd**, which by itself automatically puts her back in her home directory (*/home/tracy*) no matter where she is. Or she can type **cd ..** (yes, that's *cd* and then two periods), which will change her current directory to the parent of the one she's currently in (up one level). Remember these two "change directory" commands in case you find yourself deep in your directory tree.

Back to the David Letterman example. If he decides to organize his joke files a bit, he could create a directory called *jokes*. To do this, he types:

```
mkdir jokes
```

The next thing he should do is move the two joke files he has in his home directory to the jokes directory. To do this, he'll type the following commands:

```
mv LightBulbJokes jokes
mv tonights-jokes jokes
```

He is using the "rename" command to move the files, but they do keep their original names in the jokes directory. To change directories to the jokes directory, David will type:

```
cd jokes
```

Now his current directory is */home/letterman/jokes*. If he types **ls**, he'll see:

```
LightBulbJokes tonights-jokes
```

He can then edit or look at the two files in that directory. If he decides to change back to the parent directory, he types **cd ..**, and he'll be one level above (*/home/letterman*).

If he decides later on to remove the jokes directory, he needs to use the "rm -r" command:

```
rm -r jokes
```

This will recursively delete every file in the jokes directory, and the jokes directory entry as well. Your system may be thoughtful enough to prompt you before each file is deleted, but don't count on it. Whatever the case, be careful if you decide to use this command!

These instructions are the bare minimum, but they should get you started moving, removing, renaming, and looking at files and directories.

Creating Files

Perhaps one of the reasons Unix doesn't have a good reputation for being "user-friendly" is the choices of editors. They're not that hard to use—it's just that in most cases you can't use your mouse to point, click, and insert text. The three most common editors available to you are **vi, PICO**, and **emacs**. Or, you can create a file on your PC or Macintosh, and upload it (transfer it from your PC or Mac to the Unix system). The following section provides very brief survival guides for each of these.

Uploading Files to the Unix System. If you decide "to heck with learning another editor," and you'd rather upload files you created with your easy-to-use word processor on your PC, here's what you need to do. This section assumes you're dialed-in to the Unix system using a communications package like Kermit, PROCOMM, or WhiteKnight. Most of these packages come with the Kermit file transfer protocol (which is different from the Kermit communications package—confusing, yes). This section demonstrates how to transfer using Kermit. There may be other protocols available to you, such as Zmodem. Ask around if Kermit won't work for you.

Most likely the files you've created on your home computer are not text files. For example, a word-processed file is not a text file because there are a lot of codes and symbols in it known only to your word processor program. You should decide before you start transferring the file whether you need to do a binary or a text transfer. This is similar to what was described for the FTP program in Chapter 4. You can also convert a word-processed file to a text file by saving it as "text with line breaks" or "text with no line breaks."

To transfer a text file from your own computer to the Unix computer, initiate Kermit on the Unix system by typing **kermit -r**; the "-r" option means that the Unix system is going to receive the file. You should then "escape" back to your PC or Macintosh and initiate the sending process on your home computer by specifying what file you're sending, either through the menu system (choose "Send file") or by typing a command (for example, **send file1.txt**). Unfortunately, there are so many communications packages that it is impossible to tell you here what to do in your particular situation. Refer to your communications manual for the specifics. If everything goes according to plan, your text file should transfer nicely, and then it will be "on" the Unix system. You can then email it, post it on USENET news, or just look at it from time to time.

If you decide to transfer a binary file, such as software or a word-processed document, you can do that too. On the Unix side, type **kermit -ir**. Here the "i" option indicates that the Unix system is prepared to receive a binary file. You need to specify on your PC or Mac that you're going to send a binary file also. This may be set through a menu or a command. Again, if everything goes according to plan, you should have successfully transferred your binary file to the Unix system.

Vi. Vi (VIsual) is a display-oriented, interactive text editor, and it's very hard for newbies to figure out on their own. It's not the beginner's fault, mind you. Vi is not very helpful or intuitive at all.

Here's your basic survival guide. The first thing you should know is that it's pronounced "vee eye," not "vie." To create or edit an existing file, you type **vi** *filename*, where *filename* is the name of the file you want to create or modify.

When you fire up vi, you'll recognize a vi session because your screen doesn't contain much explanatory information, just the text in the file or, if the file is empty, a bunch of ~'s in the first column of every line. There are two vi modes you should know about: **command mode** and **insert mode**.

Upon initiating a vi session, you'll automatically be put into command mode. This means that most of the keys you type are interpreted as *commands* to vi. If you're creating a file, use the "insert" command, or **i**. (There are other single letters that will also put you into insert mode, such as **a, o**, and **O**.)

When you type **i**, it won't show up on your screen, but you will instantly be put into insert mode. (There are no status messages to indicate which mode you're in.) Now everything you type goes into vi's temporary editing buffer. When you're finished typing, press your ESC key one time to return to command mode. (If the ESC key doesn't work, try holding down the control or alt key and typing a "[". This is written as ^[.)

Here's a way to tell if you're in command mode or insert mode. If you type ESC while you're already in command mode, your terminal will beep or flash at you. So just hit the ESC key a couple of times to reorient yourself in command mode, and proceed from there.

You can move around and position your cursor by using the arrow keys. These may work when you're in insert mode, but most of the time you use them in command mode. You can also use the letters *h, j, k, l* (in command mode only) to move left, down, up, and right, respectively.

To delete characters when you're in command mode, position the cursor over the character to be deleted and type **x**. To delete a word, position the cursor at the beginning of the word and type **dw** (for "delete word"). To delete an entire line, type **dd**.

It's possible to include other files in a vi session. Suppose that you've typed a lot of material, and you want to add the contents of another file to it. Make sure you're in command mode first, then position the cursor where you want the file insertion to begin. Type:

:r *filename*

where *filename* is the name of the file located in your current directory. Notice that when you type a colon in command mode, the cursor automatically positions itself at the bottom of the screen. That's so you can type additional information required by the command.

Finding out how to leave vi is the biggest question most newbies have right after they start it up. To quit, type **:q**. To write changes and quit, type **:wq**. To quit without saving changes, type **:q!**. A shortcut command to writing changes and quitting is to type **ZZ** without a colon (which is just *really* obvious!).

PICO. PICO stands for PIne COmposer, and it's the default editor used with the email application PINE, which is described below. PICO is a full-screen editor, and it's very popular among new users. If you shudder when you hear vi mentioned, see if PICO is available.

SUMMARY OF VI COMMANDS

Command Mode

Insert Commands:
i	insert before the cursor
a	insert after the cursor
o	"open" or start inserting in the line below the cursor
O	"open" or start inserting in the line above the cursor

Delete Commands:
dd	delete the current line
dw	delete word under the cursor
x	delete the character under the cursor

Exiting Commands:
:w	write or save file
:q!	quit without saving changes
:wq	write (save) changes and quit
ZZ	write changes and quit (shortcut)

Other:
:r *filename*	include filename in buffer
ESC	returns to Command Mode

To edit a file with PICO, simply type **pico** *filename*. Your screen will split into several parts. The top line is a status line, the third line from the bottom is used for informational messages, and the bottom two lines provide a summary of the commands you can execute. Unlike vi, you are automatically put into insert mode, so you can begin typing immediately. To position the cursor, simply use the arrow keys.

To perform functions, PICO makes use of the control commands mentioned above. For example, to delete a line, position the cursor on the line, and type **CTRL-k** (hold down the control key and press the "k" key). To delete a character, again position the cursor, and type **CTRL-d**. Be sure to look at the help facility by typing **CTRL-g** (**^G**) for more information on commands. See the box below for a summary of commonly used commands.

To quit PICO, type **CTRL-x** (**^X**). The message line (three lines from the bottom) will ask you if you want to save your creation or changes before exiting. All you have to do is type **y** for yes or **n** for no. Unless you don't want to save your changes for some reason (perhaps you made too many mistakes and would like to recover the old version), you should always save. The next prompt will ask you what file name to write the changes to. It will default to the *filename* you specified at startup, so just press return if you want to write over that file. Otherwise, type a new filename.

SUMMARY OF PICO COMMANDS

^G	Get Help
^X	Exit
^O	WriteOut (save changes)
^J	Justify (format) the current paragraph
^R	Read file (insert a file at cursor position)
^W	Where is (position the cursor at a specified text string)
^Y	Previous page (position the cursor at the previous screen page)
^V	Next page (position the cursor at the next screen page)
^K	Delete line
^U	Undelete line
^C	Current position of cursor
^T	Spell

Emacs. Emacs stands for "editor macros," and a lot of people prefer using it over vi. There's a good tutorial available in emacs that will step you through all the commands you need to know. To get started, type:

> **emacs** *filename*

To learn about emacs, check out the online tutorial by typing **^H T**. This means that you type CTRL-H and then the character "t."

ELECTRONIC MAIL

There are lots of email applications choices available for Unix users. This section offers an introduction to ELM and PINE.

Here's how they work in general. All Unix mail readers access a "spool" file called the **inbox**. The inbox is where incoming email is stored automatically. The inbox file is probably stored elsewhere on the Unix system. When you execute an email application, it checks your inbox to see if you have any mail. If you do, your email program will display the messages you've received. You can then read, respond, and send email.

ELM

ELM is a very popular and intuitive email application. To begin using it, just type **elm**. Message summaries will appear on your screen that will look similar to this:

```
Mailbox is '/usr/spool/mail/letterman' with 4 messages
[ELM 2.3 PL11]


->  1 Feb 14 Connie Chung      (26)    Your Mother in Norway
    N 2 Feb 15 Larry Bud Melman (38)    A great Light Bulb Joke
    N 3 Feb 15 Paul Schaffer    (1039) New Song Lyrics
    N 4 Feb 16 Hal Gurnee       (10)    Tonight's Top Ten List


You can use any of the following commands
                        by pressing the first character:
d)elete or u)ndelete mail, m)ail a message,
                        r)eply or f)orward mail, q)uit
To read a message, press <return>.
                        j = move down, k = move up, ? = help

Command:
```

In this example, there are four messages in David Letterman's inbox. This screen is ELM's "index" of messages. The first column indicates the status of the messages, whether they've been read or not. Here, messages two through four have not been read. To read a message, position the arrow or the cursor on the desired message using the arrow keys, or type "j" for down and "k" for up. The arrow in this example is pointing at message one. To view this message requires that you only hit the <return> key. You can then page through the message by hitting the space bar to continue each page (or type **q** to quit the paging process).

If David wanted to reply to Connie Chung, he would position the arrow or cursor line on message 1 and type **r**. ELM will ask him if he wants to include a copy of the original message, to which he types "y" or "n." (The default is "n.") It will then let him edit the subject of the message (at the "Subject of message:" prompt); he can leave it the way it is (by pressing <return>), or change it. The next prompt, "Copies to:", lets him specify other recipients of this message by typing in other email addresses (he might decide that Larry Bud and Hal need to be in on this). After completing this last question, he's whisked into an editor, which will probably be one of the three mentioned above. When he finishes editing, ELM gives him the following prompt:

```
Please choose one of the following options
                        by parenthesized letter: s

e)dit message,   edit h)eaders,  s)end it,  f)orget it.
```

The default command is "s" for send, so if he types **s** or <return>, his message will be sent. Typing **f** aborts the sending process, a very handy command to have. Also, the **h** command is very important—it lets you view your headers, which specify whom the message is going to, among other things. (You should get in the habit of checking the "To:" and "Cc:" headers to make sure that this message is going to end up where you want. Or break out the Maalox, as recommended in Chapter 3.) Finally, the **e** command will put him right back into the editor.

After Dave has sent the message, there are several things he can do: save this message, forward it to someone, delete it, or do nothing. To delete it, all he has to do is type **d**, and the letter "D" should appear to the left of the message. To save it, he types **s**. ELM will ask if he wants to save it in a file that is named for the sender of the message. It will attach a "=" (equals sign) to the beginning of the filename, which means that it will save it in the mail directory (which is most likely named "Mail" or "mail"). In this particular case, it asks if he wants to save the mail folder as "=cchung". If he just types <return>, it will be saved in the mail directory as *cchung* (this is also written as *Mail/cchung*). He can, of course, name it anything he wants.

You should save important messages in folders, which are named either by subject or sender. You can then refer to them later in the mail program by typing **c** for "change folder," and then typing the name of the folder (prefixed by "=" to indicate the standard mail directory). For more information about changing folders, type **?** at the "Change to which folder" prompt. The help screen will show you the names of the folders in your mail directory.

Once you get more proficient with ELM, you may want to customize it a bit to suit you better. You can do that by typing **o** for options at the index command level. Some of the things you can set include your editor, your default mail directory (where you save your mail messages), your name, your user level, and how ELM sorts your messages (by date, by sender, by size, by subject, and so on).

ELM also lets you create aliases, or your own email directory of names and addresses. Aliases are a really nice feature—they eliminate the need to type long and complicated email addresses. Once you've created an alias in ELM, all you have to do is use *that* name instead of the long address. To enter the alias database, at the index command level, type **a**. To "make" an alias, type **m**. ELM will prompt you for the alias name (the nickname), the full name of the person, and the email address for the person. There are quite a few other things you can do here; type **?** for more information.

To quit ELM, at the mail index, type **q**. If you haven't emptied your inbox, ELM will ask you what you want to do with read or unread messages. It's up to you whether you want to keep them in your inbox (so they're shown next time you read email) or move them to a "received" folder. Answer the questions ELM asks you, based on what you want to do with your inbox messages. You can also bail out and not save any changes that you've made to your inbox by typing **x**.

PINE

Another very popular email application, **PINE,** was developed by the University of Washington, and stands for "Pine Is No-longer Elm." (It used to stand for "Pine Is Nearly Elm.") PINE is an extremely easy mail agent with lots of help and menus.

To execute PINE, type **pine**. This will bring up the PINE main menu which looks similar to this:

```
PINE 3.89       MAIN MENU     Folder: INBOX 4 Messages

? HELP              - Get help using Pine
C COMPOSE MESSAGE   - Compose and send a message
I FOLDER INDEX      - View messages in current folder
L FOLDER LIST       - Select a folder to view
A ADDRESS BOOK      - Update address book
S SETUP             - Configure or update PINE
Q QUIT              - Exit the Pine program

Copyright 1989-1993. PINE is a trademark of the
University of Washington
     [Folder "INBOX" opened with 4 messages]
? Help                    P PrevCmd      R RelNotes
O OTHER CMDS   L [ListFldrs}  N NextCmd      K KBLock
```

The very first thing you should do, of course, is take advantage of PINE's help facility, so type **?** to get started.

To compose and send a message, type **c**. This will put you into PINE's editor, PICO, which was described above.

```
PINE 3.89    COMPOSE MESSAGE Folder: INBOX 4 Messages

To      :
Cc      :
Attchmnt :
Subject :
----- Message Text -----
```

As you can see, there are four fields to complete for the email message. Use the arrow keys or tab key to jump from field to field. You need to specify who you're sending the message to, the subject, and any carbon copies. PINE has the MIME capability, which was mentioned in Chapter 3, so you can send non-text (binary) files very easily. Just type the name of the file in the "Attchmnt:" field. If it's a file you created on your PC or Macintosh, remember that you need to upload it first to the Unix system using a file transfer protocol such as Kermit before you can attach it to your message.

Once you've filled in all the blanks, you can start typing your message in the "Message Text" buffer. When you're done, type **^X** to send. PINE will ask you if you want to send the message—type "y" or "n." If in the middle of editing, you decide you want to cancel the whole process, just type **^C**, and then respond with **y** to indicate that you really want to abort the sending process.

PINE has a nice feature that eliminates the need to send yourself a carbon copy. It automatically appends every message you send in the *sent-mail* folder. The first time you run PINE, it will probably ask you if you'd like to create a *sent-mail* folder. Type **y** to create it, and all your outgoing email will be saved in this folder. You can then call it up by changing email folders (see the PINE main menu for that option).

The next option on the PINE main menu is the Folder Index. Type **i** to look at your inbox. The screen will look very similar to ELM's above, and many of the commands are the same. Use your arrow keys to position the cursor on the message you wish to read, and hit <return>. You can delete this message by typing **d**, save the message by typing **s**, reply to it by typing **r**, and so on. Make sure that you type **?** to read the help manual. To return to the main menu, type **m**.

Another neat feature about PINE is the Folder List menu item. From the PINE main menu, type **l**. PINE will list all of your saved mail; each file is actually a mail folder. You can select which one to open by using your arrow keys to position the cursor on the folder. Then hit <return>, and the folder's index is displayed. It will look a lot like your inbox index. If you saved email from your mother in a folder called *mom*, you could then use this feature to reference all the email your mother sent to you. Or you could ignore it until she calls you asking why you never write her email.

Next on the PINE main menu is an "Address Book" feature that lets you create an address book. Type **a** to enter this directory. If this is your first time, you probably won't have any addresses listed. To create an entry for David Letterman, type **a** for add. At the New full name (last, first): prompt, type **Letterman, David** <return>. You'll be asked for a nickname, so type **dave** <return>. And lastly, you need to input the email address for Dave at the Enter new e-mail address: prompt, so type **letterman@sullivan-theater.cbs.com**. And there you go! Now when you send email, you don't have to type **letterman@sullivan-theater.cbs.com** every time in the To: field; you can just type **dave**! For more information on creating an address book, type **?**.

Last on the PINE main menu is the "Other" menu. Here you can check on the status of your disk space or set your printer. This is a really nice feature if you're dialed-in. Setting the printer to **attach-to-ansi** will, in many cases, let you print directly to your own printer. Be sure to read the help files while in the "Other" menu to find out more.

Quitting PINE is easy. From the main menu, all you have to do is type **q**. PINE will ask you if that's really what you want to do. Type **y** if it is.

READING USENET NEWS

The last section in this Unix survival guide will help you get started in reading USENET news. By just using your news reader, you're able to read articles that have originated from all over the world. Don't worry how they got to your computer, though. That's another book.

The news reader discussed here is called **tin**. There are many other news readers, so if you don't like this one, ask your Internet provider what other applications are available and try them out.

The First Amendment Upheld on the Internet

"Those who want to censor pornography on the Net at the source have missed the point. For the first time in history, we can provide the digital tools to individuals to censor what they receive on their screens according to their own values, while letting those who produce exercise freedom of speech. Which is no longer, as it has been in Broadcast, an obligation to listen. That's why I think computer bulletin boards, locally tailored by parents, teachers, or guardians of young people, can make ideal 'front ends' to the Internet. We can have it both ways now."

Source: Dave Hughes in post on the Com-Priv Internet Maillist, January 8, 1994.

News Reader Basics

Every Unix news reader accesses a file in your home directory called *.newsrc*. Notice that this filename is prefaced by a dot. This means that it's an "invisible" file, and it probably doesn't show up when you list your files (using ls). But it's there, and if it isn't, your news reader will create it the first time you execute it.

The *.newsrc* file lists each and every newsgroup that is accessible on your machine, one newsgroup per line. Part of the file looks similar to this:

```
rec.arts.anime:
rec.arts.books: 1-73875,78896,80480
rec.arts.drwho:
rec.arts.int-fiction:
rec.arts.misc:
rec.arts.movies:
rec.arts.movies.reviews:
rec.arts.poems:
rec.arts.sf-lovers:
rec.arts.tv:
rec.arts.tv.soaps:
rec.arts.wobegon:
```

When you first start reading news, you are automatically "subscribed" to every single newsgroup in your *.newsrc* file. The operative subscription character in that file is the colon after each name—that indicates a subscription. There are several ways to "unsubscribe" from newsgroups. One is through your news reader. The other is a "brute force" way—that is, by editing your *.newsrc.*

Why do you care about unsubscribing anyway? Because you may be a bit overwhelmed by the sheer number of newsgroups—thousands and thousands. You simply cannot read all of them regularly, so don't even try! Paring down to the ones you want to participate in and adding others later on will make reading news a bit more manageable.

To edit *.newsrc,* use your favorite editor, and replace all the colons of the newsgroups with an exclamation point, "!". You can do this really quickly with vi. Type the following commands:

```
vi .newsrc
:1,$s/:/!/
```

For those who are interested, the second command means, "from lines 1 through the end of the file (**1,$**), substitute (**s/**) every colon (**:/**) with an exclamation point (**!/**)."

You can then subscribe to the newsgroups you want by replacing the exclamation points with colons. This may take you awhile, because some sites carry thousands and thousands of newsgroups. You certainly don't have to do this all in one sitting; you can edit your *.newsrc* at a later time when you hear about newsgroups that interest you. (Or you can subscribe to a newsgroup using your newsreader.)

If you decide to go ahead and page through all of these newsgroups, there's an easy way to search for keywords using vi. In command mode, type */keyword,* where *keyword* is the word for which you're searching. For example, using vi to search for the keyword "music," type **/music**. The cursor will position you at the next occurrence of that word, and you can then change the exclamation point. To keep searching for that word, just type **n** (for next). When you're finished editing, you can exit and write your changes by typing **:wq**.

Tin is a full-screen news reader that lets you read and post to USENET newsgroups. It's a very powerful application, and this section cannot cover all the various options and commands—it will only give you enough information to get started. Be sure to check out the manual page, **man tin**, to find out more about this news reader.

Here's how tin works in general. When you fire it up, you'll be at the top level, the Group Selection level. This is a newsgroup table of contents from which you pick a newsgroup to read. When you've selected the desired newsgroup, you advance to the next level, the Article level or Thread Selection list. Here you can select articles within a chosen newsgroup to read (the reading level). You can post an article at any time during your tin session. To use this news reader, type **tin**. You'll see some messages that look like this:

```
tin 1.2 PL2 [UNIX] © Copyright 1991-93 Iain Lea.
Reading news active file . . .
Reading attributes file . . .
Reading newsgroups file . . .
```

If there are newsgroups that have been added since your last session, tin will ask you if you want to subscribe to each of them. Type **y** or **n**.

After any newsgroup additions, you'll see the Group Selection screen, a newsgroup table of contents. The Group Selection screen shows you every newsgroup you're subscribed to, one per line. If you want to quit when you're at the Group Selection screen, type **q**. To get complete command help listings at the Group and Article screens, type **h**.

Navigating. In order to read a newsgroup, you must first select it. When you start tin, the first newsgroup will be highlighted. To select another newsgroup, move the highlighter bar up and down the screen. You can do this by using the up and down arrow keys, or by typing **j** (for down) and **k** (for up). You can jump directly to a newsgroup by typing the corresponding number. Finally, you can search forward for a newsgroup by typing

/keyword, where *keyword* is a word you're looking for in a newsgroup name. In the example above, if you wanted to position the highlighter bar on the *soc.culture.japan* newsgroup, you could type **/japan** or **/soc.culture.japan**.

Let's read the *alt.fan.dave_barry* newsgroup. Since this group is already highlighted, all you need to do is type <return>, and you'll be at the next level of tin, the Article or "Thread" level. You'll then see a screen that looks similar to the Group Selection screen above. This one, however, lists all the articles in the *alt.fan.dave_barry* newsgroup instead of listing newsgroup names.

To advance to the next unread article from the Group Selection index, you can also press the <TAB> key instead of <RETURN>. You can use the <TAB> key within the newsgroup to advance to unread articles. In this case, when you hit the <TAB> (or <RETURN>) key, you'll get the article index screen for the *alt.fan.dave_barry* newsgroup:

```
alt.fan.dave_barry (105T 409A 0K 0H R)                       h=help


1  +     Where's Dave's World?              Mike Steele

2  +     The funniest joke . . .           Rocky Frisco

3  + 5   .signature                        Rose Marie Holt

4  +     Cows May Get Fluorescent Leggings Cheryl Kaye Bryant

5  + 13  Be amazed. Be very amazed.        Nep Smith

6  + 2   Child development milestones      gordon hlavenka

7  + 2   Hey                               Dave Barry

8  + 14  Interesting cuisine ideas         Andy Moise

9  +     Letter #5, "Dear Dave . . ."      Richard Evans

10 + 3   This is Dave's feed,              Eric A. Seiden

11 +     Not Making Up Thesis Title . . .  Rangerus Pernickle

12 + 3   New Menace: TWINKIE VAMPYRES      Roger A. Hunt

13 + 8   REQ: Exploding Whale Video Available? Jack Parker

14 + 6   Sad news for Chuckletrousers fans Brad 'Templeton

15       Dave's skivvies                   John G. Skosnik

16 + 6   POP TARTS BURSTING INTO FLAME     Allen A. Hinrichs,


        <n>=set current to n, TAB=next unread, /=search pattern,
    ^K)ill/select, a)uthor search, c)atchup, j=line down, k=line up,
      K=mark read, l)ist thread, |=pipe, m)ail, o=print, q)uit,
            r=toggle all/unread, s)ave, t)ag, w=post
```

As you can see, this screen looks a lot like the title screen of newsgroups. Moving around works the same way, using numbers or the arrow key (or the "j" and "k" keys). In this case, the highlighted selector is pointing at the very first unread article.

This level—the Thread or Article level—will let you follow discussion threads. A thread is two or more postings devoted to one topic in a discussion. For example, you might post an article to the *alt.fan.dave_barry* newsgroup about Dave Barry's dogs, Earnest and Zippy. People who are reading your article can then respond to what you said. This creates a discussion thread. At this article level, discussion threads are normally referenced by the original poster's article. From there you can follow the thread and post a follow-up, if you wish.

In the above *alt.fan.dave_barry* example, the first line indicates the name of the newsgroup, followed by some numbers in parentheses. These refer to the number of threads (in this case, 105), the number of articles (409), the number of "killed" (thrown-away) articles (0), and the number of "hot" (preselected according to a certain standard) articles (0). If you have the "R" switch toggled to "on"—meaning, show only articles that haven't been read—that will be indicated here too, in this case, by the "R."

The next section lists the articles in this newsgroup. The first column specifies the article number. If there's a "+" sign after the article number, then there are articles in the thread that haven't been read. If there's another number, it indicates the number of articles—follow-up discussions—in the thread. The next column is the subject of each particular news thread. The last column specifies the author of the original thread.

At this point, if you wish to return to the Group Selection index, either type **q** (for quit the Article/Thread index), or use the left arrow key.

Navigating and Reading News. Navigating this level is the same as the Group Selection level. You can either start at the beginning or move the highlighter bar down to a desired article/thread. Once the article is selected, hit either the <RETURN> or <TAB> key. The <RETURN> key will advance you to the first ar-

ARTICLE/THREAD COMMAND SUMMARY

The bottom of the screen lists a summary of some of the commands
you can use in this level. Here's a brief explanation:

<n>	Set current article selector to article number <n>.
<TAB>	Position the selector at the next unread article.
/keyword	Search forward in the article index for keyword.
^K	Kill specified threads (for you only).
a author	Search forward for articles by author.
c	Mark all articles in newsgroup as read (catchup).
j	Move selector down.
k	Move selector up.
K	Mark the selected thread as read.
l	List the thread (all the articles in the thread).
I	Pipe the current article to a Unix command (advanced command).
m	Mail the article or thread to someone.
o	Print the thread or article.
q	Quit; return to Group Selection level.
r	Toggle: show all or just unread.
s	Save article or thread.
w	Post an article.

ticle in that thread. The <TAB> key will place you at the next
unread article. When you're reading an article, you page through
it just like you do using the "more" program mentioned above—
that is, by using your space bar. If you want to return to the
Article/Thread index level, type **q**.

(If you haven't realized by now, the "quit" command can be
used at any level to return you to the previous level. When you
use it at the Group Selection index, you exit tin.).

Posting. At some point, you'll want to tell the world what you
think by posting your own articles. There are several ways to do
this in tin. To post an article "from scratch"—you're not following
up on another discussion—is very easy. At any level, type **w** (for
write). You'll be asked for a subject. Type the subject (be descriptive), and hit return. Tin will put you in an editor, probably one of

SUMMARY OF COMMON UNIX COMMANDS AND APPLICATIONS

To find out more about a command, use the **man** (for manual)
command. For example, to find out about the change directory
command, *cd,* type **man cd.**

File Commands
ls	list files
more, page	display a file at your terminal
cp	copy a file
mv	move or rename files
rm	remove files
vi	editor
emacs	editor

Directory Commands
cd	change current directory
mkdir	make a new directory
rmdir	remove a directory
pwd	print working directory

Command Information
apropos	locate commands by keyword lookup
whatis	display a command description
man	displays manual pages online

Useful Information Commands
cal	print calendar
date	print date and time
who	print who and where users are logged in

Email Applications
elm	email
PINE	email

News Applications
rn, trn, tass, tin, nn, vnews

the three editors described above. At this point you can type your
article. Make sure you leave a blank space between the headers
(*Subject:, Newsgroups:, Organization:, Summary:, Keywords:,* etc.) and
the text of your article. When you're finished, exit the editor. Tin
will then prompt you to do the following:

```
    q)uit, e)dit, p)ost:
```

If you want to abort this article, type **q**. If you want to go back and edit the article again, type **e**. And if it's ready to be posted, just type **p**.

The next common way to post an article is by following up a discussion. So, when you're reading an article, you can type **f** (which will include the text of the message to which you're replying), or **F** (which won't include the text of the article).

If instead of posting your reply to the entire world you'd rather keep it private between you and the poster of the article, you can send him or her private email. To do this, type **r** (includes the text of the article), or **R** (won't include the text of the article).

Finally, when you're done using tin, you can either keep typing **q** until you exit the program, or you can type **Q**, which will let you make a quick exit.

You may feel as though you've earned an Internet advanced degree by now. But, unless you already have access through your office or college, you're probably itching to get connected to the Internet. The next chapter deals with the nitty-gritty of getting on the Internet: finding the right modem and software, deciding what kind of access *you* need, and locating commercial or alternative Internet access. So stay tuned—you're almost at home on the Internet!

Chapter 7

GETTING CONNECTED

*N*ow that you know what you want to do on the Internet, or at least where you want to go exploring, you'll want to get connected. There isn't just one place you can go to get access; paths and roads to the Internet are many. The best one for you will depend on your circumstances, your needs, and—to some extent—your pocketbook. This chapter tells you what you need to get started, your choices for individual access, where to go for services, and the basics for connecting a business organization. Many of the details apply only to the U.S. market, but most of the general information applies to the rest of the world, as well. Demand for Internet access is increasing worldwide, but there are more connectivity choices for individuals and businesses in the United States because of the many competing provider services there.

EASY STREET

If you work for an institution or a company with full-time access through a network connection to the Internet, you have the shortest path of all. All you need to do is sit down at your office terminal or workstation and, using the instructions and Internet applications supplied by your in-house computer gurus, log on and get going. Most Internet connections have been made just like that—as connections between two networks, rather than between two computers. For example, a college's local-area network (LAN) might get access to the Internet by making a connection through a leased phone line to a regional network. Once that connection is made, in most cases, every computer on the local-area network has "full-time" access—meaning, the Internet is available all the time, day and night. More and more businesses are getting connections, and most universities provide access. Be sure to inquire locally before starting your search.

ALL YOU NEED TO GET STARTED DIALING INTO THE INTERNET

Fortunately, these days there are more and more ways to get access to the Internet if you're an individual computer user or small business. All you need is a personal computer (Mac, PC, whatever), a modem, communications software, and a phone line. Connecting an entire business or organization's network is more complex than can be covered in detail here, but an overview of the major steps is included later in this chapter (see "Connecting Your Business or Organization"). Some sources for more information are given, as well.

Modems

If you're in the market for a modem, then read this section before whipping out your credit card. A little planning and research in the modem department on your part will make your journey to the Internet a bit easier.

Modems are, simply put, computer appliances that convert the digital signal from your computer into an analog sound wave that can be transmitted over telephone lines. A modem at the other end converts the analog signal back into a digital signal that is understood by the computer you're talking to. Exciting advances are being made in modem technology, with faster speeds and more error-free data transmission. High-speed modems can reduce errors from line noise and even do data compression. As with any computer-related purchase, you should buy the very best modem you can afford—perhaps even a bit better than you can afford. Technology changes fast, and five years from now, today's high-speed modems will be as obsolete as that dinosaur of modems, the 300bps acoustic coupler.

If you've already got a slower modem, don't despair just yet. Many individuals are still using 2400bps (or slower) modems that they've had for several years to access the Internet and other services. All of the access and information systems support them, and, for the occasional user, the difference in online and/or long-distance charges may not be too significant. (The higher your modem speed, of course, the less time it takes you to get information.) Using a 2400bps modem, you can access electronic mail, Telnet, FTP, and the terminal client gopher application. However, the bigger the message or file, the longer it will take to show on your screen or transfer to your computer. If you've got a 2400bps modem, you're pretty much limited to text-based communication, unless you have *a lot* of patience.

If you plan to spend a lot of time online and run applications like Mosaic, or if you need quick, error-free access, spring for a high-speed modem with error correction and data compression. Many of the new Internet applications incorporate multimedia, and require you to drive in the fast lane of the infobahn. You *can* use Mosaic if you're dialing into the Internet with a modem, but you must be using a modem that runs at least 9.6Kbps, preferably at 14.4Kbps (or faster). Prices for these high-speed modems keep falling; they're available today from $100-$200 (U.S.). That's pretty reasonable, and you can probably show savings immediately in connect-time charges alone. (The faster your modem, the faster you can transfer information.) See the "Full-Access Dial-up Connection" section to learn how to use Mosaic and other client applications via a dial-up link.

The ideal modem for telecommunications not only communicates at high speeds but also has error correction and data compression features. Error correction protocols help filter out line noise, which throws "garbage" characters—like "{{pdf{{{"—on your screen, and they ensure an error-free transmission. Most file transfer programs also have a mechanism to ensure accurate file transfers. Data compression, while a useful feature, may not help you much on some bulletin boards and information services that have already compressed their files because *your* modem can't compress them any further. Shopping for a modem gets you into a complexity of feature combinations: speed, modulation protocols, data compression, and more. Claims, particularly for speed, may not be what they appear to be. So it would be wise, especially if you are planning to spend a lot for a high-speed modem, to check some independent sources before you buy. The information box (opposite) decodes some of the seemingly cryptic modem standards.

Communications Software

The second required component is software that will enable communication. Communications software, which is installed on your personal computer, sets up the three-way conversation between your computer, the modem, and the remote computer or terminal server. Since you are dialing into the Internet, there are many types of communication packages available, enabling three different kinds of connections. These are terminal emulation, offline access, and SLIP/PPP.

TYPES OF CONNECTIONS

The following sections explain the three basic access options you have as an individual/independent user. All of these are commonly used and available from a large number of Internet providers. The best choice for you depends on your existing equipment situation and how much you're willing to spend.

Terminal Emulation

What It Is. Terminal emulation is the easiest type of dial-up Internet access to understand. Using your modem and free or commercial communications software, such as Kermit, PROCOMM, WhiteKnight, or MicroPhone, you can dial into an Internet-connected computer or communications server and basically turn your PC or Mac into a dumb terminal that will most

COMMON MODEM STANDARDS AND TYPICAL SPEEDS

The following specify some common modem standards. Many of these—the ones that begin with a "V"—are defined by the Consultative Committee for International Telegraph and Telephone (CCITT), an international organization that develops communications standards.

The third column estimates the time it would take to transfer a 100K file (the average size of many documents or image files on the Internet).

Modulation	Standard Speed	Approx. Time for 100K File Transfer
V.22	1200bps	14 minutes
V.22bis	2400bps	7 minutes
V.32	9.6Kbps	2 minutes
V.32bis	14.4Kbps	1 minute
V.34	28.8Kbps	30 seconds

Standard Type	
V.42	Error Correction
V.42bis	Data Compression
MNP 4	Error Correction
MNP 5	Data Compression

Notes:

Speeds are represented here in bits per second (bps), not in baud. Baud rates and bps are different terms, and faster modem speeds are always measured in bps.

Be aware that the other end must support the same standards in order to achieve the desired connection rate.

V.34 is also known as "V.fast," and is supposed to be available in the summer of 1994.

A popular high-speed modem these days is one that conforms to V.32bis with V.42 and V.42bis. You should expect to spend in the neighborhood of $120-$200 for a good modem.

There are many other standards. See the "Getting Connected" section in the Appendix for more information about modems.

likely emulate a VT100, a venerable terminal produced in the millions by Digital Equipment Corporation (DEC). (You can get communication software from a number of places. Some mo-

With terminal emulation, your personal computer becomes a terminal on an Internet computer.

dems come bundled with communications software. You can also buy it from any software store. And there are a number of free implementations, like Kermit, that are widely distributed through various channels, such as user groups, bulletin board systems, and the Internet.) Once connected, everything you type is from the perspective of the remote computer into which you have dialed. When you read email or news, you are using email and news applications that reside on the remote computer. Similarly, remote logins, file transfers, and other tools, are all executed on the remote computer. Your PC or Mac provides only the display.

When you use FTP or Gopher to transfer a file, be aware that you are transferring the file to the Internet-connected computer you are dialed into, *not* to your own computer. If you want the file to reside on your PC or Mac, then you have to execute *another* transfer process by downloading it using a different kind of file transfer protocol, such as Kermit, Xmodem, Ymodem, or Zmodem. This is perhaps one of the biggest stumbling blocks for new users—the confusion about where the file actually is and how to make it show up where you want. In this situation, when you're transferring files, just think of this Internet-connected computer as the "middle guy." When you transfer a file to the middle guy using FTP or Gopher, remember that you then need to tell the middle guy to transfer it to your own computer. Think of it as a "two-step transfer" dance.

For example, suppose that you're using Kermit to dial into an Internet-connected computer on the Zilker Parknet (a commercial Internet provider located in Austin, Texas). You're zipping around the planet checking out the scene, when you find an archive of online books available via anonymous FTP on host *vtucs.cc.vt.edu* in the *Files/infores/books* directory (the URL is *ftp:// vtucs.cc.vt.edu/Files/infores/books*). After you browse the digital shelves looking for a book you can curl up with on your laptop and read, you decide on *Walden* by Henry David Thoreau. To get this, you have to change to the *walden* directory (**cd walden**), and then get the file (**get walden**).

At this point, *Walden* is on the Zilker Parknet computer (the middle guy), *not* on your own computer. You need to initiate another transfer (using Kermit, Xmodem, Ymodem, or Zmodem, for example) from Zilker Parknet to your PC or Mac.

Here's how to do this if the middle-guy computer and your computer both have Kermit. First, fire up Kermit on the middle-guy computer, in this case, the Zilker Parknet computer. If you're using a Unix system, you can type, **kermit -s walden** (the "-s" means send). Then, on your own computer, you need to select the "receive file" option. You can do this a number of ways—it depends on what system you're using. Refer to your communication software documentation for the exact details. (FYI, this online book archive is also available via Gopher on host *gopher. vt.edu*, path *Eris Information Services/Eris Files/Information Resources/ Books*.)

"Offline" Software Access

What It Is. Offline software access brings some of the Internet functions, such as electronic mail, USENET news, and file transfer, straight to your computer, but lets you work offline. This means that you're not actively dialed-in while you're working (or playing), only when the need arises. When that happens, the software makes the connection, performs the required functions, such as transferring email back and forth, and then disconnects. Providers or services supply you with special software, called **client** or **agent software**. This type of software may conform to the Post Office Protocol mentioned in Chapter 3, and it may also offer newsreader capability. There are implementations available in both the commercial and the public domains.

Although you're not *interactively* using the Internet, you can still do a lot of useful things, such as download electronic mail and news, reading messages and postings at your leisure on your home computer rather than tying up a phone line or running up connection charges. But be aware that not all of the Internet's applications, particularly remote login, Gopher, and Mosaic, are available to you, since you can't issue commands and receive information interactively when you're not connected. Despite this limited functionality, these client connections are recommended for novice users, because they are more user-friendly than many of the public-access systems. With such access, you work with a familiar graphical application on your PC or Macintosh, not on a foreign computer account. You also don't have to worry about taking the extra step of transferring files from a middle-guy Internet computer to your home computer (as you do with dial-up terminal emulation access)—the software does all of this for you.

Full-Access Dial-up Connection

What It Is. A more advanced client connection uses client networking software and a high-speed modem to actually *become* a "directly connected" computer on the Internet. This type of ac-

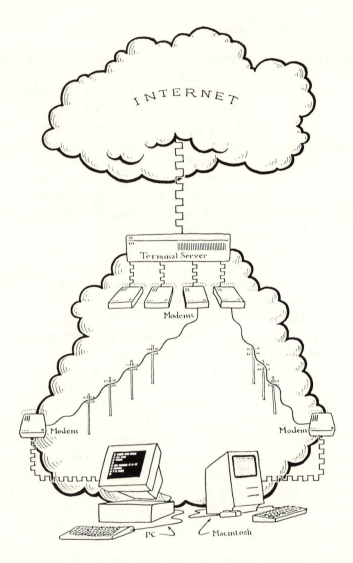

With SLIP or PPP, your computer *becomes* a host on the Internet.

cess differs from the services above because you are skipping the terminal-emulation middle guy, so to speak, and you're interactively using the Internet, not working offline.

What makes this happen is a fast modem (the fastest you can get, at least 9.6Kbps), and software that conforms to Serial Line Internet Protocol (SLIP) or Point-to-Point-Protocol (PPP). Either of these, used in conjunction with graphical Internet client applications like Gopher and Mosaic, brings the power and flexibility of the Internet straight to your home computer over an ordinary telephone line. SLIP and PPP are different, but each performs essentially the same function—that is, they make your computer a **peer** computer on the Internet. A SLIP or PPP connection is a great way to connect, but it can be more expensive and a bit more difficult to configure.

When you use this type of connection, you are actually executing Internet applications on your own computer, not on an Internet-connected computer that you've dialed into. For example, if you want to transfer a file using FTP from a public-access site, you transfer that file straight to your home computer instead of working with the terminal-emulation middle guy. Similarly, you can use a client Gopher application that lets you point and click your way through Gopherspace. The Gopher menus appear as folders on some systems, which is very intuitive. Or, try exploring the WorldWideWeb using Mosaic. It's much more interesting when the Web is in color (if you've got a color monitor, of course).

How It Works. You must dial into another computer or terminal server that is running SLIP (if your computer is running SLIP) or PPP (if your computer is running PPP) to make this connection. (These remote ends are known as SLIP or PPP servers. They help you get set up at the beginning of the connection, but they are essentially "invisible" after you get going.) You'll also need a unique Internet Protocol (IP) address, because your computer must be identified on the network. Your IP address may stay the same, or it may change every time you connect. Your provider will most likely assign you an address, or the remote SLIP/PPP server will assign you a number to use when you make the connection. You may want a registered hostname as well, but as with the IP address and any other required information and

Internet to the Rescue!

Tired of those busy signals when you're trying to reach technical support for your computer? One high-tech company gets much of its hardware and software technical support over the Internet. Over the past year, they've gotten bug fixes and patches for their SUN Microsystems workstations and technical support from their router vendor, Cisco Systems. Another hardware vendor uses the Internet to login to their system for problem diagnosis and resolution.

One of the company's software engineers told us about how the Internet recently saved the day (and night) for him when his boss needed a network monitoring problem fixed by Friday morning (and it was 4:59 p.m. on Thursday)! A quick search into the Internet produced a gold mine of network monitoring programs. He chose one of the simpler ones, customized it, and within an hour was done and on his way home. "Another victory for Truth, Connectedness, and the Internet Way!"

Source: Peter Ho, Unocal Corp. (Note: All opinions are Ho's and in no way reflect Unocal's positions.)

parameters, your network provider will probably be able to assist you. The "Getting Connected" section in the Appendix lists some SLIP and PPP implementations, as well as some popular client applications.

CHOOSING AN INDIVIDUAL ACCESS PROVIDER

Network access for individuals is a new and evolving market, one that is growing very quickly. So finding the services you want, the access, and the right price is not as simple as picking a long-distance phone carrier, or getting phone service through your local phone company. Internet access is offered by private companies, universities, academic/research networks, and public-private partnerships. Service packages vary a great deal and change constantly, as do rates. Your options are not limited to what is described in this chapter. Use the information here and in the "Providers" section of the Appendix as a general guide to starting your own research.

Public Dial-up Internet Access Systems

Lots of companies offer dial-in access to their large Internet-connected computer systems, giving you terminal emulation or (if available) SLIP/PPP access to the Internet. All of these services offer file transfer, remote login, Gopher, and news services, in addition to electronic mail and (depending on the system) a variety of other services, including commercial databases. Access is usually via a phone call to the system's local number, although some systems also offer access via public data networks, such as CompuServe Public Network (CPN). (Other alternative access methods are discussed below.)

Many public-access providers are expanding and adding access points in more cities, so you may want to contact them for their latest local dial-in information. Some of them also offer assistance with buying and installing modems and communications software. Pricing structures vary widely, with monthly access fees, connect charges, or a combination. The services all provide for a wide range of modem speeds.

More often than not, the type of computer into which you're dialed is running the Unix operating system. Don't fret, though, if you don't know Unix. Many providers also offer menu systems that eliminate the requirement of a "computer science Unix internals degree" and simplify things greatly. If you are forced to wade through the Unix muck, be sure to refer to Chapter 6, which includes information on some common commands, applications, and how to get help if you get stuck. To be fair, Unix isn't all that bad, and once you get the hang of the system, it can be quite fun to use. It's just not very intuitive to the novice.

See the "Providers" section in the Appendix for a list of public access dialup systems compiled by Peter Kaminski.

U.S. National and Mid-level Individual Access Providers

As mentioned in Chapter 2, there are lots of regional academic/ research and national commercial Internet providers that offer individual access to their networks. The commercial providers, such as CERFnet, UUNET, ANS CO+RE, Sprint, Netcom, and PSI, offer a wide range of access for individuals, from terminal emulation to full-time SLIP or PPP access. Many mid-level and state networks also offer public and commercial access. The Appendix has pointers to lists of providers.

Everything-but-the-Kitchen-Sink Providers

You've probably been shaking your head at all the background work you have to do just to find "graphical, user-friendly" interfaces, and to find an Internet provider. Well, be on the lookout for commercial products that combine full Internet access, an Internet provider, and all the parts needed to make graphical client applications like Gopher, WAIS, and Mosaic work. You, of course, supply the computer, modem, phone line, and a standard kitchen sink. One such product is slated to be available in the summer of 1994 from O'Reilly and Associates and Spry. Called *Internet-In-A-Box*, it even throws in a complimentary subscription to an online hypermedia newsletter, *Global Network Navigator*. See the Appendix for contact information.

Special Interest/Professional Groups

You may be eligible for inexpensive Internet access through a special interest or professional group. Librarians and educators, for example, have led the way in providing Internet access in member groups. Who knows? A group you belong to might be offering a low-cost Internet connection. Check around. More and more teachers are using computer networking in the classroom and for their own education and curriculum development. Several states—Texas, Florida, California, and Virginia, to name a few— offer low-cost access to K–12 educators. If you are a teacher and are interested in finding out more about access to the Internet, then contact your district's computer coordinator or regional computing consortium to find out about your access options.

Community Networks

Community networks are springing up in cities all over the world. In addition to acting as online town halls, providing information about city government and local functions, they often offer email and perhaps full access to the Internet. Many of these systems are known as Freenets.

See the Appendix to find out if there's a community network or Freenet in your area.

Alternative Phone Access

The services listed above are great if you live in a big city with local dial-in access points. However, if you live in a rural area, you travel frequently, or your chosen system is an expensive long-distance call away, you should investigate other access methods. Some major options are mentioned below.

CompuServe Packet Network (CPN). CompuServe has hundreds of local-access phone numbers all over the world. You need not subscribe to CompuServe's information service to use CPN—you'll be billed for your use through your provider. If your chosen system allows access via CPN, use your modem to dial CompuServe's information service, (800) 848-4480 in the United States, to find your closest CPN access number. Hit <RETURN> to get to the HOST NAME: prompt, and enter the command **phones** to use their number look-up service. If you're outside the United States, call +1 614-529-1340 to obtain access information using a voicemail system.

Toll-Free Service. There are some Internet providers in the United States that offer a "toll-free" 800 number that gets you access to a communications or terminal server. This is a very

TeleOlympics

Kids around the world caught the Olympic spirit last year as they participated in their own worldwide "virtual" Olympics. The Academy One TeleOlympics, organized by NPTN (National Public Telecomputing Network), had more than 12,000 kids from nine countries competing in track and field events in their own schoolyards. All of the events were held on the same day, after an opening ceremony that included a real-time chat hosted by the Cleveland FreeNet and an exchange of email among all the participating schools. Events included 50-, 400-, 800-, and 1600-meter runs (for different age groups), a long jump, and a tennis ball throw. Results were posted to the network, and medalists in each event and age category shared an electronic victory platform. The teachers made the most of the accompanying educational opportunities, and the kids had fun!

Source: Linda Delzeit, Cleveland FreeNet.

flexible option that can be used for travel or remote areas. Be aware, however, that 800 numbers are not free, and the cost is passed on to you, just like a long-distance charge. Typically, the costs range from $7 to $10 per hour, so be sure to inquire about rates before jumping aboard. The last thing you need is a big surprise on your bill, because those blissful Internet hours can add up quickly. Providers offer terminal emulation, SLIP/PPP access, or both.

Major City Dial-in Service. Some commercial providers offer dial-in "ports" around the world, giving telecommuters and travelers local access in major cities. Access is usually made via the local phone system to a **terminal server** or **communications server** connected directly to the Internet. A terminal server is basically a "bouncing off" point to the Internet, a computer that accepts connections and allows you to use the Internet to remotely login to other computers. Terminal servers have modems attached to them so that users can dial in and, from there, remotely login to any computer on the Internet, or initiate a SLIP/PPP connection to become directly connected.

Who does it: UUNet's TAC Access, EUnet's Traveller (major cities in Europe), and PSI's Global Dialing Service (GDS) offer local dial access in many cities.

Electronic Mail and News Services

The wonder of the Internet is its many connecting points. If the methods above don't suit you for some reason, an outernet (or indirect) connection may. Some of the so-called indirect (email and news only) access paths are mentioned below; to discover other available options, just ask around. Keep in mind that new services, new software, and new technology are being made available almost on a daily basis, creating new opportunities to connect directly or indirectly to the Internet.

Email Access Through Commercial Networks. If electronic mail is all you need, you have plenty of choices for an Internet connection. Most commercial online services, such as Delphi, America Online, CompuServe, MCIMail, and Prodigy, have an electronic mail gateway to the Internet. If you have an account on one of these systems, you can send and receive email to and from anyone on the Internet. Note, however, that these services may have a per-message charge for both inbound and outbound Internet email. These charges can add up, so be sure to inquire about prices and then shop around for the best deal.

Wireless Email. Some services allow email to be forwarded from the Internet to alphanumeric pagers, portable computers, and personal communication devices equipped with radio modems. For example, RadioMail is a gateway service from Anterior Technology that provides two-way email between RadioMail subscribers and the Internet (and other commercial networks), and one-way delivery of email (from the Internet and other networks) to pagers, facsimile machines, public and private databases, and information services. The two-way RadioMail service provides a transparent connection between the worldwide wide-area land-based networks and wide-area wireless networks. For people who don't want to be tied to their office or home computer, RadioMail and similar services have a real advantage. They are also useful for mobile Internet users who travel frequently. Subscriptions are available for a flat monthly rate, and include unlimited wireless messaging. See the Appendix for contact information.

Email Access Through the UUCP Worldwide Network. UUCP stands for Unix-to-Unix Copy Program. Basically, it is used as a method for computers to talk to each other over phone lines. Versions of UUCP are available for VMS and DOS operating systems, as well as for Unix computers.

UUCP provides for file transfer between machines. The files that are transferred often contain commands to be executed on a remote system, including printing on a remote computer or sending email. The UUCP network consists of thousands of computers all over the world that have agreed to communicate with each other via the phone lines. Because of these agreements, it is possible to send email from one computer to another by specifying exactly which computers the email must travel through to get to its destination. This process is called **source routing**. Many UUCP nodes are starting to register in the Internet domain name system (by using MX records), so that they look as if they're directly connected to the Internet (when, in fact, they have an agreement with an Internet-connected computer to act as a "post office," transferring email back and forth).

Although no central authority controls the UUCP network, a public registry maintains information about computers whose administrators have volunteered (or remembered) to submit information. There are many email gateways between the UUCP network and the Internet, so it is easy to send and receive email. USENET news runs over the UUCP network, so that may also be available. However, UUCP does not allow for remote login or interactive file transfer.

Going the UUCP route is usually much less expensive than other kinds of access, but it may require more research and up-front work. The equipment is simple—your PC or Mac, a modem, and a phone line. The software is usually free or very inexpensive. Your expenses may include some long-distance charges. The hard part may be finding someone to agree to connect you, either letting you dial them up for information or having them dial you up, or both. If you ask, you may find someone in a local computer user group who'll agree to let you send information back and forth from/to their computer.

Although some universities may offer similar services, user support and reliability is not always guaranteed, because people are usually connecting you out of the kindness of their hearts. If you don't want to struggle to find someone to help you or spend time debugging problems, you should go with a commercial UUCP email provider, where hand holding and ongoing support are available. (Although, even with hand holding, it can still be hard to set up.)

Bulletin Board Systems. Many local bulletin board systems also provide some type of mail access to the Internet. Through these systems, you may be able to exchange UUCP and USENET news, or you may be able to dial-up the system (using terminal emulation) and access mail and news interactively on the BBS system.

Another network that's similar to UUCP is called FidoNet. FidoNet is primarily a hobbyist network whose principal applications are electronic mail and conferences (called "echoes"). It consists of thousands of computers from all over the world, located mostly in the United States, Europe, and Australia. Messages are transferred over dial-up phone lines, just like the UUCP network. The FidoNet technology is being used for many different networks; one of these is K12net, a primary and secondary education network that connects schools all over the United

Serious Games

Paralleling world events such as the 1990 Persian Gulf
War, university-sponsored computer simulations play out
real-world political dramas on the Internet stage. In early
1990 these computer simulations started in the Middle East
politics classes at Melbourne University in Australia, connected with foreign relations classes at the University of
Texas and Macquarie University, Australia.

Students were divided into teams of one to five people
each (simulations generally had 40 to 150 teams), and each
team assumed the role of a political leader in the Middle East
or of another vitally interested country, such as the United
States, the United Kingdom, or France. One team played
Yasser Arafat, while others played President Bush, the prime
minister of Israel, and the king of Saudi Arabia. The teams
extensively researched their characters to help them play the
assigned roles in a realistic fashion.

The controllers (usually the class lecturers) then set an
initial scenario (typically the assassination of a prominent figure, an invasion, or whatever seemed like fun), and the various teams responded, using email (and "talk" where possible)
to communicate with each other. Each team tried to advance
its own goals and strategies, almost always at the expense of
someone else.

The amount of mail flying back and forth was tremendous. Over the three-week simulation period, most teams

(Continued)

States. There are email gateways between most FidoNet networks and the Internet.

Find these systems by asking local computer gurus at user
group meetings, or by consulting the NIXPUB list, which currently includes about 127 systems and their services worldwide.

received 1,500 to 2,000 messages. Many general "press release" type of missives went out to all players, supplemented by roughly 200 to 250 personal messages for each team. Aside from the mail, lots of the wheeling and dealing took place over "talk" as well.

In a sense, the Internet became the stage on which these games of global diplomacy were played out. In the past, such simulations used letters that "runners" carried back and forth. Using email and the Internet improves the concept tremendously. Most of the standard advantages of email apply, including speed, imperviousness to distance, and the ability to login from almost anywhere, rather than being confined to one specific location.

During the 1990 Mideast computer simulation, the participants managed to *talk* Saddam Hussein into leaving Kuwait without going to war. Otherwise, events in the simulations tended to mirror real life to an astonishing degree. At one point, one of the "characters" was killed off in a simulation, only to have his real-life counterpart die a few weeks later. Players threaten, cajole, bribe, fall in love, blackmail, and occasionally shoot at each other. A lot of hot air is vented, and things generally don't change very much in the end, which is pretty much the way the Middle East is in reality.

The concept's popularity is growing; other simulations occurred in 1991, and probably are going on right now, as you read this, holding the mirror up to nature and playing out alternate scripts to reality on the Internet.

Source: Joseph D'Cruz, Research Assistant at Melbourne University, Australia.

NIXPUB is an access list that's maintained by a volunteer and made available via anonymous FTP and dial-up UUCP. See the Appendix for instructions on getting the NIXPUB list. (If you don't have direct Internet access, you may have to ask someone with Internet access to retrieve it for you.)

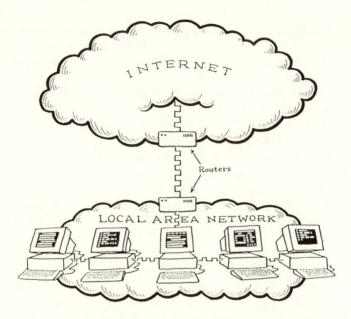

Your business or organization can connect its local area network to the Internet.

CONNECTING YOUR BUSINESS OR ORGANIZATION

The types of connections discussed above work great for individuals, but if you're interested in offering Internet access to every computer in your business, school, or organization, do not run out and buy a large number of modems and phone lines. What you need is a **full-time connection** from your local-area network (LAN) to the Internet. This is the "traditional" way of connecting to the Internet—that is, interconnecting LANs and wide area networks (WANs). The steps down this path are many and involved, and unfortunately this book is not large enough to fill you in on all the details. Indeed, whole books are written on this subject (see the Appendix at the end of this chapter for information), but the major steps are outlined below.

The first thing you should do is to make sure you're set up locally. This means that the LAN (or LANs) that you're interconnecting needs to be running appropriate software. Remember that the Internet, for the most part, is based on TCP/IP protocols. All computers that are participating must be running the necessary TCP/IP communications programs and applications, or else they won't be able to "talk" to any other computer on the Internet. TCP/IP implementations, both commercial and public domain, exist for almost every type of computer platform around. The Appendix will get you pointed in the direction of some of these. You may need network consulting assistance to help you find the best solution for your particular situation.

Along with installing the software (if it's not already available on the computers), you're going to need to do some network administration. You will need your own Internet Protocol network number (for example, 131.108), and a domain name (such as *cisco.com*). The IP network number will be one of several classes, depending on how big your network is in terms of number of networks and computers.

Once you obtain this network number, you can assign separate, unique IP addresses based on it to each computer on your network. Similarly, with a domain name, you can uniquely identify your organization and each of your computers by giving them a logical name within that domain. You can obtain these key identifiers from the InterNIC registration services operated by Network Solutions, Inc. (explained in Chapter 5). Some countries provide their own registration services; you can contact the InterNIC to find out who to contact. You will need to complete several registration forms to apply for your IP number and domain name, and send them in to the InterNIC. These registration forms ask for certain information about your network, such as how many computers are connected to it, as well as administrative and technical contact information. If you have problems answering any of the questions on these registration forms, ask your network provider or the InterNIC for assistance. (Your network provider may provide registration services as part of the connection fee.)

You'll also need to provide the names of two computers that will act as domain nameservers for host information on your network. You will recall from Chapter 2 that a domain nameserver is a computer that has a database of information about the computers on your network. (The type of information in this database includes each computer's name, Internet address, and computer type.) Two servers are required for reliability purposes, one designated primary, the other secondary. (Your organization can have more than one secondary nameserver.)

If one server (perhaps the primary one) is unavailable (probably for hardware reasons or because the network is down), the other will be able to answer queries for computer addresses and names. For this reason, it is recommended that one of these nameservers be located at some place other than your own network. Some network providers offer name service as part of their services or will act as a domain "dating service" for you, helping you to find an off-site secondary server.

Making the Connection

Equipment. The next step involves connecting to "the world." To do this, you need some special equipment, which will be owned, maintained, and configured by your organization, by your Internet provider, or by a combination of both. A key piece of equipment you will need is a router, a special computer that connects to your local area network and also has a connection to your Internet service provider. The router takes care of forwarding and routing packets to the proper destination, in addition to providing security, circuit bandwidth management, and other useful features. You will also need equipment called CSU/DSUs for the local and remote ends to handle the connections between the phone company circuit (mentioned below) and the routers.

Phone Circuit. The next step involves "lashing" your network up to an Internet provider. This requires obtaining a wide-area network circuit from your local Bell Operating Company, a long-distance provider, or both. Your Internet provider may do this for you or assist you with this. There are many different types of circuits and bandwidth choices. Your solution will depend on what's available in your area, what you can afford, and basically what makes sense for your situation.

A phone circuit can be dedicated (full-time) or dial-up. A dial-up "dedicated" solution is similar to the individual SLIP/PPP service mentioned above; in fact, it probably uses SLIP or PPP. Using these protocols and the fastest modem around, it is possible to serve a couple of users on a local-area network. This is an on-demand type of connection, and the connection will have to be established each time before it can be used. If you have more than a couple of users, and you're planning on running applications like Mosaic or CU-SeeMe, you will want a faster, dedicated circuit, running at least 56Kbps. Bandwidth refers to the speed of your connection, or how much data can be pumped through a circuit at a given time. The speed you need depends on the combination of users, applications, and amount of money you have to spend. Your organization's connection may be running as slow as 9.6Kbps or as fast as 155Mbps. See the "Circuit Choices" box for a list of common circuits and typical speeds.

Internet connections are being made with just about anything these days, and some wacky engineers have even demonstrated transmitting TCP/IP over a string connecting two tin cans. A phone company circuit may not be the best solution for you, so be aware that there are other options, such as wireless, microwave, or satellites. One Internet provider, PSI, is offering access to the Internet through local cable companies; call PSI to inquire about availability in your area.

The Internet Provider. You can buy the equipment and obtain a circuit, but you're not going anywhere unless you've got an Internet provider. In the United States, your choices in providers and service offerings are many. The members of the Commercial Internet Exchange (CIX) have already been mentioned (CERFnet, PSI, Sprint, and UUNET). Another commercial provider, Advanced Network and Services, Inc. (ANS), also offers commercial access. Many academic and research mid-level networks will connect you. Most of the NSFNET mid-level networks are good sources for connections. You can get an up-to-date list and access information from InterNIC's Information Services (IS) (mentioned in Chapter 5) from the indexes listed in the books suggested below or from the Appendix in this book.

Circuit Choices

The chart below lists common circuits and typical speeds you can obtain from your local or long-distance telephone companies. Your circuit will begin at your site and terminate at an Internet provider's Point of Presence (POP), the closest telephone company location. Circuit costs are a recurring charge, billed monthly, and most commonly are based on speed and distance. Depending on your situation, you may have to lease circuits from both a local phone company and a long-distance service.

The type of services include both digital and analog; the lower speeds are usually analog, and the higher speeds are usually digital. Keep in mind that if you use an analog service, you'll need a modem (explained at the beginning of this chapter) to convert the digital bits to analog for the analog circuit. If you're using a leased digital circuit, you'll need a CSU/DSU instead of a modem.

These choices may look complicated, but the good news is that a lot of the Internet service providers will act as one-stop shopping outlets, recommending solutions and packaging the equipment that you need to make the connection. This assistance is not only easier on you, but it can also frequently save you money, not to mention time.

Costs. Costs of connecting your organization's network can vary widely (or wildly) from provider to provider. Obviously, providers who do much of the work for you will charge more in administrative and monthly or yearly fees. Start-up expenses include special equipment and administrative fees. CSU/DSUs can cost anywhere from $400 to $2500 each, depending on the speed of your connection (you'll probably have to buy two of them, one for each end of the circuit). Router prices are falling, but

POINT-TO-POINT CIRCUITS

Type	Typical Speeds	Notes/Explanation
DDS	up to 56Kbps	Dataphone Digital Service
T1	1.5Mbps	
FT1	128Kbps-768Kbps	Fractional T1
T3	45Mbps	
E1	2.048Mbps	European equivalent of T1
E3	34Mbps	European equivalent of T3

PACKET-SWITCHED CIRCUITS

Type	Typical Speeds	Notes/Explanation
X.25	9.6Kbps	CCITT Standard
Frame Relay	1.544 Mbps-2Mbps	
SMDS	64Kbps–N*64Kbps	Switched Multimegabit Data Service
ATM	1Mbps-155Mbps	Asynchronous Transfer Mode

CIRCUIT-SWITCHED CIRCUITS

Type	Typical Speeds	Notes
POTS (Plain Old Telephone Service)	modem speeds	analog service
Switched 56	56Kbps	Digital Circuits
BRI-ISDN	64Kbps	Integrated Services Digital Network, Basic Rate Interface (BRI)
PRI-ISDN	1.544Mbps	ISDN Primary Rate Interface (PRI)

you'll spend at least a couple of thousand dollars for a good, low-end access router. After your network is connected, recurring costs include monthly administrative fees and circuit charges. Remember, though, that the information traffic on your circuits isn't metered—you won't get a monthly long-distance bill on top of everything else for every file transfer an employee or student made from a computer in Norway, or every email message sent to someone in Alaska. (However, this situation could change, and it may not be the case for Internet providers that charge by the packet, not a flat rate charge.)

Other Connection Issues

Once you're connected, there are several issues that you may have to address constantly. One is technical support. If your network provider doesn't monitor, configure, and upgrade your network's connection, then you will have to pay someone to do it (or do it yourself). Someone has to maintain the domain nameservers and establish an electronic mail system for your organization. Also, you may want to provide a Gopher or WWW server for your organization's public information; as has been mentioned throughout this book, quite a few businesses offer public information archives that include their catalogs, pricing information, tutorials, books, and so on.

User Support. An Internet connection does your business or school no good if no one knows how to use it. Don't underestimate the amount of support and training you'll need; this is one of the most important components of an Internet connection, and unfortunately one of the first things to be ignored. You can get help from the millions of people, the thousands of email lists, and the megabytes of documentation available on the Internet, but more than likely you'll need some hand holding for your users. Your network provider may assist in training, and Internet seminars are springing up all over the world. No matter what you do, everyone in your organization needs a copy of this book. :-)

Security. Finally, you or your network provider will be responsible for maintaining security on your network and computers. Security includes making sure you know which users on your network are accessing the Internet (by using proper authoriza-

hacker (originally, someone who makes furniture with an ax) n. 1. A person who enjoys exploring the details of programmable systems and how to stretch their capabilities, as opposed to most users, who prefer to learn only the minimum necessary. 2. One who programs enthusiastically (even obsessively), or who enjoys programming rather than just theorizing about programming. 3. A person capable of appreciating hack value. 4. A person who is good at programming quickly. 5. An expert at a particular program, or one who frequently does work using it or on it; as in 'a Unix hacker.' (Definitions 1 through 5 are correlated, and people who fit them congregate.) 6. An expert or enthusiast of any kind. One might be an astronomy hacker, for example. 7. One who enjoys the intellectual challenge of creatively overcoming or circumventing limitations. 8. [deprecated] A malicious meddler who tries to discover sensitive information by poking around. Hence *password hacker, network hacker.*

It is better to be described as a hacker by others than to describe oneself that way. Hackers consider themselves something of an elite (a meritocracy based on ability), though one to which new members are gladly welcome. There is thus a certain ego satisfaction to be had in identifying yourself as a hacker (but if you claim to be one and are not, you'll quickly be labeled bogus).

Source: *The New Hacker's Dictionary,* edited by Eric S. Raymond, with assistance and illustrations by Guy L. Steele, Jr. © 1991 Eric S. Raymond. Published by The MIT Press, Cambridge and London, 1991. Reprinted with permission.

tion mechanisms, such as accounts and passwords on computers and terminal servers) and keeping intruders out of your systems. A router can be configured to allow outside access to all, some, or none of your internal networks. There are quite a few businesses who use their routers as "firewalls," only allowing a certain type of traffic to enter their internal networks.

FOR MORE INFORMATION

There are two very good books that provide information on buying
and implementing a network connection:
- *Connecting to the Internet: An O'Reilly Buyer's Guide,* by Susan
  Estrada, published by O'Reilly & Associates
- *The Internet Connection,* by John S. Quarterman and Smoot Carl-
  Mitchell, published by Addison-Wesley

There it is. Whether you're a retiree or a recluse, whether
you have a gigabit-per-second connection or a tin can and a
string, *you* can be a part of the Internet. And once you're connected, you can behold the fabulous sites in cyberspace. Some
good advice: keep trying when you're frustrated, keep looking
when you can't find it, and keep your sense of humor. You probably couldn't ride a bicycle perfectly the first time you tried
either!

The world of the Internet is immense, and so, too, is the body
of information about it! The biggest task in writing this book was
sorting out what you, the new Internet user, most needed to
know to get started. The listing of resources that follows in the
Appendix is the most fitting conclusion to this book, because it
gives you places to look for even more information. Hopefully,
you're excited about further adventures. You've now been given
the map, the rules of the road, and the keys to the kingdom.
Enjoy your Internet journey!

Appendix

This appendix contains pointers to popular resources available on the Internet. The Uniform Resource Locators (URL) system (explained in Chapter 4) was used to describe these resources. Here are some quick examples of how you would use each type of URL:

URL	Commands
telnet://flounder.rutgers.edu:5150	**telnet flounder.rutgers.edu 5150**
ftp://quartz.rutgers.edu/ *pub/baseball/jazz*	**ftp quartz.rutgers.edu** **cd pub/baseball** **get jazz**
gopher://sunsite.unc.edu	**gopher sunsite.unc.edu**
http://galaxy.einet.net/galaxy.html	Use entire URL in your web browser. For example, Choose *Open URL* in Mosaic and type in the URL.

N.B.: Some URLs and commands are split between lines because of their length.

Many of the FTP URLs specify directories of files, not filenames. In this appendix, FTP URLs that end with a "/" are directories. In those cases you'll need to type **dir** to get a listing of files that are available. Remember to read any instructions shown on the screen and check for "readme" files in each directory that will provide more clues.

Remember, the Internet is a moving target. Computer names change. Sites disappear. What works today may not work tomorrow. You're welcome to send comments and corrections to: *tracy@editorial. com*

SECTION 1: STARTING YOUR INTERNET TOUR
Selected Resources for Navigating the Internet

Lists and Guides for Online Library Catalogs, BBSs, and Databases

Accessing On-line Bibliography Databases, maintained by Billy Barron and Marie-Christine Mahe. Directory of online library catalogs and databases. *ftp://ftp.utdallas.edu/pub/staff/billy/libguide; gopher://squirrel1. utdallas.edu* (Choose *Libraries.*)

AT&T InterNIC Directory and Database Services. Includes white pages, yellow pages, and access to a large number of databases and Internet documents. *gopher://gopher.internic.net; ftp://ds.internic.net/8dirofdirs*

Campus-Wide Information Systems (CWIS), compiled by Judy Hallman (*Judy_Hallman@unc.edu*). *ftp://sunsite.unc.edu/pub/docs/about-the-net/ cwis/cwis-l*

Internet-Accessible Library Catalogs & Databases, by Art St. George and Ron Larsen. Listing of over 100 online library catalogs and databases. *ftp://ariel.unm.edu/library/internet.library*

The Internet Yellow Pages, by Harley Hahn and Rick Stout. Osborne McGraw-Hill, 1994.

SURAnet Guide to Selected Internet Resources, by the SURAnet Network Information Center. This is a monthly updated guide to new and unique Internet resources. *ftp://ftp.sura.net/pub/nic/how.to.get.SURAnet. guide* or call (301) 982-4600 to order.

Special Internet Connections, compiled by Scott Yanoff (*yanoff@ csd4.csd.uwm.edu*) This is a list of Internet services organized by subject. *ftp://cds4.csd.uwm.edu/pub/inet.services.txt*

Network Information Centers

Asia-Pacific: Asia Pacifica Network Information Center (APNIC), c/o Computer Center, University of Tokyo 2-11-16; Yayoi, Bunkyo-ku, Tokyo 113 Japan Phone: 81-3-3580-3781, 81-3-3580-3784 Fax: 81-3-3580-3782 Email: *admin@apnic.net* Information: *gopher:// apnic.net*

Australia: Australian Academic and Research Network (AARNET), GPO Box 1142, Canberra ACT 2601 Australia Phone: 61-6-249-3385 Fax: 61-6-249-1369 Email: *aarnet@aarnet.edu.au* Information: *gopher://plaza.aarnet.edu.au; http://aarnet.edu.au*

Canada: The CA❁NET Network Operations Centre (NA-NOC), University of Toronto, 255 Huron St., Room 367, Toronto, Ontario M5S 1A1, Canada Phone: (416) 978-4621 Email: *noc@canet.ca*

Europe: RIPE Network Coordination Centre (RIPE-NCC), Kruislaan 409, NL-1098 SJ Amsterdam, The Netherlands Phone: 31-20-592-5065, Fax: 31-20-592-5090 Email: *ncc@RIPE.NET*

United States: InterNIC Information Services Phone: (800) 444-4343, (619) 455-4600 Email: *info@internic.net* Information: *telnet:// gopher.internic.net* (login **gopher**); *gopher://gopher.internic.net*

Information Services: General Atomics, P.O. Box 85608, San Diego, CA 92186-9784 Phone: (800) 444-4345, (619) 455-4600 Fax: (619) 455-4640 Email: *info@is.internic.net* Information: *telnet://is.internic.net* (login **gopher**); *ftp\gopher://is.internic.net/; http://www.internic.net*

Directory and Database Services: AT&T Phone: (800) 862-0677, (908) 668-6587 Fax: (908) 668-3763 Email: *admin@ds.internic.net* Information: *ftp\gopher://ds.internic.net*; *http://www.internic.net*
Registration Services: Network Solutions Inc. (NSI), Attn: InterNIC Registration Services, 505 Huntmar Park Dr., Herndon, VA 22070 Phone: (703) 742-4777 Email: *admin@rs.internic.net* Information: *telnet\ftp\gopher://rs.internic.net*; *http://www.internic.net*

Commercial Networking
Organizations and Consortiums
CommerceNet, 459 Hamilton Ave., Palo Alto, CA 94301 Phone: (415) 617-8790 Fax: (415) 617-1516 Email: *info@commerce.net* Information: *ftp://ftp.commerce.net/*; *http://www.commerce.net*
The Commercial Internet Exchange (CIX) Association Trade Association of Commercial Internet Providers, 3110 Fairview Park Dr, Suite 590, Falls Church, VA 22042 Phone: (303) 482-2150 Fax: (303) 482-2884 Email: *info@cix.org* Information: *ftp\gopher://cix.org/*
Enterprise Integration Networking (EINet), Microelectronics and Computer Technology Corporation (MCC), 3500 West Balcones Center Dr., Austin, TX 78759 Phone: (512) 338-3569 Fax: (512) 338-3897 Email: *info@einet.net*; Email server: *einet-info@einet.net*

Commercial Information Services
ClariNet Communications Corporation, 4880 Stevens Creek Blvd., Suite 206, San Jose, CA 95129 Phone: (408) 296-0366, (800) USE-NETS Fax: (408) 296-1668 Email: *info@clarinet.com ftp://ftp.clarinet.com/clarinet_info/main_info*
Dialog Information Services Phone: (415) 858-3785, (800) 3-DIALOG; Fax: (415) 858-7069
Dow Jones News/Retrieval, Dow Jones Information Services Phone (customer service): (800) 522-3567
Lexis-Nexis, Mead Data Central, Inc. Phone: (800) 227-4908

Books and Periodicals
Cronin, Mary. *Doing Business on the Internet: How the Electronic Highway Is Transforming American Companies*. Van Nostrand Reinhold, 1994.
Internet Business Journal. Subscriptions $149/12 issues (year). Write to: Strangelove Press, 60 Springfield Rd., Suite 1, Ottawa, Ontario, Canada, K1M 1C7. For more information, see: *ftp://nstn.ns.ca/pub/internet-business-journal/subscription.info* or *gopher://gopher.fonorola.net* (Choose *Internet Business Journal*.)
Internet Business Report. Subscription information available from CMP Publications, Inc., 600 Community Dr., Manhasset, N.Y. 10030.

Hypercard Tours

A Cruise of the Internet. Developed by Steve Burdick in collaboration
with Laura Kelleher and Mark Davis for Merit Network, Inc. *ftp://
nic.merit.edu/resources/* (Choose directory *cruise.dos* or *cruise.mac.*) For
more information, contact Merit Network, Inc., Information Services, 2901 Hubbard, Pod G, Ann Arbor, MI 48105. Email address:
cruise2feedback@merit.edu

Tour of the Internet. Developed by the NSF Network Service Center
(NNSC), BBN Laboratories, Inc. *ftp://ftp.es.net/pub/networking-info/
internet-tour/* Get the *internet-tour-readme.txt* file for instructions on
getting and installing this HyperCard stack.

Books and Online Documents

See elsewhere in the Appendix for a listing of Internet resource guides,
both hardcopy and online.

Resource Catalogs and Lists

Finding Sites

New Internet Sites is a database of new WorldWideWeb, Gopher,
hytelnet, and WAIS sites. *gopher://liberty.uc.wlu.edu* (Choose *Explore
Internet Resources.*)

Nova-Links Internet Access, maintained by Rob Kabacoff, is a
WorldWideWeb navigator of available WWW, Gopher, and hytelnet
sites that is updated daily. It also provides software libraries and a
"fun and games page." *http://alpha.acast.nova.edu/start.html*

Sites to Lose Yourself In

NASA. NASA has a large number of Web, Gopher, FTP, WAIS, and
Telnet sites. In the NASA sites, you can view the latest Hubble Space
Telescope photographs, read the notebook logs of the JASON project,
and access NASA's immense databases of astrophysics, oceanogra-
phy, and geosciences information. For a hypertext gateway to all of
NASA's resources, try *http://www.jsc.nasa.gov/NASAInternetConnection.
html* Otherwise, connect to the Goddard Space Flight Center: *ftp://
ftp.gsfc.nasa.gov/*; *gopher://gopher.gsfc.nasa.gov/*; *http://www.gsfc.nasa.
gov/NASA_homepage.html*

SunSITE. Telnetting to SunSITE will provide public access to all of the
most frequently used clients, including lynx, WAIS, and Gopher;
there is also a large anonymous FTP archive. The SunSITE
WorldWideWeb site archives the White House papers, has a large
number of multimedia "exhibits," serves the Cisco K-12 Educational
Archive and Resource Catalog, and provides Dr. Fun, a daily cartoon; it is so popular that it receives 100,000 visitors per day.
telnet\FTP\gopher\http://sunsite.unc.edu/

For More Information

The Clearinghouse for Networked Information and Retrieval (CNIDR)
provides information on and promotes the use of Network Information and Retrieval (NIDR) tools. *gopher://gopher.cnidr.org; http://
cnidr.org/welcome.html*

The mailing list, *NEWNIR-L,* discusses new Network Information and
Retrieval Services. List address: *NEWNIR-L@ITOCSIUM.BITNET.* To
subscribe: *LISTSERV@ITOCSIUM.BITNET*

The mailing list, *Net Happenings,* distributes announcements of interest,
including new Internet resources, conferences, and publications. To
subscribe, send a message to *majordomo@is.internic.net* and in the
body of the message type: **subscribe net-happenings**

Telnet Resources

List of Sites. A good list of Telnet sites is included in Scott Yanoff's
Special Internet Connections (see the "Starting Your Internet Tour"
section of this Appendix).

Greatest Hits. **Dartmouth Library.** Access Dante's *Divine Comedy* and
all the criticism written on it, *The King James Bible,* and Shakespeare's
Sonnets. *telnet://library.dartmouth.edu*

Library of Congress. Access a database of all of the Library of
Congress' holdings, or find the most up-to-date legislative and
copyright information. *telnet://locis.loc.gov*

Anonymous FTP Resources

List of Sites. List of Anonymous FTP Sites, originally by Tom Czarnik, now
maintained by Perry Rovers (*Perry.Rovers@kub.nl*). *ftp://ftp.edu.tw/
documents/networking/guides/ftp-list/sitelist*

How to Find Sources and Lists of Mail Servers, originally by Jonathan
Kamens, now maintained by Kent Lanfield (*kent@sterling.com*).
Includes a list of anonymous FTP sites that allow files to be accessed
via email. Posted regularly to the USENET newsgroups: *comp.sources.
wanted, alt.sources.wanted, comp.answers, alt.answers,* and *news.answers*
To get a current copy, send email to: *send-finding-sources-faq@
sterling.com*

Greatest Hits. **Entertainment Archives.** Includes the largest humor
archive on the Internet, as well as directories for TV and music,
puzzles, books, cyberculture, Disney, and baseball, among many
others: *ftp://quartz.rutgers.edu/pub* Send email to *pirmann@
cs.rutgers.edu* for more information.

NCSA. The home of Telnet, Mosaic, and a large virtual reality archive:
ftp://ftp.ncsa.uiuc.edu/

UUNET Archives of Everything. All the software you could possibly need can be found here: *ftp://ftp.uu.net/* For more information, send email to *archive@uunet.uu.net*

Gopher Resources

Lists of Sites. Gopher Jewels, maintained by David Riggins (*david.riggins@tpoint.com*). Lists Gopher sites by category. *gopher:// cwis.usc.edu* (Choose *Other Gophers and Information Servers*); *http:// galaxy.einet.net/GJ/index.html* David Riggins also maintains a mailing list for sharing interesting Gopher finds: *GOPHERJEWELS@ EINET.NET* To subscribe, send a message to *listproc@einet.net* and put the following command in the body: **subscribe gopher jewels** *firstname lastname*

All the Gopher Servers in the World (the name says it all). Gopher sites are listed by geographical location: *gopher://gopher.tc.umn.edu* (look in the directory *Other Gopher and Information Servers*).

Gopher-Mail is a guide for accessing Gopher resources via electronic mail. For more information, send email to *gophermail-admin@ calvin.edu*

Greatest Hits. **The Internet Wiretap**. This gargantuan Gopher site maintains a video game archive, archives the White House press releases, and has a large Etext library. *gopher://wiretap.spies.com* Send email to *gopher@wiretap.spies.com* for more information.

UIUC Weather Machine. This Gopher site provides up-to-the-minute weather forecasts for every part of the United States, along with the latest satellite images. *gopher://wx.atmos.uiuc.edu*

The World. The home of the Online Book Initiative, a project for publishing electronic texts, as well as a shopping mall and an archive of newsgroups and mailing lists. Also provides gateways to a large number of other Gopher and Telnet sites. *gopher://gopher.std.com*

Additional Information and Discussion. **Mailing list:** GOPHERN, also called "Let's Go Gopherin'," is dedicated to discussing new and interesting Gopher sites. List address: *GOPHERN@UBVM.CC. BUFFALO.EDU* To subscribe: *LISTSERV@UBVM.CC.BUFFALO.EDU*

Veronica FAQ: Compiled and maintained by Steven Foster and Fred Barrie: *gopher://veronica.scs.unr.edu* (Choose *Search All of Gopherspace Using Veronica.*)

USENET: See *comp.infosystems.gopher* or *alt.gopher*

WAIS

List of Sites. Master Directory of WAIS Servers. Indexes all the WAIS sites. *ftp://quake.think.com/pub/wais/; http://info.cern.ch/hypertext/DataSources/ WAIS/ByHost.html*

Newsgroup-Related Indexes, by Edward Vielmetti. Lists WAIS sites that index some or all of USENET newsgroups. *http://info.cern.ch/hypertext/ Products/WAIS/Sources/NewsGroupRelated.html*

Greatest Hits. **CIA World Factbook**. This immense resource is searchable via gopher and WAIS at *gopher://gopher.uwo.ca* (Choose *Selected Internet Resources,* then *Books, Serials, Music.*)

White House Papers. A WAIS search of all the Clinton papers is available at *telnet://sunsite.unc.edu* (login as **politics**).

Additional Information and Discussion. **USENET:** *comp.infosystems.wais* is a general discussion of WAIS.

WorldWideWeb

Lists of Sites. CUI Catalog. A powerful searching tool of WorldWideWeb resources: Also regularly announces "what's new" in the Web: *http:// cui_www.unige.ch/w3catalog*

MKGray@MIT.EDU's New 'Wow, It's Big!' Comprehensive HTTP Site List, compiled and maintained by Matthew K. Gray (*mkgray@mit.edu*). Lists every WWW site, and provides information on the growth of the web: *http://www.mit.edu:8001/people/mkgray/compre3.html*

Virtual Library. Lists WorldWideWeb servers by subject: *http:// info.cern.ch/hypertext/DataSources/bySubject/Overview.html*

W3 Servers. A geographical listing of WorldWideWeb servers: *http:// info.cern.ch/hypertext/DataSources/WWW/Geographical.html*

Greatest Hits. **Doctor Fun**. The Web's own daily cartoon, as well as archives of every Doctor Fun, and a place to grab Doctor Fun thumbnails for your own home pages: *http://sunsite.unc.edu/Dave/ drfun.html*

EINet Galaxy. This huge WWW site searches the Internet for any topic imaginable, from multimedia and fun stuff to education, business, medicine, and law, and provides pointers to virtually all the information you could need: *http://galaxy.einet.net/galaxy.html* For more information, send email to: *galaxy@einet.net*

Online BookStore. Find the Mosaic version of the first Stephen King story to be published on the Internet, or order a copy of: *The Internet Companion. http://marketplace.com/0/obs/obshome.html*

Wired. The WWW site of the popular alternative magazine archives back issues, provides discussion on ongoing topics, and has subscription forms: *http://wired.com* To receive update announcements, send email to *infobot@wired.com* with the message **subscribe hotwired**. For more information, send email to: *www@wired.com*

Additional Information and Discussion. **List of FAQs and Guides to WWW**. Starting from here, you should be able to find the answer to any question about anything in the WorldWideWeb: *http://cui_www.unige.ch/OSG/FAQ/www.html*

URL Specifications. The official specifications are available at: *http://info.cern.ch/hypertext/WWW/Addressing/URL/URL_TOC.html*

WWW FAQ, maintained by Thomas Boutell (*boutell@netcom.com*). Posted regularly to *comp.infosystems.www*, and archived at: *http://siva.cshl.org/~boutell/www_faq.html*

USENET: *comp.infosystems.www* is a general discussion of all WWW issues; *comp.os.lynx* discusses lynx, a WWW text browser.

Software, Games, and Video Archives

Merit/University of Michigan Software Archives, maintained by Fred Swartz (*archive-admin@archive.umich.edu*). *gopher://gopher.archive. merit.net* (Choose *Merit Software Archives.*)

MPEG Archives. MPEG videos that can be accessed through the WorldWideWeb: *http://w3.eeb.ele.tue.nl/mpeg/index.html*

PC Game Archives, maintained by Brian O'Neill (*oneill@cs.uml.edu*): *ftp://ftp.ulowell.edu/msdos/Games/* (See the *README* file in this directory.)

Other large software archives (for all systems) can be found at: *ftp://ftp.uu.net/systems/*, *ftp://wuarchive.wustl.edu/*, and *ftp://oak.oakland.edu/pub/* or *pub2/*

Communication Directories, Resources, and Lists

Email Directories of Addresses

How to Find People's E-Mail Addresses FAQ, by Jonathan Kamens, and maintained by David Lamb (*dlamb@qucis.queensu.ca*). Posted regularly to the USENET newsgroups: *comp.answers, soc.answers, news.answers, comp.mail.misc, soc.net-people,* and *news.newusers.questions* Archived at: *ftp://rtfm.mit.edu/pub/usenet/news.answers/finding-addresses*

InterNIC White Pages. Email questions to *admin@ds.internic.net. telnet://ds.internic.net* (login as **guest**); *ftp://ds.internic.net/internic.info/* (see the file *whitepages.info*); *gopher://gopher.internic.net/* (Choose *InterNic Directory and Database Services.); http://ds.internic.net/ds/dspgwp.html*

List of Internet Whois Servers, by Matt Power (mhpower@mit.edu): *ftp://sipb.mit.edu/pub/whois/whois-servers.list; gopher://sipb.mit.edu* (Choose *Internet Whois Servers.*)

NetPages, by Susan Estrada, Aldea Communications, Inc., Carlsbad CA. Email: *netpages@aldea.com* Phone: 1-800-TOALDEA or (619) 943-0101

NYSERNET/PSI White Pages. For more information, send email to: *wpp-manager@psi.com. telnet://wp.psi.com* (login as **fred**)

Stable Large Email Database (SLED). SLED registers people and provides a directory service. For more information, send email to *sled@ drebes.com* with the subject *info*.

!%@:: A Directory of Electronic Mail Addresses and Networks, by Donnalyn Frey and Rich Adams. This is a detailed resource to over 130 networks. Published by O'Reilly and Associates.

In addition, university Gopher servers often maintain directories of students and faculty. See the "Gopher" section above for lists of Gopher sites.

Online Address Services

CSO: searches "all the directory servers in the world." *gopher:// gopher.tc.umn.edu/* (Choose *Phone Books* and then *Phone Books at Other Institutions*.)

Knowbot: a uniform interface to the white pages services on the Internet: *telnet://cnri.reston.va.us*

Netfind: a program that queries the network to find addresses: *telnet:// bruno.cs.colorado.edu* (login as **netfind**). Gopher gateway to Netfind: *gopher://ds.internic.net:4320* (Choose *Network Wide E-Mail Searches.)*

X.500: to look up addresses for people and organizations. *gopher:// ds.internic.net* (Choose *Directory and Database Services*, then *White Pages*, then the X500 Gateway.)

WHOIS: another way to look up addresses for people and organiza- tions. *gopher://ds.internic.net:4320*

Lists of Mailing Lists and Misc. Documents

Directory of Scholarly Electronic Conferences, compiled by Diane K. Kovacs (*dkovacs@kentvm.kent.edu*). Provides descriptions of scholarly mailing lists of interest to scholars: *ftp://ksuvxa.KENT.EDU/library/*; (See the file: *ACADLIST.README*.) A print version is available from the Association of Research Libraries; contact Ann Okerson at: *ann@cni.org*

List of BITNET LISTSERV Lists, compiled and maintained at the BITNET Network Information Center (BITNIC), Washington, DC. Available via email by sending a message to *listserv@bitnic.cren.net* with the message, **list global**. For more information, send email to *listserv@ bitnic.cren.net* with the message **info** or contact the BITNIC, 1112 Sixteenth St. NW, Washington, D.C. 20036, (202) 872-4200.

Mailing List Search. WWW search of all available mailing lists and their descriptions: *http://alpha.acast.nova.edu/cgi-bin/lists*

Publicly Accessible Mailing Lists, compiled and maintained by Stephanie da Silva (*arielle@taronga.com*): *ftp://rtfm.mit.edu/pub/usenet/ news.answers/mail/mailing-lists*; *http://www.ii.uib.no/cgi-bin/paml*

Inter-Network Mail Guide, originally by John J. Chew, now maintained by Scott Yanoff (*yanoff@csd4.csd.uwm.edu*). A guide on how to send electronic mail: *ftp://csd4.csd.uwm.edu/pub/internetwork-mail-guide*; *http://alpha.acast.nova.edu/cgi-bin/inmgq.pl*

Smiley Server, maintained by David W. Sanderson. Online resource of all the "smilies" in the known universe: *ftp://ftp.uu.net/usenet/ comp.sources.misc/volume23/smiley*; *gopher://gopher.ora.com* (Choose *Feature Articles*, then *All the Smileys.* . . .) *Smileys* is also available in hardcopy from O'Reilly and Associates (1993).

USENET: *comp.mail.misc*

USENET News

Newsgroup Lists and Descriptions. WWW List of Internet Newsgroups. Also provides instructions for reading news with a WWW client: *http:// info.cern.ch/hypertext/DataSources/News/Groups/Overview.html*

Search USENET newsgroup descriptions (and USENET FAQs): *gopher:// owl.nstn.ns.ca* (Choose *Internet Resources*, then *Search USENET Newsgroup Descriptions.*)

USENET FAQs and Periodic Postings. USENET FAQs. Posted or emailed regularly to newsgroups and mailing lists; also regularly posted on the USENET newsgroup *news.answers.* Archives: *ftp://rtfm.mit.edu/pub/ usenet/*; *gopher://gopher.physics.utoronto.ca* (Choose *USENET News Frequently Asked Questions.*); *http://www.cis.ohio-state.edu/hypertext/faq/ usenet/FAQ-List.html Periodic Postings*, compiled and maintained by Jonathan I. Kamens. Periodic documents are posted or emailed regularly to newsgroups and mailing lists. Archives: *ftp://rtfm.mit.edu/ pub/usenet/news.answers/periodic-postings*

MUDs, MOOs, MUSEs, and MUSHs

Lists of MUDs. MUD List Archive. Also provides a MUD FAQ and descriptions of a few MUDs. Select "jack in" to login to various MUDs. *gopher://actlab.rtf.utexas.edu* (Choose *Virtual Spaces: MUD.*)

Totally Unofficial List of Internet MUDs, compiled by Scott Goehring: *ftp:// caisr2.caisr.cwru.edu/pub/mud/mudlist.txt*

Zarf's List of Interactive Games on the Web, maintained by Andrew Plotkin (*zarf@cs.cmu.edu*). *http://www.cs.cmu.edu:8001/afs/cs.cmu.edu/user/zarf/ www/games.html*

Greatest Hits. **JaysHouseMOO**. A place where friends hang out. This MOO actually has a WWW server running inside it. *telnet://jayshouse. ccs.neu.edu:1709*

lambdaMOO. This is probably the most popular of the interactive environments. Check the documentation for help and information: *gopher://oac3.hsc.uth.tmc.edu* (Choose *Computer Information*, then *OAC*

Staff Test Projects, then *Steve Newton's Goodies,* then *LambdaMoo Documentation.*) To get to lambdaMOO: *telnet://lambda.parc. xerox.com:8888.*

Nails. A MUD with a "Miami Vice" theme: *telnet://flounder.rutgers. edu:5150.* For more information, send email to *rbright@clam. rutgers.edu*

TrekMUSE. Based on the Star Trek universe. *telnet://grimmy.cnidr. org:1701.* For more information, see: *ftp://grimmy.cnidr.org/trek/docs/ trek-manual*

Additional Information and Discussion. **MUD FAQ:** This is the *rec.games.muds.misc* FAQ: *ftp://ftp.math.okstate.edu/pub/muds/misc/mud-faq/*

USENET: For newsgroups discussing various interactive systems, see: *alt.mud, rec.games.mud.announce, rec.games.mud.misc,* and *rec.games. mud.tiny* (devoted to the tinyMUDs)

SECTION 2: INTERNET GROUPS AND ORGANIZATIONS

Coalition for Networked Information (CNI), Library Networking, Joan Lippincott, Assistant Executive Director, 21 Dupont Circle, NW, Washington, D.C. 20036 Email: *info@cni.org* Information: *ftp:// ftp.cni.org*; *gopher://gopher.cni.org*

Computer Professionals for Social Responsibility (CPSR), P.O. Box 717, Palo Alto, CA 94302-0717 Phone: (415) 322-3778 Fax: (415) 322-4748 Email: *cpsr@cpsr.org* Mailing List: *CPSR-Announce_listserv@ cpsr.org*; include the message **help** Information: *ftp://ftp.cpsr.org*

Consortium for School Networking (CoSN), K-12 Networking, P.O. Box 65193, Washington, D.C. 20035-5193 Phone: (202) 466-6296 Email: *info@cosn.org* Mailing List: *COSNDISC*; to subscribe, send a message to *listproc@ukon.csen.org.* Information: *gopher://cosn.org*

The Electronic Frontier Foundation, Inc. (EFF), 1001 G St. NW, Suite 950E, Washington, D.C. 20001 Phone: (202) 347-5400 Fax: (202) 393-5509 BBS: (202) 638-6120 Email: *askeff@eff.org* Information: *ftp://ftp.eff.org/pub/EFF/*; *gopher://gopher.eff.org*; *http://www.eff.org.* Mailing Lists: *eff-news-request@eff.org*; *eff-talk-request@eff.org* USENET Newsgroups: *comp.org.eff.talk*; *comp.org.eff.news*; *alt.politics.datahighway*

Federation of Academic and Research Networks (FARNET), 114 Waltham St., Suite 12, Lexington MA 02173, Phone: (617) 890-9445 Fax: (617) 890-9345 Email: *mstone@farnet.org*

Internet Society, 12020 Sunrise Valley Dr., Suite 270 Reston, VA 22091 Phone: (703) 648-9888, (800) 468-9707 Fax: (703) 648-9887 Email: *isoc@isoc.org* Information: *ftp://ftp.isoc.org/*; *gopher:// gopher.isoc.org*

Network Information Discovery and Retrieval Tools

Client Software	Purpose	Quantity of Public Information	Positive Aspects	Negative Aspects	Where to Find Client Software (anonymous FTP)
TELNET	Remote interactive	Over 1,400 sites	Log into thousands of databases worldwide	Need to know where the databases are in advance	*ftp://ftp.ncsa.uiuc.edu/Telnet/* (choose system)
FTP	File Transfer Protocol	Gigabytes	Good for moving even large files; lots of software archives	Need to know where the files are in advance	*ftp://wuarchive.wustl.edu/systems/* (pick directory for your computer)
archie	Search and retrieve anonymous FTP	More than 2.2 million files searched	Great for finding software archives if you know an exact filename	Need to know what you are looking for	*ftp://ftp.sura.net/pub/archie/clients/*
WAIS	Multimedia search and retrieval	500+ databases	Fast search; grades quality of information received	Need to know which databases you want to search	*ftp://quake.think.com/wais/*
GOPHER	Publishes and searches information on a distributed network	More than 25,000 sites	Email or FTP results to yourself; menued information is easily navigated	Can get lost in the overwhelming amount of information; links are often poorly maintained	*ftp://boombox.micro.umn.edu/pub/gopher/*
Veronica	keyboard search of Gopher menus	all of Gopherspace	quick way to find a lot of Gopher information on a single topic	widely used and difficult to get a connection	no client available; must be accessed through a gopher client
Jughead	keyboard search of Gopher menus	single Gopher server search	often more accessible than Veronica	limited to one Gopher server	*ftp://boombox.micro.umn.edu/pub/gopher/Unix/GopherTools/Jughead/*
WORLD-WIDEWEB	Hypertext interface to Internet resources	More than 2,500 sites	Hypertext links make finding information easy	Easy to get lost or distracted	*ftp://info.cern.ch/pub/www/*

Network Information Discovery and Retrieval Tools (continued)

Client Software	Purpose	Quantity of Public Information	Positive Aspects	Negative Aspects	Where to Find Client Software (anonymous FTP)
Mosaic	Hypermedia browser of the WWW	The entire Internet	Encompasses all tools; multimedia interface	Requires dedicated line and direct Internet connection	ftp://ftp.ncsa.uiuc.edu/Mosaic/
Lynx	distributed hypertext browser	The entire Internet	Can be accessed with a dial-up connection	Text-only browser	ftp://ftp2.cc.ukans.edu/pub/lynx/
Cello	WWW hypermedia browser for Microsoft Windows	The entire Internet	Good documentation	Requires a direct Internet connection	ftp://ftp.law.cornell.edu/pub/LII/Cello/
TKWWW	WWW browser for X Windows	The entire Internet	The only WWW client currently available with a text editor	Requires a direct connection to the Internet	ftp://info.cern.ch/pub/www/src/

Source: *Netpages*, Aldea Communications, *netpages@aldea.com* or 1-800-TOALDEA, or (619) 943-0101.

SECTION 3: CLIENT SOFTWARE OR TOOLS

For an online summary of Internet tools—their uses, their advantages
and disadvantages, and where to get them—see the *Internet Tools for
NIR* list compiled and maintained by John December (*decemj@rpi.
edu*): *ftp://ftp.rpi.edu/pub/communications/internet-tools.readme*; *gopher://
nysernet.org* (check the directory *Special Collections: Internet Help*)

Tools and Clients for Accessing Information
(See chart on preceding pages.)

Email

There are many Unix email clients, each with its own advantages.
   ELM is easy to use: *ftp://ftp.uu.net/networking/mail/elm/*, or send email
   archive-server@DSI.COM with the message **help** to get more information. **PINE** is a good client for the novice user; it includes many
   features, such as folders for storing messages and a stand-alone
   editor, PICO: *ftp://ftp.cac.washington.edu/pine/* **MH** is useful because it
   allows you to access email directly from the Unix shell prompt: *ftp://
   ftp.ics.uci.edu/pub/mh/*
POPmail is a mailserver for PC and Macintosh systems: *ftp://
   boombox.micro.umn.edu/pub/* Look in the *POPmail* directory for
   Macintosh applications, and in the *pc/minuet* directories for PC.
   NUPop is an email client for Windows/Dos systems: *ftp://
   casbah.acns.nwu.edu/pub/nupop/* **Eudora** is a popular client for the
   Macintosh, and recently a Windows version has been developed: *ftp:/
   /ftp.qualcomm.com/* (choose *mac or pceudora/*)

News Readers

News-reader clients include **tin, nn, rn**, and **trn** for Unix, **thenews**
   for Mac, **trumpet** for IBM, and **NewsGrazer** for NeXt. All news
   readers are archived at *ftp://news.cis.umn.edu/pub/*

IRC Chat

This multiuser chat program enables you to talk interactively with
   other users: *ftp://cs.bu.edu/irc/clients/* (See the *README* file.)

Finger

This client enables you to find out information about specific users:
   ftp://wuarchive.wustl.edu/systems/gnu/

MUDs, MOOs, MUSEs, MUSHs

Clients for text-based, interactive, multiuser environments include
   tinytalk, tinyfugue, VT, LPTalk, SayWat, RMF, and **TinyView**,
   among others. All are archived in *ftp://ftp.math.okstate.edu/pub/muds/
   clients/*

BinHex

This software program codes Macintosh files for file transfer and emailing: *ftp://mac.archive.umich.edu/mac/util/comm/* It's also available for PCs: *ftp://boombox.micro.umn.edu/pub/binhex/MSDOS* (See the *00readme* file.)

MBONE

Information on the MBONE is archived at: *ftp://isi.edu/mbone/faq.txt* or *http://www.eit.com/techinfo/mbone/mbone.html* The multicast software needed is available at *ftp://gregorio.stanford.edu/vmtp-ip/*; see the *ipmulticast.README* file for more information. Information on MBONE is also available from the mailing list; send subscription request to: *mbone-request@isi.edu*

CU-See Me

This Macintosh video-conferencing package enables you to see and "talk" with other Internet Macintosh users. Archived at *ftp://gated.cornell.edu/pub/video/*

SECTION 4: INTERNET CONNECTIVITY, INTERNETWORKING, UNIX, AND SECURITY
Internet Organizational and Individual Access Providers

International Networks

Chinese Resource Network (CRN), P.O. Box 619, 100083 Beijing, China Phone: 86-1-201-7661 ext. 646 Email: *helpdesk@crn.cn*

Demon Internet Ltd. (United Kingdom), 42 Hendon Lane, Finchley, London, UK Phone: 44-081-349-0063 Email: *internet@demon.net ftp://ftp.demon.co.uk/pub/doc* USENET: *demon.announce*

DIALix Services (Australia), Box 7, 145 Sydney, Fairlight, NSW 2054 Australia Phone: 61-2-948-6995 BBS: 61-2-948-6918 (login **guest**) Email: *justin@sydney.DIALix.oz.au*

EUnet Ltd. (Europe), Kruislaan 409, 1098 SJ, Amsterdam NL Phone: 31-20-592-5109 Fax: 31-20-592-5163 Email: *info@eu.net ftp://ftp.EU.net; gopher://gopher.EU.net; http://www.EU.net* **EUNet Traveller**. This service, provided by EUNet, enables the business traveller to access their computer at home from most major European cities. For more information, send email to *traveller@EU.net* or try one of the following: *telnet://Traveller.EU.net* (login **new**); *ftp://ftp.EU.net/EUnet/Traveller/; gopher://gopher.EU.net/*

GARR Network Information System (Italy) Phone: 39-50-593-360 Email: *info@nis.garr.it telnet://wais.nis.garr.it* (login **wais**); *ftp://ftp.nis.garr.it/garr/doc/; gopher://gopher.nis.garr.it*

Hong Kong Supernet HKUST Rand Corporation, Ltd., Hong Kong
   University of Science and Technology, Clear Water Bay, Kowloon,
   Hong Kong Phone: 852-358-7924 Fax: 852-358-7925 Email: *info@*
   HK.Super.NET
Internet Initiative Japan, Inc. (IIJ2-DVM), Hashigaoka Bldg, 2-11-2
   Nagatocho, Chiyoda-ku, Tokyo, 100 Japan Phone: 81-3-3580-
   3781 Email: *info@IIJ.AD.JP; ftp://ftp.iij.ad.jp/pub/info/English/; gopher:/*
   /gopher.iij.ad.jp; http://www.iij.ad.jp
PIPEX Ltd. (United Kingdom), 216 Science Park, Milton Rd, Cam-
   bridge, CB4 4WA, UK Phone: 44-223-250-120 Fax: 44-223-250-
   121 Email: *pipex@pipex.net* Email server: *pipex-info-request@pipex.net*
   http://www.pipex.net
SURFnet (Netherlands), Cluetinckborch Office (3rd floor),
   Godebaldkwartier 24 Hoog Catharijne, Utrecht, NL Phone: 31-30-
   310-290 Email: *info@surfnet.nl; ftp://ftp.nic.surfnet.nl/; gopher://*
   gopher.nic.surfnet.nl

Additional Information. Information on United Kingdom networks is
   posted regularly to the USENET newsgroup *uk.nets*, and is archived
   at *ftp://ftp.demon.co.uk/pub/doc/*
The Network Access in Australia FAQ by Zik Sakeeba (*zik@aurora.*
   cc.monash.edu.au) is posted monthly to: *alt.internet.access.wanted*
Also, see Susan Estrada's *DLIST* for a comprehensive listing of international networks. (Look in the "Lists of Providers" section for instructions on getting the *DLIST*.)

National U.S. Networks
Advanced Network & Services, Inc. (ANS) and ANS CO+RE
   100 Clearbrook Road, Elmsford, NY 10523 Phone: (800) 456-8267,
   (313) 663-7610; Fax: (914) 789-5310 Email: *info@ans.net*
   Information: *ftp://ftp.ans.net/*
California Education & Research Federation Network (CERFnet)
   A Division of General Atomics
   P.O. Box 85608, San Diego, CA 92186-9784
   Phone: (619) 455-3900, (800) 876-2373
   Email: *sales@cerf.net ftp://ftp.cerf.net/cerfnet/cerfnet_info* Information:
   gopher://gopher.cerf.net; http://www.cerf.net
NETCOM On-Line Communications Services, Inc.
   4000 Moorpark Ave., Suite 200, San Jose, CA 95117
   Phone: (408) 554-8649, (800) 501-8649
   Email: *info@netcom.com*
Performance Systems International, Inc. (PSI)
   Attn: Inside Sales, P.O. Box 592, Herndon, VA 22070

Phone: (703) 709-0300, (800) 82-PSI-82; Fax: (703) 904-1207
Email: *all-info@psi.com* Information: *ftp://ftp.psi.com*; *gopher://gopher.psi.com*; *http://www.psi.com*
Sprint Bob Doyle, Sprintlink
13221 Woodland Park Road, Herndon, VA 22071
Phone: (703) 904-2167; Fax: (703) 904-2680
Email: *bdoyle@icml.icp.net*
UUNET Technologies, Inc.
3110 Fairview Park Drive, Suite 570, Falls Church, VA 22042
Phone: (703) 204-8000, (800) 4-UUNET-3; Fax: (703) 204-8001
Email: *alternet-info@uunet.uu.net* Information: *ftp://ftp.uu.net/uunet-info*

Radiomail

Radiomail Corporation
2600 Campus Dr., San Mateo, CA 94070
Phone (800) 597-MAIL
Email: *info@radiomail.net*

Public Access Systems

Source: most of the following information and provider listings were obtained from *Public Dialup Internet Access List (PDIAL)*, compiled by Peter Kaminski, and used with permission. Send additions and corrections to: *kaminski@netcom.com* See the "Lists of Providers" section in this Appendix for information on obtaining the latest online list.

Many of these systems run the UNIX operating system. All provide dial-up terminal emulation. Ask about UUCP, SLIP, or PPP access. Typical services include USENET, IRC, BBS, and games. Most of these systems offer local-area dial-up access. (See the "Dial-up" field for the local modem number and a new user login name, if one exists.) A summary of services by area code is provided. (See "Local Dial-up Access Providers Summary.")

A good number of systems also provide access for users outside their local areas. Wide-area access is usually offered via a public data network or PDN (contact information listed below), and is specified in the "Long Distance" field. "800" means that the provider is accessible via a "toll-free" U.S. phone number. The phone company will not charge for the call, but the service provider will add a relatively large surcharge to cover the high cost of the 800 service. Please note that prices, access, and services for each of these may change; use the prices listed here for guidance only and not as the definitive pricing structure for each organization.

Local Dial-up Access Providers Summary.

201 GES
202 CAPCON; ClarkNet; Express;
    MichNet; TMN
203 GES
205 Nuance
206 Eskimo; Halcyon; Netcom;
    NW Nexus; Olympus
212 echonyc; Maestro; MindVOX;
    PANIX; Pipeline
213 CRL; DIAL n' CERF;
    KAIWAN; Netcom
214 Texas Metronet; Netcom
215 GES; PREPnet
216 OARnet; wariat
217 Prairienet
301 CAPCON; ClarkNet; Express;
    MichNet; TMN
302 ssnet
303 CNS; CSN; Netcom; Nyx
305 gate.net
310 CLASS; CRL; DIAL n' CERF;
    KAIWAN; Netcom
312 InterAccess; MCSNet;
    Netcom; XNet
313 MichNet; MSen
401 IDS; GES
403 UUNET-Canada
718 Maestro; MindVOX; Netcom;
    PANIX; Pipeline
404 CRL; Netcom
407 gate.net; PSS
408 a2i; Netcom; Portal
410 CAPCON; ClarkNet; Express
415 a2i; CLASS; CRL; DIAL n'
    CERF; IGC; Netcom; Portal;
    WELL
416 hookup.net; UUNET-Canada;
    UUnorth
419 OARnet
503 agora.rain.com; Netcom;
    Teleport

504 Sugar
508 NEARnet; North Shore;
    NovaLink
510 CLASS; CRL; DIAL n' CERF;
    HoloNet; Netcom
512 Realtime
513 FSP; OARnet
514 CAM.ORG; UUNET-Canada
516 GES
517 MichNet
519 hookup.net; UUNET-Canada;
    UUnorth
602 CRL; Data.Basix; Evergreen;
    indirect
603 MV; NEARnet
604 UUNET-Canada
609 GES
613 UUNET-Canada; UUnorth
614 OARnet
616 MichNet
617 DELPHI; NEARnet; Netcom;
    North Shore; NovaLink; World
619 cg57; CLASS; crash.CTS.com;
    Cyberspace; DIAL n' CERF;
    Netcom
703 CAPCON; ClarkNet; Express;
    MichNet; Netcom; TMN
704 CONCERT; Vnet
707 CRL
708 InterAccess; MCSNet; XNet
713 Black Box; nuchat; Sugar
714 CLASS; DIAL n' CERF;
    Express; KAIWAN; Netcom
717 PREPnet
719 CNS; CSN; oldcolo
804 Wyvern
810 MichNet; MSen
814 PREPnet 412 PREPnet;
    Telerama
815 InterAccess; MCSNet; XNet
817 Texas Metronet

818 CLASS; DIAL n' CERF;   907 alaska.edu
   Netcom   908 Express; GES
904 PSS   910 CONCERT
905 UUNET-Canada   916 Netcom
906 MichNet   919 CONCERT; Vnet

International Access Providers Summary
+44 (0)81 Demon; dircon; ibmpcug   +61 2 connect.com.au
+49 Individual.NET   +61 3 connect.com.au
+49 23 INS   +301 Ariadne
+49 069 in-rhein-main   +353 1 IEunet
+49 089 mucev

a2i Communications Dial-up: 408-293-9010 (v.32bis), 415-364-5652
   (v.32bis), 408-293-9020 (PEP); login **guest** Area Codes: 408,
   415 Long Distance: provided by user Fees: $20/month or $45/3
   months or $72/6 months Email: *info@rahul.net* Phone: 408-293-
   8078 *ftp://ftp.rahul.net/pub/BLURB*
APK—Public Access UNI* Site (wariat) Dial-up: 216-481-9436
   (V.32bis, SuperPEP on separate rotary) Area Code: 216 Long
   Distance: provided by user Fees: $15/20 hours, $35/monthly, $20
   signup Email: *zbig@wariat.org* Phone: 216-481-9428
Ariadne—Greek Academic and Research Network Dial-up: +301 65-
   48-800 (1200-9600 bps) Area Code: +301 Long Distance: provided
   by user Fees: 5900 drachmas per calendar quarter, 1 hr/day
   limit. Email: *Dial-up@leon.nrcps.ariadne-t.gr* Phone: +301 65-13-
   392 Fax: +301 6532910
The Black Box Dial-up: (713) 480-2686 (V32bis/V42bis) Area Code:
   713 Long Distance: provided by user Fees: $21.65 per month or
   $108.25 for 6 months Email: *info@blackbox.com* Phone: (713) 480-
   2684 or 2685.
Communications Accessibles Montreal *CAM.ORG* Dial-up: 514-931-
   7178 (v.32 bis), 514-931-2333 (2400bps) Area Code: 514 Long
   Distance: provided by user Fees: $25/month Cdn. Email:
   info@CAM.ORG Phone: 514-931-0749 *ftp://ftp.CAM.ORG/*
CAPCON Library Network Dial-up: contact for number Area Codes:
   202, 301, 410, 703 Long Distance: various plans available/recom-
   mended; contact for details Fees: $35 start-up + $150/yr + $24/mo
   for first account from an institution; $35 start-up + $90/yr + $15/mo
   for additional users (member rates lower); 20 hours/month included,
   additional hours $2/hr Email: *capcon@capcon.net* Phone: 202-331-
   5771 Fax: 202-797-7719

Clark Internet Services, Inc. (ClarkNet) Dial-up: 410-730-9786, 410-995-0271, 301-596-1626, 301-854-0446, 301-621-5216 login **guest** Area Codes: 202, 301, 410, 703 Long Distance: provided by user Fees: $23/month or $66/3 months or $126/6 months or $228/year Email: *info@clark.net* Phone: Call 800-735-2258, then give 410-730-9764 (MD Relay Svc) Fax: 410-730-9765 *ftp://ftp.clark.net/pub/clarknet/fullinfo.txt*

Colorado SuperNet, Inc. (CSN) Dial-up: contact for number Area Codes: 303, 719, 800 Long Distance: provided by user or 800 Fees: $1/hour off-peak, $3/hour peak ($250 max/month) + $20 signup, $5/hr surcharge for 800 use Email: *info@CSN.org* Phone: 303-273-3471 Fax: 303-273-3475 *ftp://CSN.org/CSN/reports/DialinInfo.txt* Off-peak: midnight to 6 a.m.

Community News Service (CNS) Dial-up: 719-520-1700 login **new**, password **newuser** Area Codes: 303, 719, 800 Long Distance: 800 or provided by user Fees: $2.75/hour; $10/month minimum + $35 signup Email: *service@cscns.com* Phone: 719-592-1240 *ftp://cscns.com/*

CONCERT-CONNECT Dial-up: contact for number Area Codes: 704, 910, 919 Long Distance: provided by user Fees: SLIP: $150 educational/research only Email: *info@CONCERT.net* Phone: 919-248-1466 *ftp://ftp.CONCERT.net/*

connect.com.au pty ltd Dial-up: contact for number Area Codes: +61 3, +61 2 Long Distance: provided by user Fees: AUS$2000/year (1 hour/day), 10% discount for AUUG members; other billing negotiable Email: *connect@connect.com.au* Phone: +61 3 5282239 Fax: +61 3 5285887 *ftp://ftp.connect.com.au/*

Cooperative Library Agency for Systems and Services (CLASS) Dial-up: contact for number. Note: CLASS serves libraries and information distributors only. Area Codes: 310, 415, 510, 619, 714, 818, 800 Long Distance: 800 service available at $6/hour surcharge Fees: $4.50/hour + $150/year for first account + $50/year each additional account + $135/year CLASS membership. Discounts available for multiple memberships. Email: *CLASS@CLASS.org* Phone: 800-488-4559 Fax: 408-453-5379

CR Laboratories Dial-up Internet Access (CRL) Dial-up: 415-389-UNIX Area Codes: 213, 310, 404, 415, 510, 602, 707, 800 Long Distance: 800 or provided by user Fees: $17.50/month + $19.50 signup Email: *info@CRL.com* Phone: 415-381-2800

CTS Network Services (CTSNET) *crash.CTS.com* Dial-up: 619-637-3640 HST, 619-637-3660 V.32bis, 619-637-3680 PEP login **help** Area Code: 619 Long Distance: provided by user Fees: $10-$23/month flat depending on features, $15 startup, personal $20/month flat depending on features, $25 startup, commercial Email:

info@crash.CTS.com (server), *support@crash.CTS.com* (human) Phone: 619-637-3637 Fax: 619-637-3630

CyberGate, Inc *gate.net* Dial-up: 305-425-0200 Area Codes: 305, 407 Long Distance: provided by user Fees: $17.50/month on credit card; group discounts; SLIP/PPP: $17.50/month + $2/hr Email: *info@gate.net* or *sales@gate.net* Phone: 305-428-GATE Fax: 305-428-7977

The Cyberspace Station Dial-up: 619-634-1376 login **guest** Area Code: 619 Long Distance: provided by user Fees: $15/month + $10 startup or $60 for six months Email: *help@cyber.net*

Data Basix Dial-up: 602-721-5887 Area Code: 602 Long Distance: provided by user Fees: $25 month, $180 year; group rates available Email: *info@Data.Basix.com* (automated); *sales@Data.Basix.com* (human) Phone: 602-721-1988 *ftp://Data.Basix.COM/services/dial-up.txt*

DELPHI Dial-up: 800-365-4636 login **JOINDELPHI**; password: **INTERNETSIG** Area Code: 617, PDN Long Distance: Sprintnet or Tymnet: $9/hour weekday business hours, no charge nights and weekends Fees: $10/month for 4 hours or $20/month for 20 hours + $3/month for Internet services Email: *walthowe@delphi.com* Phone: 800-544-4005

Demon Internet Systems (DIS) Dial-up: +44 (0)81 343 4848 Area Code: +44 (0)81 Long Distance: provided by user Fees: GBPounds 10.00/month; 132.50/year (inc 12.50 startup charge). No online time charges. Email: *internet@demon.co.uk* Phone: +44 (0)81 349 0063

DIAL n' CERF or DIAL n' CERF AYC Dial-up: contact for number Area Codes: 213, 310, 415, 510, 619, 714, 818 Long Distance: provided by user Fees: $5/hour ($3/hour on weekend) + $20/month + $50 startup OR $250/month flat for AYC Email: *help@cerf.net* Phone: 800-876-2373 or 619-455-3900 *ftp://nic.cerf.net/cerfnet/dial-n-cerf/* Off-peak: Weekend: 5 p.m. Friday to 5 p.m. Sunday

DIAL n' CERF USA Dial-up: contact for number Area Code: 800 Long Distance: included Fees: $10/hour ($8/hour on weekend) + $20/month Email: *help@cerf.net* Phone: 800-876-2373 or 619-455-3900 *ftp://nic.cerf.net/cerfnet/dial-n-cerf/* Off-peak: Weekend: 5 p.m. Friday to 5 p.m. Sunday

The Direct Connection (dircon) Dial-up: +44 (0)81 317 2222 Area Code: +44 (0)81 Long Distance: provided by user Fees: Subscriptions from GBPounds 10.00 per month, no online charges. GBPounds 7.50 sign-up fee. Email: *helpdesk@dircon.co.uk* Phone: +44 (0)81 317 0100; Fax +44 (0)81 317 0100

E & S Systems Public Access *Nix (cg57) Dial-up: 619-278-8267
   (V.32bis, TurboPEP), 619-278-8267 (V32) 619-278-9837 (PEP) Area
   Code: 619 Long Distance: provided by user Fees: BBS free; shell—
   $30/3 months, $50/6 months, $80/9 months, $100/year Email:
   steve@cg57.esnet.com Phone: 619-278-4641
Echo Communications (echonyc) Dial-up: (212) 989-8411 (v.32, v.32
   bis) login **newuser** Area Code: 212 Long Distance: provided by
   user Fees: Commercial, $19.95/month; students/seniors, $13.75/
   month Email: *horn@echonyc.com* Phone: 212-255-3839
Eskimo North Dial-up: 206-367-3837 300-14.4k, 206-362-6731 for
   9600/14.4k, 206-742-1150 World Blazer Area Code: 206 Long
   Distance: provided by user Fees: $10/month or $96/year Email:
   nanook@eskimo.com Phone: 206-367-7457
Evergreen Communications Dial-up: (602) 955-8444 Area Code:
   602 Long Distance: provided by user or call for additional
   information Fees: individual: $239/yr; commercial: $479/yr; special
   educational rates Email: *evergreen@libre.com* Phone: 602-230-
   9330 Fax: 602-955-5948
Express Access—A Service of Digital Express Group Dial-up: 301-220-
   0462, 410-766-1855, 703-281-7997, 714-377-9784, 908-937-9481
   login **new** Area Codes: 202, 301, 410, 703, 714, 908 Long Distance:
   provided by user Fees: $25/month or $250/year Email:
   info@digex.net Phone: 800-969-9090, 301-220-2020
Freelance Systems Programming (FSP) Dial-up: (513) 258-7745 to 14.4
   Kbps Area Codes: 513 Long Distance: provided by user Fees: $20
   startup and $1 per hour Email: *fsp@dayton.fsp.com* Phone: (513) 254-
   7246
Global Enterprise Service (GES)—Dialin' Tiger Dial-up: contact for
   number Area Codes: 201, 203, 215, 401, 516, 609, 908 Long
   Distance: provided by user Fees: $99/month + $99 startup (PC or
   Mac SLIP software included—shell is additional $21/month) Email:
   info@jvnc.net Phone: 800-35-TIGER, 609-897-7300 Fax: 609-897-
   7310
Global Enterprise Service (GES)—Tiger Mail & Dialin' Terminal (JVNC)
   Dial-up: contact for number Area Codes: 800 Long Distance:
   included Fees: $19/month + $10/hour + $36 startup (PC or Mac
   SLIP software included) Email: *info@jvnc.net* Phone: 800-35-TIGER,
   609-897-7300 Fax: 609-897-7310
Halcyon Dial-up: 206-382-6245 login **new**, 8N1 Area Code: 206 Long
   Distance: provided by user Fees: $200/year, or $60/quarter + $10
   start-up Email: *info@halcyon.com* Phone: 206-955-1050 *ftp://halcyon.
   com/pub/waffle/info*

HoloNet Dial-up: 510-704-1058 Area Code: 510, PDN Long Distance:
(per hour, off-peak/peak) Bay Area: $0.50/$0.95; PSINet A: $0.95/
$1.95; PSINet B: $2.50/$6.00; Tymnet: $3.75/$7.50 Fees: $2/hour
off-peak, $4/hour peak; $6/month or $60/year minimum Email:
info@holonet.net Phone: 510-704-0160 *ftp://holonet.net/info/* Off-peak:
5 p.m. to 8 a.m. + weekends and holidays

HookUp Communication Corporation *hookup.net* Dial-up: contact for
number Area Codes: 800, PDN, 416, 519 Long Distance: 800 access
across Canada, or discounted rates by HookUp Fees: Cdn$14.95/mo
for 5 hours; Cdn$34.95/mo for 15 hrs; Cdn$59.95/mo for 30 hrs;
Cdn$300.00/yr for 50 hrs/mo; Cdn$299.00/mo for unlimited
usage Email: *info@hookup.net* Phone: 519-747-4110 Fax: 519-746-
3521

The IDS World Network Dial-up: 401-273-1088, 401-785-1067 Area
Code: 401 Long Distance: provided by user Fees: $10/month or
$50/half year or $100/year Email: *info@ids.net* Phone: 401-884-
7856 *ftp://ids.net/ids.net*

IEunet Ltd., Ireland's Internet Services Supplier Dial-up: +353 1
6790830, +353 1 6798600 Area Code: +353 1 Long Distance:
provided by user, or supplied by IEunet Fees: IEP25/month
Basic Email: *info@ieunet.ie, info@Ireland.eu.net* Phone: +353 1
6790832 *ftp://ftp.ieunet.ie/pub/*

Individual Network e.V. (IN) Dial-up: contact for number Area Code:
+49 Long Distance: provided by user Fees: 15-30 DM/month
(differs from region to region) Email: *in-info@individual.net* Phone:
+49 2131 64190 (Andreas Baess) Fax: +49 2131 605652 *ftp://ftp.fu-
berlin.de/pub/doc/IN/*

Individual Network—Rhein-Main (in-rhein-main) Dial-up: +49-69-
39048414, +49-69-6312934 (+ others) Area Code: +49 069 Long
Distance: provided by user Fees: SLIP/PPP/ISDN: 40 DM, 4 DM /
Megabyte Email: *info@rhein-main.de* Phone: +49-69-39048413

INS—Inter Networking Systems Dial-up: contact for number Area
Code: +49 23 Long Distance: provided by user Fees: For commercial
institutions and any others: uucp/e-mail,uucp/usenet:$60/month;
ip:$290/month minimum Email: *info@ins.net* Phone: +49 2305
356505 Fax: +49 2305 25411

Institute for Global Communications/IGC Networks (PeaceNet, EcoNet,
ConflictNet, LaborNet, HomeoNet) Dial-up: 415-322-0284 (N-8-1),
login **new** Area Codes: 415, 800, PDN Long Distance: (per hour,
off-peak/peak) SprintNet: $2/$7; 800: $11/$11 Fees: $10/month +
$3/hr after first hour Email: *support@igc.apc.org* Phone: 415-442-
0220 *ftp://igc.apc.org/pub/*

InterAccess Dial-up: 708-671-0237 Area Codes: 708, 312, 815 Long
Distance: provided by user Fees: $23/mo shell, $26/mo SLIP/PPP, or
$5/mo +$2.30/hr Email: *info@interaccess.com* Phone: 800-967-
1580 Fax: 708-671-0113 *ftp://interaccess.com:/pub/interaccess.info*

Internet Direct, Inc. (indirect) Dial-up: 602-274-9600 (Phoenix); 602-
321-9600 (Tucson); login **guest** Area Code: 602 Long Distance:
provided by user Fees: $20/month (personal); $30/month (business) Email: *info@indirect.com* (automated); *support@indirect.com*
(human) Phone: 602-274-0100 (Phoenix), 602-324-0100 (Tucson)

KAIWAN Public Access Internet Online Services Dial-up: 714-539-
5726, 310-527-7358 Area Codes: 213, 310, 714 Long Distance:
provided by user Fees: $15.00/signup + $15.00/month or $30.00/
quarter (3 months) or $11.00/month by credit card Email:
info@kaiwan.com Phone: 714-638-2139 *ftp://kaiwan.com/pub/
KAIWAN*

Maestro Dial-up: (212) 240-9700 login **newuser** Area Codes: 212,
718 Long Distance: provided by user Fees: $15/month or $150/
year Email: *info@maestro.com* (autoreply); *staff@maestro.com,
rkelly@maestro.com, ksingh@maestro.com* Phone: 212-240-9600

MCSNet Dial-up: (312) 248-0900 V.32, 0970 V.32bis, 6295 (PEP),
follow prompts Area Codes: 312, 708, 815 Long Distance: provided
by user Fees: $25/month or $65/3 months untimed, $30/3 months
for 15 hours/month Email: *info@genesis.mcs.com* Phone: 312-248-
UNIX *ftp://genesis.mcs.com/mCSNet.info/*

Merit Network, Inc.—MichNet project Dial-up: contact for number or
telnet://hermes.merit.edu and type **help** at *Which host?* prompt Area
Codes: 202, 301, 313, 517, 616, 703, 810, 906, PDN Long Distance:
SprintNet, Autonet, Michigan Bell packet-switch network Fees: $35/
month + $40 signup ($10/month for K-12 & libraries in Michigan)
Email: *info@merit.edu* Phone: 313-764-9430 *ftp://nic.merit.edu/*

The Meta Network (TMN) Dial-up: contact for numbers Area Codes:
703, 202, 301, PDN Long Distance: SprintNet: $6.75/hr; FTS-2000;
Acunet Fees: $20/month + $15 signup/first month Email:
info@tmn.com Phone: 703-243-6622

Millennium Online Dial-up: contact for numbers Area Code:
PDN Long Distance: PDN Fees: $10 monthly/.10 per minute
domestic, .30 internationally Email: *jjablow@mill.com* Phone: 800-
736-0122

MindVOX Dial-up: 212-989-4141 login **mindvox, guest** Area Codes:
212, 718 Long Distance: provided by user Fees: $15-$20/month. No
startup. Email: *info@phantom.com* Phone: 212-989-2418 or 4141

MSen Dial-up: contact for number Area Codes: 313, 810 Long
Distance: provided by user Fees: $20/month; $20 startup Email:
info@msen.com Phone: 313-998-4562 Fax: 313-998-4563 *ftp://
ftp.msen.com/pub/vendor/msen/*

muc.de e.V. (mucev) Dial-up: contact for numbers Area Code: +49
089 Long Distance: provided by user Fees: From DM 20. (Mail
only) up to DM 65. (Full Account with PPP) Email: *postmaster@
muc.de ftp://ftp.muc.de/public/info/muc-info.**

MV Communications, Inc. Dial-up: contact for numbers Area Code:
603 Long Distance: provided by user Fees: $5.00/month minimum
+ variable hourly rates. See schedule. Email: *info@mv.com* Phone:
603-429-2223 *ftp://ftp.mv.com/pub/mv/*

NEARnet Dial-up: contact for numbers Area Codes: 508, 603,
617 Long Distance: provided by user Fees: $250/month Email:
nearnet-join@nic.near.net Phone: 617-873-8730 *ftp://nic.near.net/docs/*

NeoSoft's Sugar Land Unix Dial-up: 713-684-5900 Area Codes: 504,
713 Long Distance: provided by user Fees: $29.95/month Email:
info@neosoft.com Phone: 713-438-4964

Netcom Online Communication Services Dial-up: 206-547-5992, 214-
753-0045, 303-758-0101, 310-842-8835, 312-380-0340, 404-303-
9765, 408-241-9760, 408-459-9851, 415-328-9940, 415-985-5650,
503-626-6833, 510-274-2900, 510-426-6610, 510-865-9004, 617-
237-8600, 619-234-0524, 703-255-5951, 714-708-3800, 818-585-
3400, 916-965-1371 Area Codes: 206, 213, 214, 303, 310, 312, 404,
408, 415, 503, 510, 617, 619, 703, 714, 718, 818, 916 Long Distance: provided by user Fees: $19.50/month + $20.00 signup Email:
info@netcom.com Phone: 408-554-8649, 800-501-8649 Fax: 408-
241-9145 *ftp://ftp.netcom.com/pub/netcom/*

North Shore Access Dial-up: 617-593-4557 (v.32bis, v.32, PEP) login
new Area Codes: 617, 508 Long Distance: provided by user Fees:
$9/month includes 10 hours connect, $1/hr thereafter, higher
volume discount plans also available Email: *info@northshore.
ecosoft.com* Phone: 617-593-3110 *ftp://northshore.ecosoft.com/pub/flyer*

Northwest Nexus, Inc. Dial-up: contact for numbers Area Code:
206 Long Distance: provided by user Fees: $10/month for first 10
hours + $3/hr; $20 start-up Email: *info@nwnexus.wa.com* Phone:
206-455-3505 *ftp://nwnexus.wa.com/NWNEXUS.info.txt*

NovaLink Dial-up: (800) 937-7644 login **new** or **info**; 508-754-4009
2400, 14400 Area Codes: 508, 617, PDN Long Distance: CPS: $1.80/
hour 2400, 9600; SprintNet $1.80/hour nights and weekends Fees:
$12.95 sign-up (refundable and includes 2 hours) + $9.95/mo
(includes 5 daytime hours) + $1.80/hr Email: *info@novalink.com*
Phone: 800-274-2814 *ftp://ftp.novalink.com/info*

Nuance Network Services Dial-up: contact for number Area Code: 205 Long Distance: provided by user Fees: personal $25/month + $35 start-up, corporate: call for options Email: *staff@nuance.com* Phone: 205-533-4296 *ftp://ftp.nuance.com:/pub/NNS-INFO*

Nyx, the Spirit of the Night Dial-up: 303-871-3324 Area Codes: 303 Long Distance: provided by user Fees: none; donations are accepted but not requested Email: *aburt@nyx.cs.du.edu* Phone: login to find current list of volunteer 'phone' helpers

OARnet Dial-up: send Email to *nic@oar.net* Area Codes: 614, 513, 419, 216, 800 Long Distance: 800 service Fees: $4.00/hr to $330.00/month; call for code or send Email. Email: *nic@oar.net* Phone: 614-728-8100 Fax: 614-292-7168

Old Colorado City Communications (oldcolo) Dial-up: 719-632-4111 login **newuser** Area Code: 719 Long Distance: provided by user Fees: $25/month Email: *dave@oldcolo.com; thefox@oldcolo.com* Phone: 719-632-4848, or 719-636-2040 Fax: 719-593-7521

Olympus—The Olympic Peninsula's Gateway to the Internet Dial-up: contact phone number below Area Code: 206 Long Distance: provided by user Fees: $25/month + $10 startup Email: *info@pt.olympus.net* Phone: 206-385-0464

PANIX Public Access Unix Dial-up: 212-787-3100 login **newuser** Area Codes: 212, 718 Long Distance: provided by user Fees: $19/month or $208/year + $40 signup Email: *alexis@panix.com* Phone: 212-877-4854 (Alexis Rosen)

The Pipeline Dial-up: 212-267-8606 login **guest** Area Codes: 212, 718 Long Distance: provided by user Fees: $15/month (inc. 5 hrs) or $20/20 hrs or $35 unlimited Email: *info@pipeline.com, staff@pipeline.com* Phone: 212-267-3636

The Portal System Dial-up: 408-973-8091 high-speed, 408-725-0561 2400bps; login **info** Area Codes: 408, 415, PDN Long Distance: SprintNet: $2.50/hour off-peak, $7-$10/hour peak; Tymnet: $2.50/hour off-peak, $13/hour peak Fees: $19.95/month + $19.95 signup Email: *cs@cup.portal.com, info@portal.com* Phone: 408-973-9111 Off-peak: 6 p.m. to 7 a.m. + weekends and holidays

Prairienet Freenet Dial-up: (217) 255-9000 login **visitor** Area Code: 217 Long Distance: provided by user Fees: Free for Illinois residents, $25/year for non-residents Email: *jayg@uiuc.edu* Phone: 217-244-1962

PREPnet Dial-up: contact for numbers Area Codes: 215, 412, 717, 814 Long Distance: provided by user Fees: $1,000/year membership. Equipment: $325 onetime fee plus $40/month Email: *prepnet@cmu.edu* Phone: 412-268-7870 Fax: 412-268-7875 *ftp://ftp.prepnet.com/prepnet/general/*

PSILink—Personal Internet Access Dial-up: North America, send email to *CLASSa-na-numbers@psi.com* and *CLASSb-na-numbers@psi.com*; Rest of World, send email to *CLASSb-row-numbers@psi.com* Area Code: PDN Long Distance: (per hour, off-peak/peak) PSINet A: included; PSINet B: $6/$2.50; PSINet B international: $18/$18 Fees: 2400: $19/month; 9600: $29/month (PSILink software included) Email: *all-info@psi.com, psilink-info@psi.com* Phone: 703-709-0300; Fax: 703-620-4586 *ftp://ftp.psi.com/*

PSI's World-Dial Service Dial-up: send email to *numbers-info@psi.com* Area Codes: PDN Long Distance: (per hour, off-peak/peak) V.22bis: $1.25/$2.75; V.32: $3.00/$4.50; 14.4K: $4.00/$6.50 Fees: $9/month minimum + $19 startup Email: *all-info@psi.com, world-dial-info@psi.com* Phone: 703-703-0300; Fax: 703-620-4586 *ftp://ftp.psi.com/* Off-peak: 8 p.m. to 8 a.m. + weekends and holidays

PSS Internet Services, Inc. Dial-up: 904-239-8355 V.42bis; login **newuser**, password **signup** Area Codes: 904, 407 Long Distance: provided by user Fees: $19.50/mo + $20.00 sign-up Email: *info@ america.com* Phone: 904-253-7100; Fax: 904-253-1006

RainDrop Laboratories *agora.rain.com* Dial-up: 503-293-1772 (2400) 503-293-2059 (v.32, v.32 bis) login **apply** Area Codes: 503 Long Distance: provided by user Fees: $6/month (1 hr/day limit) Email: *info@agora.rain.com ftp://agora.rain.com/pub/gopher-data/agora/agora*

RealTime Communications (wixer) Dial-up: 512-459-4391 login **new** Area Code: 512 Long Distance: provided by user Fees: $75/year. Monthly and quarterly rates available. Email: *hosts@wixer. bga.com* Phone: 512-451-0046 (11 a.m.-6 p.m. Central Time, weekdays) Fax: 512-459-3858

South Coast Computing Services, Inc. (nuchat) Dial-up: (713) 661-8593 (v.32)—(713) 661-8595 (v.32bis) Area Code: 713 Long Distance: provided by user Fees: Dial-up—$3/hour, UUCP—$1.50/hour or $100/month unlimited, dedicated—$120, unlimited access Email: *info@sccsi.com* Phone: 713-917-5000 *ftp://sccsi.com/pub/ communications/*

Systems Solutions (ssnet) Dial-up: contact for info Area Code: 302 Long Distance: provided by user Fees: full service $25/month $20/startup; personal slip/ppp $25/month + $2/hour, $20/startup; dedicated slip/ppp $150/month, $450/startup Email: *sharris@marlin. ssnet.com* Phone: (302) 378-1386, (800) 331-1386

Teleport Dial-up: 503-220-0636 (2400) 503-220-1016 (v.32, v.32 bis) login **new** Area Code: 503 Long Distance: provided by user Fees: $10/month (1 hr/day limit) Email: *info@teleport.com* Phone: 503-223-4245 *ftp://teleport.com/about*

Telerama Public Access Internet Dial-up: 412-481-5302 login **new**
(2400) Area Code: 412 Long Distance: provided by user Fees: 66
cents/hour 2400bps; $1.32/hour 14.4K bps; $6 min/month Email:
info@telerama.pgh.pa.us Phone: 412-481-3505 *ftp://telerama.pgh.pa.us/
info/general.info*

Texas Metronet Dial-up: 214-705-2901/817-261-1127 (V.32bis),214-
705-2929(PEP), login **info** or 214-705-2917/817-261-7687 (2400)
login **signup** Area Codes: 214, 817 Long Distance: provided by
user Fees: $5-$45/month + $10-$30 startup Email: *info@
metronet.com* Phone: 214-705-2900, 817-543-8756 Fax: 214-401-
2802 (8 a.m.-5 p.m. CST weekdays) *ftp://ftp.metronet.com/pub/
metronetinfo/*

UK PC User Group (ibmpcug) Dial-up: +44 (0)81 863 6646 Area Code:
+44 (0)81 Long Distance: provided by user Fees: GBPounds 15.50/
month or 160/year + 10 startup (no time charges) Email: *info@
ibmpcug.co.uk* Phone: +44 (0)81 863 6646

University of Alaska Southeast, Tundra Services *alaska.edu* Dial-up:
907-789-1314 Area Code: 907 Long Distance: provided by user
Fees: $20/month for individual accounts; discounts for 25+ and 50+
to public, government, and non-profit organizations. Email:
JNJMB@acad1.alaska.edu Phone: 907-465-6453 Fax: 907-465-6295

UUNET Canada, Inc. Dial-up: contact for numbers Area Codes: 416,
905, 519, 613, 514, 604, 403 Long Distance: provided by user Fees:
(All Cdn$ + GST) TAC: $6/hr; UUCP: $20/month + $6/hr, IP/UUCP:
$50/month + $6/hr, ask for prices on other services Email: *info@
uunet.ca* Phone: 416-368-6621 Fax: 416-368-1350 *ftp://ftp.uunet.ca/*

UUnorth Dial-up: contact for numbers Area Codes: 416, 519,
613 Long Distance: provided by user Fees: (All Cdn$ + GST) $20
startup + $25 for 20 hours Off-peak: + $1.25/hr OR $40 for 40 hours
up to 5/day + $2/hr OR $3/hr Email: *uunorth@uunorth.north.net*
Phone: 416-225-8649 Fax: 416-225-0525

Vnet Internet Access, Inc. Dial-up: 704-347-8839, 919-406-1544, 919-
851-1526 'new' Area Codes: 704, 919 Long Distance: Available for
$3.95 per hour through Global Access. Contact Vnet offices for more
information. Fees: $25/month individual. $12.50 a month for
telnet-in-only. SLIP/PPP/UUCP starting at $25/month. Email:
info@char.vnet.net Phone: 704-334-3282

The Whole Earth 'Lectronic Link (WELL) Dial-up: 415-332-6106 login
newuser Area Code: 415, PDN Long Distance: Compuserve Packet
Network: $4/hour Fees: $15.00/month + $2.00/hr Email: *info@well.
sf.ca.us* Phone: 415-332-4335

The World Dial-up: 617-739-9753 login **new** Area Code: 617,
PDN Long Distance: Compuserve Packet Network: $5.60/hour Fees:

$5.00/month + $2.00/hr or $20/month for 20 hours Email: *office@world.std.com* Phone: 617-739-0202 *ftp://ftp.std.com/world-info/*
Wyvern Technologies, Inc. Dial-up: (804) 627-1828 Norfolk, (804) 886-0662 (Peninsula) Area Codes: 804 Long Distance: provided by user Fees: $15/month or $144/year, $10 startup Email: *system@ wyvern.com* Phone: 804-622-4289 Fax: 804-622-7158

Public Data Networks Contacts (PDN)

BT Tymnet. For information and local access numbers, call 800-937-2862 or 215-666-1770.

Compuserve Packet Network. You do not have to be a Compuserve member to use the CPN to dial other services. For information and local access numbers, call 800-848-8199.

PSINet. For information, call 800-82-PSI-82 or 703-620-6651, or send email to *all-info@psi.com*. For a list of local access numbers, send email to: *numbers-info@psi.com*

Freenets and Groups Offering Internet Access

California Online Resource for Education (CORE), Keith Vogt, Administrator, P.O. Box 3842, 4665 Langson Ave., Seal Beach, CA 90740 Phone: (800) 272-8743 Email: *kvogt@ctp.org*

Institute for Global Communications (IGC) (Peacenet, Econet, Conflictnet, Labornet), 18 De Boom Street, San Francisco, CA 94107 Phone: (415) 442-0220 Fax: (415) 546-1794 Email: *support@igc.apc.org* Information: *ftp://igc.apc.org/*; *gopher:// gopher.igc.apc.org*

Missouri Research and Education Network (MOREnet), Scott Fritz, User Service Coordinator, 200 Heinbel Bldg., Columbia, MO 65211 Phone: (314) 882-2000 Fax: (314) 884-5240 Email: *nic@more.net* Information: *ftp://ftp.more.net*; *gopher://gopher.more.net*

National Public Telecomputing Network (NPTN) (Freenets), Box 1987, Cleveland, OH 44106 Phone: (216) 247-5800 Fax: (216) 247-3328 Email: *info@nptn.org* Information: *ftp://nptn.org/pub/info.nptn*

Public Education Network (PEN), Dr. Harold Cother, Administrator, P.O. Box 2120, Richmond, VA 23216 Phone: (804) 225-2921 Email: *hcothern@pen.k12.va.us*

SENDIT, North Dakota K-12 Education Telecommunications Net, Gleason Sackman, Administrator Box 5164, North Dakota State University, Computer Center, Fargo, ND 58105 Phone: (701) 237-8109 Email: *sackman@sendit.nodak.edu*

The Texas Education Network (TENET), The Texas Education Agency (TEA), 1701 N. Congress Ave., Austin, TX 78701 Phone: (512) 463-0828 ext. 39091 Fax: (512) 463-9090 Email: *tea@tenet.edu* Information: *gopher://gopher.tenet.edu*

For Additional Information. A list of freenets is accessible at *gopher://
gopher.tamu.edu* (Choose *Hot Topics:*, then *A&M's Most Popular Items*,
then *Freenets.*) For additional information, send email to
gopher@tamu.edu

MTLNET is an email list that discusses freenet issues. List address:
MTLNET@VM1.MCGILL.CA. To subscribe: *LISTSERV@VM1.MCGILL.CA;*
in the body of the message type **sub mtlnet** *your name.*

Lists of Providers

Dedicated Line Internet Providers (DLIST). Compiled by Susan Estrada,
made freely available by O'Reilly and Associates. Send email to
dlist@ora.com to get a copy.

Internet Access Providers. Compiled by SRI International Network
Information Systems Center (NISC). Archived at: *ftp://nic.merit.edu/
internet/providers/* and *gopher://nic.merit.edu:7043* (Choose *internet,* then
providers.) Also available in hardcopy form in *Internet: Getting Started,*
published by Prentice Hall.

Network Service Providers Around the World. Compiled by Barry
Raveendran Greene. Archived at *ftp://nic.merit.edu/internet/providers/
providers.around.the.world* and *gopher://nic.merit.edu:7043* (Choose
internet, then *providers.*) Or send email to *p00128@psilink.com* for more
information.

Open Access Unix Sites: NIXPUB List. Compiled by Paul Eschallier. Posted
regularly to the USENET newsgroups *comp.misc, comp.bbs.misc,* and
alt.bbs. Archived at *gopher://gopher.ilc.com*

Public Dialup Internet Access List (PDIAL). Compiled and maintained by
Peter Kaminski. Posted regularly to the following USENET
newsgroups: *alt.internet.access.wanted, alt.bbs.lists* and *ba.internet.*
Archived at *ftp://nic.merit.edu/internet/providers/pdial* and *gopher://
nic.merit.edu:7043 (Choose internet,* then *providers.*) Or send a message
to *info-deli-server@netcom.com* with the subject, **Send PDIAL**.

Internet Connectivity Information and Products

Mailing List

INFO-NETS@THINK.COM. This mailing list is for general discussion of
networks, focusing on internetwork connectivity. Focuses on general
worldwide networking questions, connections to particular sites, and
announcements of new networks and services. Subscription requests
and questions should be sent to *info-nets-request@
think.com.* Also see the USENET group *info.nets.* Archives are WAIS-
indexed: *info-nets.src*

Getting Started Packages

The Internet Companion Expanded Book. The Voyager Company, 1993. The first expanded book to offer readers a live link into the Internet, using CERFnet's popular software. For more information, contact The Online BookStore, Whistlestop Mall, Rockport, MA 01966, (508) 546-7346. Or, send email to OBS@marketplace.com. Other online options are *ftp://ftp.std.com/OBS/The.Internet.Companion; gopher://gopher.std.com* (Choose *Internet Information and Resources/The Internet Companion*.)

Internet in a Box. O'Reilly and Associates, 1994. For more information, contact O'Reilly and Associates, Inc., 103A Morris St., Sebastopol, CA 95472, (800) 998-9938 or (707) 829-0515. *gopher://gopher.ora.com* (Choose *News Flash!* and then *What is Internet in a Box?*) Or send email to *nuts@ora.com*

The Internet Membership Kit. Ventana Media, 1994. For either Macintosh or PC systems, this "kit" includes *The Internet Yellow Pages*, *The Internet Tour Guides*, a guide to downloading and configuring Mosaic, and software for a SLIP or PPP connection, which is provided by CERFnet. For more information, contact Ventana Media at P.O. Box 2468, Chapel Hill, NC 27515, (919) 942-0220, Fax (919) 942-1140. Or send email to: *help@vmedia.com*

SLIP and PPP Implementations

SLIP and PPP implementations for the PC are available commercially from the following companies. Frontier Technologies: (414) 241-4555 FTP Software: (508) 685-4000 or send email to *info@ftp.com* Netmanage: send email to *info@netmanage.com* Novell, Inc.: (801) 429-5588 or see *http://www.novell.com* PC Spry, Inc.: (206) 447-0300 or send email to *info@spry.com*

SLIP and PPP implementations for the Macintosh are available commercially from the following companies. Hyde Park Software: (800) 531-5170 or send email to *info@hydepark.com* InterCon Systems: (703) 709-9890 or send email to *sales@intercon.con* Synergy Software: (215) 779-0522

Freeware PPP implementations are available at *ftp://nic.merit.edu/pub/ internet.tools/ppp/* See the *dos/* directory for DOS systems. See the *mac/* directory for Macintosh systems.

Books and Documents

Estrada, Susan. *Connecting to the Internet: A Buyer's Guide*. O'Reilly and Associates, 1993.

Knowing About Modems, by Patrick Chen. This resource is a good introduction to modems and modem standards. *gopher://gopher-chem.ucdavis.edu* (Choose *Index*, then *Modems-General*.)

PC-MAC TCP/IP and NFS FAQ List, by Rawn Shaw (*rawn@rtd.com*): *ftp://
seagull.rtd.com/pub/tcpip/   http://www.rtd.com/pcnfsfaq/faq.html*

Quarterman, John S., and Smoot Carl-Mitchell. *The Internet Connection:
System Connectivity and Configuration*. Addison-Wesley, 1994. Email
awbook@aw.com for more information.

TCP/IP and Internetworking Information

Online Documents

Introduction to Internet Protocols, by Charles Hedrick *ftp://nic.merit.edu/
introducing.the.internet/intro.to.ip*

Network Reading List, by Charles Spurgeon. This is an annotated list of
network-related items, such as books and resources describing TCP/
IP protocol sites, Unix networking, and Ethernet local area technology: *ftp://ftp.utexas.edu/pub/netinfo/reading-list/* (See the *README* file.)

Request For Comments (RFCs and FYIs). RFCs (and the RFC index) can
be obtained via ftp and email. For an rfc-index search, try *http://
web.nexor.co.uk/rfcindex*. WWW archive at *http://www.cis.ohio-state.edu/
hypertext/information/rfc.html*. Send a message to *rfc-info@isi.edu* and in
the message body put: **help: ways_to_get_rfcs** A help message will
be returned to you. One ftp repository is *ftp://ds.internic.net/rfc/*

Mailing Lists

tcp-ip@nic.ddn.mil. This mailing list is a discussion group for TCP/IP
developers and maintainers. Send subscription requests to: *tcp-ip-
request@nic.ddn.mil*

Organizations

Internet Engineering Task Force (IETF). This organization is an arm of the
Internet Architecture Board and is concerned with protocol engineering, development, and standardization. To subscribe to a mailing
list of IETF announcements, send email to *ietf-announce-
request@cnri.reston.va.us* To subscribe to a general discussion mailing
list, send email to *ietf-request@cnri.reston.va.us*. Futher information is
available at: *ftp://cnri.reston.va.us/ietf/*

Books and Periodicals

Arick, Martin R. *The TCP/IP Companion: A Guide for the Common User*.
QED Publishing Group, 1993.

Black, Uyless. *TCP/IP and Related Protocols*. McGraw Hill, 1992.

Comer, Douglas E. and David L. Stevens. *Internetworking with TCP/IP:
Principles, Protocols and Architecture, Second Edition*. Three volumes.
Prentice Hall, 1992.

ConneXions: The Interoperability Report. For subscription information,
write to Interop Company, a Division of ZP Expos, 303 Vintage Park

Dr., Suite 201, Foster City, CA 94404-1138 Phone: (415) 578-
6900 Fax: (415) 525-0194. For further information, send email to
connexions@interop.com or see *http://programs.interop.com/interop/
connexions.html*

Hunt, Craig. *TCP/IP Network Adminstration*. O'Reilly and Associates,
1992.

Unix Books

Gilly, David, and ORA Staff. *UNIX in a Nutshell*. O'Reilly and Associates, 1992.

Hahn, Harley. *A Student's Guide to UNIX*. McGraw Hill, 1993.

Libes, Don, and Sandy Ressler. *Life with UNIX: A Guide for Everyone*.
Prentice-Hall, 1989.

Norton, Peter and Harley Hahn. *Peter Norton's Guide to UNIX*. Bantam
Books, 1991.

Sobell, Mark G. *A Practical Guide to UNIX Systems*. Benjamin Cummings
Publishing Co., 1989.

SSC Staff. *Beginning UNIX Commands*. Specialized Systems Consultants,
Inc., 1992.

Todino, Grace, and John Strang. *Learning the UNIX Operating System*.
O'Reilly & Associates, Inc., 1989.

Security

Online Documents

Ethics and the Internet, by the Internet Activities Board, 1989. *ftp://
ds.internic.net/rfc/rfc1087.txt*.

Quadralay's Cryptography Archive, maintained by Brain Combs
(*combs@quadralay.com*). This is an archive of security and cryptography resources: *http://www.quadralay.com/www/Crypt/Crypt.html*

Site Security Handbook, by Paul Holbrook and Joyce K. Reynolds, 1991.
ftp://ds.internic.net/rfc/rfc1244.txt. Also known as FYI8.

Virus Information Documents. Public virus informational documents are
maintained by Ken Van Wyk (*krvw@cert.org*), and are available at:
ftp://ftp.cert.org/pub/virus-l/docs

Mailing Lists

COMP-PRIVACY. Discusses how technology impacts privacy. List
address: *comp-privacy@pica.army.mil* To request a subscription: *comp-
privacy-request@pica.army.mil*

HACK-L The Hack Report. Reports new occurrences of hacking and
computer security violation. List address: *HACK-L@alive.crsys.
edmonton.ab.ca* To subscribe: *majordomo@alive.ampr.ab.ca* and in the
body of the message type: **subscribe hack-l**

RISKS@csl.sri.com. The *RISKS Digest* is a moderated discussion group on general computer security issues. To subscribe, send a message to: *risks-request@csl.sri.com*

VALERT-L. This list shares urgent virus warnings. It is cross-posted to the *VIRUS-L Digest.* To subscribe, send a message to *listserv@lehigh.edu* and include this command in the message body: **sub valert-L** *your name*

VIRUS-L@ibm1.cc.lehigh.edu. VIRUS-L is an electronic mail discussion forum devoted to sharing information about computer viruses. To subscribe, send an email message to *LISTSERV@lehigh.edu* and include this command in the message body: **SUB VIRUS-L** *your-name.* Also, see the archives: *ftp://ftp.cert.org/pub/virus-l/*

USENET Newsgroups

The following USENET newsgroups discuss matters of computer security: *alt.security, comp.risks* (the same as the RISKS mailing list digest), *comp.security.announce* (distribution of CERT advisories), *comp.security.misc,* and *comp.virus* (the same as the mailing list VIRUS-L).

Organizations

Computer Emergency Response Team/CERT, Coordination Center Software Engineering Institute, Carnegie-Mellon University, 4500 Fifth Ave., Pittsburgh, PA 15213 Phone: (412) 268-7090 Fax: (412) 268-6989 Email: *cert@cert.org ftp://ftp.cert.org/* Mailing lists: *cert-advisory-request@cert.org; cert-tools-request@cert.org*

Electronic Mail Protection

PEM (Privacy Enhanced Mail). Client is available at: *ftp://ftp.tis.com/pub/PEM/* For more information, see the *PEM FAQ* at *ftp://ftp.tis.com/pub/PEM/FAQ* or send email to: *tispen-support@tis.com* There is also a *PGP/PEM FAQ* at: *http://hoohoo.ncsa.uiuc.edu/docs/PEMPGP.html*

PGP (Pretty Good Privacy) Mail. Client is available at: *ftp://ftp.uu.net/pub/security/pgp/* For more information, see the *PGP FAQ,* posted to the USENET newsgroup *alt.security.pgp* and archived at: *http://www.quadralay.com/www/Crypt/PGP*

Books

Curry, David. *UNIX System Security: A Guide for Users and System Administrators.* Addison-Wesley, 1992.

Garfinkel, S. and E. Spafford. *Practical UNIX Security.* O'Reilly & Associates, 1991.

Hafner, Katie and John Markoff. *Cyberpunk: Outlaws and Hackers on the Computer Frontier.* Simon & Schuster, 1991.

Russell, Deborah and G.T. Gangemi, Sr. *Computer Security Basics.* O'Reilly and Associates, 1992.

Sterling, Bruce. *The Hacker Crackdown: Law and Disorder on the Electronic Frontier.* Bantam Books, 1992.

Stoll, Clifford. *The Cuckoo's Egg: Tracking a Spy Through the Maze of Computer Espionage.* Doubleday, 1989.

Index